Volume 7

THE EUROPEAN COMMUNITY

T0382915

THE EUROPEAN COMMUNITY

A Superpower in the Making

JOHAN GALTUNG

Routledge
Taylor & Francis Group

LONDON AND NEW YORK

First published in 1973 by George Allen & Unwin, Ltd.

This edition first published in 2021
by Routledge
2 Park Square, Milton Park, Abingdon, Oxon OX14 4RN

and by Routledge
52 Vanderbilt Avenue, New York, NY 10017

Routledge is an imprint of the Taylor & Francis Group, an informa business

© 1973 Johan Galtung

British Library Cataloguing in Publication Data
A catalogue record for this book is available from the British Library

ISBN: 978-0-367-68499-0 (Set)
ISBN: 978-1-00-316169-1 (Set) (ebk)
ISBN: 978-0-367-71091-0 (Volume 7) (hbk)
ISBN: 978-0-367-71098-9 (Volume 7) (pbk)
ISBN: 978-1-00-314927-9 (Volume 7) (ebk)

Publisher's Note
The publisher has gone to great lengths to ensure the quality of this reprint but points out that some imperfections in the original copies may be apparent.

Disclaimer
The publisher has made every effort to trace copyright holders and would welcome correspondence from those they have been unable to trace.

JOHAN GALTUNG

The European Community:
A Superpower in
the Making

Universitetsforlaget
Oslo

George Allen & Unwin, Ltd.
London

PRIO STUDIES FROM THE INTERNATIONAL
PEACE RESEARCH INSTITUTE, OSLO

No. 1. Johan Galtung: The European Community: A Superpower in the Making. 1973

Published simultaneously in the United Kingdom by George Allen & Unwin, Ltd.,
London, and in Norway by Universitetsforlaget

Also as PRIO publication no. 22–21 from the International Peace Research Institute,
Oslo

Cover design: Erik Ellegaard Frederiksen IDD

Printed in Norway by
A.s Joh. Nordahls Trykkeri, Oslo

Preface

This book is an effort to see the European Community in a global perspective. Although written by a European it is not directed to the question found in the literature published by the European Community herself: what does it mean to us? to our member states? Instead, two other perspectives are offered: what does the European Community mean to the masses of the world, to the world proletariat? And what does it mean to the world community in general?

The analysis in the present book is critical of the European Community, from either perspective. This critical view derives not so much from what the European Community is today, as from what it may become if present trends continue, with further extension of membership and further deepening of integration. Of course the future is uncertain, no social or human future is absolutely determined. It is therefore mandatory that analyses also pronounce themselves on the future, rather than becoming mere accounts of present and past, as used to be the case in the social sciences. When one leaves the safe harbor of data, the analysis becomes speculative. But it goes without saying that any such analysis is also written with the hope that it may be self-denying, that there will be increasing consciousness about the nature of the European Community, and that counterforces will become operative.

The stimulus provided by dialogues with audiences exposed to the book in lecture form has been invaluable for the writing of this book. These dialogues are reflected in the analyses given throughout. Since early 1971 I have had the privilege of discussing the EC with audiences in sixteen countries, in member and non-member states in Western Europe, in Eastern Europe (Poland, Yugoslavia), in Third World countries (India, Egypt, Uganda), in the US. The audiences have been diverse indeed: trade union groups, foreign ministry officials, university seminars and courses, scientific conferences, small political opposition groups, big establishment arrangements. The form has been that of the lecture, introduction to discussions with a counter-introduction (sometimes from the Commission), the panel – but usually with extremely lively audience participation. One general impression from these discussions is that the European Community still operates largely in a vacuum where political consciousness is concerned, even to the point that there seems to be more interest concerning the Community outside than inside the Community itself. But this consciousness formation is vital, and the book is intended as a minor and certainly far from final contribution in that direction. The major contribution will never come from intellectual analyses, but from the highly concrete social processes that the European Community itself will stimulate, for good and for bad, around the world.

Although written by a Norwegian, this work presents no special analysis of the problems in connection with the Norwegian (and Danish) application for membership. This is partly because so much good literature is now available about these problems in the candidate countries. But the main reason for avoiding such a specific analysis is that the European Community will not be greatly changed by the presence or absence of these two countries. The European Community is a phenomenon on a global scale; and it is every individual's duty to form his view of it and act upon that view, regardless of whether the country of which he is a citizen happens to be inside or outside the Community.

Although written by a social scientist, the book is quite explicit in its critical attitude. That is not because I regard the book as some kind of extra-curricular activity, but because I regard social critique as an indispensable ingredient of social science analysis. So-called 'objective information' is usually conservatism in disguise. For the critique to be 'scientific', a minimum requirement is that the value-patterns be made very explicit and the contrast with facts and trends reasonably thorough. To what extent that is done in the present book the reader will have to judge. I would be most grateful for comments.

Incidentally, almost any statement about the European Community is true – and false. It is such a many-sided phenomenon that there is no end to the number of words, articles, books, even journals devoted to its description, analysis, criticism, and/or praise. In the present book an effort has been made to pursue one particular theme, given in the title of the book. But in so doing, many side-themes appear and reappear, some in the text, some in the relatively extensive footnotes. The reader in search of more elaboration might therefore find the footnotes worth looking at – they do not consist only of references.

My expressions of thanks go first of all to discussants in various coun-

6

tries, particularly to opponents who have taught me much about how the European Community conceives of herself. Then, to the School of International Studies of the Jawaharlal Nehru University in New Delhi, and particularly to Professor K. P. Misra for stimulating this attempt to make a book out of all those oral presentations when I was a visiting professor in the School, spring 1971. Then, to the colleagues and friends at the International Peace Research Institute in Oslo for numerous and always stimulating debates on all these issues – particularly to Asbjørn Eide, Nils Petter Gleditsch, Helge Hveem, Knut Hongrø, Tord and Susan Høivik, Sverre Lodgaard, and Marek Thee.

And finally to Fumiko Nishimura Galtung, who has taught me more than anybody else what Europeans, left or right, establishment or anti-establishment, may look like from other parts of the world.

Oslo, 1 May 1972
Johan Galtung

Preface to this edition

An Epilogue has been added with some comments on the outcome of the referenda in Norway and Denmark.

Oslo, Autumn 1972
Johan Galtung

Contents

Contents

Chapter 1.
The background

These years and months, every week and every day, a new superpower is gradually taking shape in Western Europe: the European Community (EC). This is a long and problematic process. Many would not agree that extension and deepening the Community inevitably will lead to a superstate, and that such a superstate is bound sooner or later to end up as a superpower – in the present world, with its present structure and the present leadership. But people have become so overexposed to the US and Soviet giants that it took them a long time before they started taking a serious look at China, and some also at Japan. Moreover, the focus has often been on the weaknesses of the European Community, e.g. its 1965–66 deadlock when it was boycotted by France after the June 30 crisis, rather than on its strengths. What has been well publicized are failures to come to some agreements, rather than the smooth day-to-day workings of the machinery: journalism focusses on drama rather than on permanence. More recently, the focus has been on the problems of candidate countries rather than on the countries that are already in – with lengthy lists of arguments pro and con from the view of the present, never debating seriously what the future role of the Community may be.

The significance of this can hardly be overstated. Candidate countries are discussing problems which member countries have already been through, since they have to join on the basis of the Paris and Rome Treaties, particularly on the treaty establishing the European Common Market. In addition they have to accept the implementations of these treaties in the practice of the European Community – where for instance mainly in the field of agriculture, and in the year 1970 alone, the Commission put into force 2,448 regulations.[1] That this leads to questions of adjustments to an existing reality is obvious: and these questions are the major subjects of at last that part of the negotiations which reaches the public. But the EC itself has a considerably more forward-looking focus, as evidenced in the communiqué from the Hague summit meeting of

1–2 December 1969, the meetings of foreign ministers, and those higher up, and above all the Davignon and Werner Plans.[2]

This means that the candidate countries and their publics may now be going through a learning process where over-emphasis on adjustment details is combined with under-emphasis on underlying principles and prospectives. Factions will emerge in the candidate countries, not necessarily along traditional party lines; and they will still be interested in proving themselves right relative to the debate that has gone on. Adherents will point out that adjustment was more easy, antagonists that it was less easy – which will give *some* time dimension to the imprint these countries have so far received. But almost nowhere are there raised such basic problems as the future role of the EC in the total world community, its adjustment to the world as a whole and the world to it – problems that may be of considerably more consequence for present and future member states than the adjustment of joining nations to the EC and the EC to them.

This essay is concerned with the future world role of the EC. We shall base ourselves on what has happened up to now, on world trends at present and in the near future, and on (hopefully educated) guesses about the future.

The thesis is that a new superpower is emerging. In a stronger version, the thesis is that the European Community is an effort to recreate:

1) a Eurocentric world, a world with its center in Europe,
2) a unicentric Europe, a Europe with its center in the West.

Now, this is in fact more or less how the world looked for a long period, perhaps from the Great Discoveries, or at least from the beginning of Western colonization till around the end of World War II. Thus, our thesis could also be formulated as saying that the Community is an effort to turn history backwards, only adding a dimension of modern technology.

We say 'effort', because we think it will only succeed in the short run. It is a logical effort, easy to explain and foresee with elementary knowledge of Western European history and some social theory. The Community is nevertheless a counter-historical approach, an effort to run against more basic world processes between and with nations. Since Western Europe is strong, it will take years, even decades of expansion before counterforces become sufficiently strong and the new giant suffers the fate of all giants before it.

What happened around 1945 that the European Community can be considered an effort to undo? Evidently, Hitler's Third Reich was defeated by the mightiest military alliance the world had ever seen. But that was not basic. The world has seen very, very many wars among European powers – three of them with Germany in three generations. By definition, wars among European powers have been the most 'important' wars, if the most important wars are those fought by the most important powers. In that sense, the war fought against Hitler was a 19th century war a century delayed, fought in the spirit of that utterly 19th century figure, Winston Churchill. It was an intra-European tribal warfare between nation-states;[3] it was not a 20th century war of national liberation from colonialism or a people's war of liberation from exploitation, foreign and domestic. Although the war against Hitler turned out differently in its consequences, it was essentially a horizontal war between sovereign nations. It was a classical war, not a class war, but also a war mobilizing the total nation on either side.

What made this war different was its technology and its scale. Never before had the world seen so much technology mobilized in a war that increasingly took the shape of genocide on both sides: genocide inside the conquered territories justified by the ideology of Nazism, and genocide across the fronts, justified by the ideology of war. The genocide committed by the losing party, for instance with gas, is still generally held to be much more a crime against humanity than the genocide committed by the winning party, for instance by saturation bombing. Modern technology made depth and extension of warfare possible on a scale hitherto undreamt of. But the structure of the war was the old one.

Nor was participation by itself, of the powerful periphery of Europe – the United States and the Soviet Union – anything new; both had participated in World War I. But this time the impact of periphery participation was different; it was decisive. Europe was overrun, Britain alone could at most defend herself but not defeat the Axis powers. The entry of the Soviet Union and the United States in 1941, challenged into the war by Germany and Japan respectively, spelt defeat not only for Germany, *but also for Europe*. Europe, from Brest (in Bretagne) to Brest (Litovsk) was no longer able to handle her own affairs. In 1945 victors and vanquished alike were exhausted, run-down, bankrupt – the populations cold and hungry, walking along the roads, picking in the ruins. There were three war machines left: US, UK, and USSR; all the others were defeated or reduced to small units trained and stationed abroad, partisan, maquis, and other resistance forces, and so on. The true victors were the US and the USSR; even the UK was worn out.[4]

Europe as such was defeated by the war, not only Germany. But there were important variations. In Western Europe, the regimes were still by and large legitimate in the eyes of the population: Nazi Germany had ruled through quisling governments, the occupied *nations* had resisted (with France as a borderline case with much collaboration), and the powers of the *state* had taken refuge in London. But in Eastern Europe (Bulgaria, Romania, Hungary, Slovakia), many regimes were made Hitler's allies, obviating any need for puppet governments; and large parts of the nations had cooperated. Whereas Western Europe was politically and socially intact but economically devastated when the power defined as legitimate returned, Eastern Europe was in chaos both politically and economically.

In a sense, this corresponded well to the capabilities of the supreme victors. The victor in the West, the United States, had fought with capital and technology more than with overriding, explicit political faith, and the war had served as a stimulus to either. The US was well fit to help the sagging economies of Western Europe, particularly since there was no socio-political issue with the regimes. In fact, the harmony and understanding were of such a nature and at such a level that it became natural for the US also to back up those regimes against the threat from forces that wanted basic social change, particularly the Communist parties. Economic reconstruction after the war therefore took the form of support to the regimes and the socio-economic structure they represented, not only the form of improving the standard of living of the population and a reconstruction of the productive forces after the war. The 'fight against Communism' was equally important.

On the other hand, there was the victor in the East, the Soviet Union. She had fought with her own and others' resources but also with a faith and with an ideological dimension reinforcing the hatred most Soviet citizens felt towards the Nazi intruder. Right after the war the Soviet Union was not in a position to offer economic assistance: on the contrary, she capitalized on the Nazi collaboration of Eastern Europe to exact war reparations of considerable magnitude. At the same time, the USSR had strong and clear ideas about *political* reconstruction, as clear as those the US had about *economic* reconstruction. Not only the Eastern European regimes, but the entire structure was considered responsible for the collaboration: the only answer was a revolution. Just as economic reconstruction in the West took the form of US investment and penetration at the top of the economic structure, socio-political reconstruction in the East took the form of a Soviet political investment with a very heavy military-political penetration at the top of these societies. Both the US and the USSR did so with a double motivation of protecting themselves and protecting vs building the type of regimes they considered best for other peoples, i.e. regimes similar to their own. Unfortunately, in the eyes of the West social construction is seen as 'ideological' and economic reconstruction as 'technological' – where both are, of course, profoundly political.

Thus, the Eurocentric pre-war world received its first blow, not only because all of Europe was defeated, but because the US and the USSR each reconstructed 'their' (as defined by the Tehran and Yalta agreements) parts in their own image – an image strengthened tremendously by the victory over the enemy. Europe became not only bicentric, but bicentric with one center in Washington and one in Moscow: *in other words, with centers located outside itself.* This is tantamount to colonization. But it was a colonization in *two* empires, and almost immediately the two parts became hostile to each other: *Europe was not only bicentric, it became bipolar,* crystallizing militarily into the NATO and the Warsaw Treaty Organization.[5]

Why? In retrospect probably for one simple reason: the changing hegemony over Eastern Europe. Western Europe had been used to exercising this privilege (although mainly through Germany) – it was now taken over by Moscow. This was interpreted in the West as an expression of the greed for power in the USSR in general and Stalin in particular – with no reference to the political bankruptcy that most of Eastern Europe had gone through, with illegitimate regimes almost everywhere. Actually, the only population that as such had really resisted German occupation was found in Yugoslavia, and even there in a fragmented and problematic way. The legitimacy of the postwar Tito regime was therefore genuine, not dependent on the outside, as clearly evidenced in June 1948. Poland might have become a second exception if her resistance had not been crushed in August 1944.

With the exception of Czechoslovakia, Eastern Europe had socio-economic systems lagging far behind with their feudal and pre-capitalistic structures. *There was a construction job to be done,* and it was in Moscow's self-interest that the job be done under Soviet supervision, often also by them. There was also an economic reconstruction job to be done in Western Europe, and it was in the interest of the US that it be done by the US. Thus, World War II provided the occasion for both of them to expand and invest and imprint their economic message and structure on either part of Europe through the Marshall Aid and the OEEC, and through the Communist parties.

15

In 1945 the Eurocentric world suffered another crack of even greater significance: *the beginning of the end of colonialism*. World War I had seen the disruption of two European empires, the German (in Africa and the Far East) and the Turkish Ottoman Empire (in the Arab world). (Spain had been the first to lose hers; most of the Latin American colonies in the 1810–1825 wars, and Cuba and the Philippines in the wars with the US around the turn of the century.) But Germany re-established some type of neo-colonial empire in Eastern Europe before World War II, and during that had proceeded towards complete colonization, exposing Eastern Europe to the type of treatment that the Red Indians had been exposed to in the Americas, or the victims of e.g. Belgian, Dutch, French, and British colonialism elsewhere – only not so well publicized. Extermination, terror, fragmentation, and extreme division of labor were basic formulas.

Six Western European powers lost their colonies in the period subsequent to the 1945 defeat: Germany (in Eastern Europe), France, Italy, Belgium (including Luxembourg), Netherlands – and Britain. Of these, the first five (or six, if we include that appendix to Belgium called Luxembourg) became the founding members of the European Community, and the last one, Britain, the leading candidate country. This leads to one basic formula for understanding the Community: 'take five broken empires, add the sixth one later, and make one big neo-colonial empire out of it all'. The accuracy of this little recipe will be explored in chapters 5–9. Here we shall only point out that Spain (whose decline as a colonial power had come a century and a half ago), Turkey (who had had her eclipse only one world war earlier), and Portugal (always behind in any development, also in losing colonies) were not included. They did not fit that formula, nor did their internal regimes fit the basic EC assumption of structural similarity either. The consequences of this will be discussed in chapter 2.

In conclusion: the world was no longer ruled from rivalling powers in Europe. The colonial powers had lost or were rapidly losing their empires at the same time as Europe itself was increasingly being ruled from the two new centers, Washington and Moscow. *And all this in the short span of a decade or two!* Anyone who does not believe that rapid world changes can take place should consider this. But one could also respond with two very forceful arguments: it took a major social catastrophe, a world war, to do it. And, even so, the social inertia in the world is so deep-rooted that regeneration efforts came into being very quickly – which is precisely our thesis about the European Community. Europe cannot be split into two parts dominated from the former periphery, and Western Europe cannot lose her traditional hold both on Eastern Europe and on the Third World without throwing aside age-old rivalries in an effort to regenerate old power.[6]

Nevertheless, the changes were real, and the humiliation of classical Europe thorough. This was concealed by the cold war, by bicentrism translated into a highly dangerous but also carefully balanced bipolarity. Both Europes were invited to play a new role, as second in command on either side − and with high probability of being the first to be sacrificed should the cold war become hot. This was certainly far from the role Western Europe was used to playing in the world. That some rethinking and re-organization took place to negate some of this *atimia* (loss of status)[7] is almost unnecessary to explain − the burden of proof rests on whoever suggests that the countries in Europe should have acquiesced forever to the role as pawns in a US–Soviet system, playing their roles in *pax americana* or *pax sovietica* respectively, increasingly turning into a joint *pax condominica*.[8]

So our interpretation of the European Common Market, as one of the Communities was once called, is that it is considerably *more* than a 'market': it is a struggle for power, for world power for Western Europe. It is also considerably *less* than 'European': it is only for those powers in *Western* Europe that meet certain requirements, above all recent loss of empires and/or NATO membership (see chapters 2 and 8). It is an effort to make the world Eurocentric and to locate the center of Europe in the West, even with an explicit peace philosophy, with a *pax bruxellana* (chapter 9) in mind. But within these limitations it is 'common', common for those who meet the bill. And that bill is written in power units more than in economic units alone. Hence an analysis of power is indispensable to understanding the European Community, and such an analysis will be presented in chapter 3 below. First let us have a brief look at some of the characteristics of the EC, as it has developed, as it appears today, and with a view to some of its prospects for the future.

Chapter 2.
The European Community:
A brief survey

The West German Chancellor, Willy Brandt, expressed in a press conference 8 October 1971[1] in very simple form some of the basic strategy in the growth of the European Community:

> Once the matter of entry has been dealt with, the way will be open for further progress towards a currency and economic union, and for closer cooperation in foreign policy.

The membership issue concerns what in EC language is called *extension*, and in social science parlance is called the *domain* of this unification of countries. The issues Brandt mentioned – currency union, economic union, cooperation in foreign policy – concern what in EC parlance is referred to as *deepening*, and in social science jargon as the *scope* of the integration.[2]

These are the two axes along which the European Community can be discussed. And Brandt's statement could just as well have been made earlier in the history of the European Community and in an inverted form: 'Once the matter of deepening has been dealt with, the way will be open for progress towards a larger membership'.

This has been the logic of EC development: deepening with constant membership, followed by extension with constant issues, followed by deepening with constant membership, and so on. We may refer to this as the staircase hypothesis (Fig. 1).

One thing at a time, not both extension and deepening simultaneously.[3] The secret of the success of the European Community so far is perhaps its ability to combine a clear view of the goal, 'une union sans cesse plus étroite entre les peuples Européens'[4] with pragmatism and a measure of restraint lest the process go too fast.

First, the background: Winston Churchill's celebrated speech in Zürich in 1946 where he said: 'We should construct some kind of United States of Europe'. The result was the Council of Europe in 1949, immediately

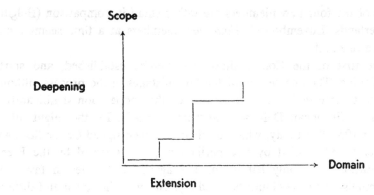

Fig. 1.

given a large domain and a broad scope, but with little real power. In its Council of Ministers, decisions *have to* be unanimous,[5] i.e. each government has a veto. The Council of Europe is only one more intergovernmental organization, nothing less, nothing more.

The plan launched in the declaration of 9 May 1950, by French foreign minister Robert Schuman in cooperation with Jean Monnet, was very different.[6] Here the domain was limited to two countries, France and Germany; the scope was limited to coal and steel, but the organization was really supranational. The unification was made on the basis of an insight often ascribed to marxists: the idea that economic organization is basic. As expressed in the *Werner Report:*[7]

> Economic and monetary union thus appears as leaven for the development of political union, which in the long run it (the Community) cannot do without.

This insight is in fact the common heritage of conservatives, liberals, and marxists alike, in an era that perhaps started around the Industrial Revolution, and is still almost equally fascinated with production and productivity.

The insight was then implemented with a textbook-like clarity starting with something very concrete, coal and steel, building power around a solid nucleus of economic organization. The next step came already 18 April 1951, when the Two became the Six: the Paris Treaty established the European Coal and Steel Community (ECSC). The scope was constant, but the domain was extended significantly and in a way typical for this process: the nucleus is very strong (France and Germany), whereas

19

three of the four new members are rather small in comparison (Belgium, Netherlands, Luxembourg). *Four* new members at a time seems almost to be a rule . . .!

The first of the Communities was thereby established, and started functioning. Then came one of the few mistakes in the process, although it almost succeeded: the effort to deepen the cooperation significantly by adding a European Defense Community (EDC). In the night of 31 August 1954 this treaty, which by then had been signed by the Six's governments and ratified by five parliaments, was rejected by the French parliament – but only barely so, 319 against 264 votes in favor (the Communists and the Gaullists voted against, on well-known and different premises). We shall return to this in chapter 8.

Efforts towards deepening did not stop for that reason – they only took a different direction. On 25 March 1957 came the two Rome treaties launching the European Economic Community (EEC) and the European Atomic Energy Community (Euratom) – matters that had been well prepared after the June 1955 conference in Messina. The major task of the EEC very quickly centered on a customs union, completed 18 months ahead of schedule (1 July 1968) with abolition of internal tariffs and a common external tariff (CET) operating around the Common Market; *and* a common agricultural policy (CAP). A decision to introduce in all six countries a uniform system of value-added tax was made 8 February 1967. And on 1 July 1967 the High Authority of the ECSC and the Commissions of the EEC and Euratom were merged so that the European Communities from that time on would have one Commission, one Council of Ministers, and one European Parliament.

In the period subsequent to the Rome treaties not only considerable deepening took place. There was also extension of membership – only that the new 'members' were not first-class European members as envisaged in the Rome Treaty § 238, but second-class non-European members according to Part IV of the Treaty. The First Yaoundé Convention was put into force 1 June 1964, associating 18 earlier dependencies of the member states with the EEC, 14 of them former French territories, 3 of them Belgian, and 1 of them Italian ('Italian Somalia').

This period is better known in Europe for another move in the direction of extension: the requests for negotiations and the applications for membership by the UK, Ireland, Denmark, and Norway. When on 14 January 1963 President de Gaulle declared that Britain was not ready for Community membership a possible interpretation, in line with the general staircase hypothesis, might be that the Community was not yet ready for British membership. Deepening had not gone far enough for extension to take place.

At the time it happened and even today, it is customary to emphasize de Gaulle's personal motives, his particular feelings towards England, and so on. But it might be equally or more fruitful to see de Gaulle's attitude as a reflection of a Community not yet ready to absorb new members – a feeling that new members will have more of an impact on the Community than it will have on them. In retrospect, de Gaulle's action may therefore well have strengthened rather than weakened the integration process. On 27 November 1967 this was still valid: de Gaulle's second rejection of the UK was announced at a press conference. By this time France, not only de Gaulle, knew very well of what it was speaking. From 1 July 1965 till 17 January 1966 France boycotted the institutions of the Community, manifestly because of the failure to reach agreement on the financing of the common agricultural policy. Evidently, the house was not in order!

The first green light since the Rome Treaties were signed in 1957 (and implemented as of 1 January 1958) that the Community was now prepared to go ahead was the communiqué from the summit meeting in The Hague, 1–2 December 1969 with general agreement to complete, enlarge, and strengthen the Community. From that point on, the growth of the EC has been accelerating, as have also the plans for its growth. On 4 March 1970 the Commission submitted a three-stage plan for full monetary and economic union by 1980; and on 31 July 1970 the foreign ministers of the Six submitted the Davignon Report to heads of government, suggesting ministerial meetings on political cooperation, particularly foreign policy harmonization, on a biannual basis. This was followed up by the meeting of 19 November 1970 in München where the foreign ministers of the Six for the first time, among other matters, emphasized the need for harmonization of voting in the United Nations.[8]

Needless to say, in the period after the Hague meeting a number of other issues were dealt with – nuclear research and also non-nuclear scientific research, the definition of medium-term economic policies, the creation of a short-term mutual-aid system of $ 2 billions, steps towards common industrial policy, power given to the European Social Fund to retrain and resettle workers, a common fishery policy, the Mansholt Plan to modernize farming, and so on. But it is characteristic of the European Community that interests have focussed on the long-range plans, particularly on the ten-year, three-stage plan for full economic and monetary union with 1980 as a target date.

The period after the Hague meeting has also been the period of negotiations with the four applicant countries, United Kingdom, Ireland, Denmark, and Norway. That does not mean that extension has been at a
standstill. In this period what we could call third class membership, looser
agreements than the Yaoundé Convention, of various kinds, became
prominent on the horizon of the Community. There had already been a
pre-history in Europe: the association agreement with Greece signed 9
July 1961, with Turkey signed 12 September 1963, both according to
§ 237 of the Rome Treaty with a view to both countries some day becoming full members of the Community. Association status in this case
could be considered a waiting room for the countries that for political or
economic reasons were not sufficiently similar with the original Member
States. After the 1967 military coup in Greece the association agreement
was practically speaking suspended. Greece was put in a frigidaire inside
the waiting-room – but with one leg outside. These agreements must
therefore be differentiated from the much looser agreements with Yugoslavia (19 March 1970), Israel and Spain (1 October 1970) and Malta
(1 April 1971).

But the real extension at the level below full membership took place
outside Europe. Nigeria signed an association agreement with the EC on
16 July 1966, and even though the agreement never took effect because
of the civil war raging in that country, it was significant as a first inroad
into Commonwealth territory. More important was the Arusha convention signed on 26 July 1968 between the EC and Kenya, Uganda, and
Tanzania – an association agreement renewed on 24 September 1969.
Its significance will be discussed in chapter 6.

That brings us up to the present situation. What is ahead on the two
axes of deepening and extension? These are the basic questions, since
these have to be answered to evaluate to what extent that superstate is
becoming a superpower: in other words, to what extent the EC's bid for
power at the very top level of the world, even to the point of making the
world Eurocentric again and creating a Europe with a center in the EC,
will become reality.

To explore this question we could imagine two types of methodology.

We could take as our point of departure politicians' expressions of
intention. The late 1940s and the early 1950s saw a plethora of statements about a coming United States of Europe; many of these statements
were carried over into the early beginnings of the EC, particularly by its
founders. Or, we could take a more recent pronouncement on how a
leading EC statesman, Chancellor Willy Brandt, sees its future role:[9]

I am sometimes amused when I read stories about the new triangular world situation into which we may get – Washington, Moscow and Peking. I myself think it will be more of a square or rectangular situation, with Western Europe the fourth corner – at least if we look as far ahead as the end of this decade.

This is not the method we shall employ here. The relationship between openly professed intentions and what is happening in the world of facts is too loose to permit any solid influence. The Council of Europe is in itself evidence of how little intentions mean when not backed up by capabilities. In addition, professed intention is one thing, the real intention quite another – and usually available only in retrospect.

But the major objection is that the quotation method attributes too much weight to intention, too little to structure. It also assumes that politicians are aware of what they are doing, that they have insight in the forces they are riding on, trying to stem, or trying to unleash. For this reason we will base ourselves much more on an analysis of the structure emerging so far, and extrapolate from this. Professed intentions may some times precede, some times antedate, some times not even touch at all what is going on.

What is going on is evidently continued deepening and extension. As to the deepening there is little reason to doubt that the goals indicated in the Werner and Davignon Plans will be reached, possibly even before the target date of 1980, with some modifications. But this is not because it is written in the plans, nor because there is a professed intention to adhere to the plans in one way or another. Rather, it is simply because the fusion process already started in the European Community *must* lead to a chain reaction. In fact, the process will have much deeper consequences than those that happen to be spelt out in the two Plans which have been the subject of so much public discussion, particularly in the applicant countries.

With fusions at various levels of major industrial organizations, e.g. in automobile and airplane production,[10] it is obvious that other aspects of capital have to merge, towards a monetary and economic union. If capital merges, labor has to do the same: European Community trade unions will be an obvious consequence of the European multinational corporation, capable of undertaking joint negotiations, launching joint strikes, and so on.

If the secondary sector of the economy of the Member States is organized so well at the Community level, something similar has to happen to the primary and tertiary sectors. So far, CAP has been run from the top; a safe prediction is that a farmers' organization for the total European Community will emerge. Correspondingly with the tertiary sector: the growth in the field of European Community INGOs (inter-nongovernmental organizations), is already explosive, as a natural mechanism in order to get into position for joint negotiations with the authorities of the Community.[11]

At the same time, if all this takes place around the basic interests individuals have because of their jobs, it will also happen at the level of values, because of shared ideology. In other words, EC parties will become more and more Community parties organized at the European Community level, and less and less coordination between the members of the European Community. Already today the members of the European Parliament are organized in the 'official' political groups: Christian Democrats, Socialists and Liberals – and in addition the European Democratic Union, which consists only of members of the French Gaullist Party. The Italian Communist Party has been represented since 1969, but its members are too few to form an official group. This process will continue outside the European Parliament.

The point here, however, is not that the European Community will be biased against radical parties to the right or to the left. The EC is built around the solid nucleus of economic and political structure that the member states have in common. With sufficiently strong communist parties in most of the countries this will probably sooner or later be adequately reflected. The point is that parties will tend to become increasingly transnational, dealing directly with the EC, and the national level will become less dominant. This will also tend to make parties in the EC countries much more similar.

These chain reaction processes are so obvious that one could rather ask the question in reverse form: which are the groupings most likely to be excluded from this general process of transnationalization? We would assume that these would be groups, or interests, that

1) are not even well articulated at the national level, or
2) are not found in a majority in the member states, or
3) do not have sufficient resources to organize transnationally.

As to the first category we would think particularly of groups in outlying districts, or in the national periphery in general; such as islanders in Northern Norway, or old and lonely people.

In the second category we could think of groups and interests related to major group conflicts, such as the conflicts found in Belgium, in the UK (Wales, Scotland, Ulster), in France (Bretagne, but also in Southeastern France[12]) and to some extent in some other countries. Since these conflicts are not found in all countries, and certainly not in the same form, it will be difficult for the groupings to find each other.

With the third case a good example might be the general situation of high school students and university students. It is not difficult for the European Community to organize meetings to discuss 'the problem of youth', 'the university crisis', and similar topics – but participants in these meetings will usually be ministers of education, bureaucrats, and others in the school systems, lecturers and professors. Those who might be interested in organizing conferences to discuss 'the problems of middle-aged males', 'professorial rest' instead of the perennial 'student unrest', would be short on resources, not only in the trivial sense of travel funds or funds to set up an organization, but also when it comes to finding people with time and opportunity to participate in such meetings *as a part of their job*.

All of this is difficult enough at the national level; it is even more difficult at the EC level. In no way does this imply that the 'problems' indicated will not be dealt with: but they will be handled by those on top, in a dominant position, with inadequate participation from the dominated side. Not even their views will be sufficiently articulated; so the stage is set for a technocratic and bureaucratic type of social engineering.

This will not last. Counterforces will be generated, organization lower down in society will take place, also at the Community level – as a measure of self-defense, starting with articulation that may sometimes take violent forms. And at this point one of the ironies of the European Community will become increasingly clear: the more forces in the EC countries strongly opposed to the centralism from Brussels organize and get into effective counter-positions, among other reasons to weaken the central powers of the European Community, the more will the EC grow in vitality. At the moment it is a vast superstructure with a European civil service approaching 10,000 persons (6,200 in the Commission, the secretariats of the Council and the Parliament, in the Court and in the European Investment Bank; 2,500 in the four Euratom research establishment).[13] This superstructure is on top of six nation-states where opposition to bureaucracy is at times very articulate.

But so far there has been practically speaking no opposition at all of a genuine transnational kind against the European Community as such

– and that is perhaps the major factor that makes the EC different from a superstate *as seen from the inside*. Clearly, it is still much closer to the con-federation of *patries* that has by and large been the French line, than to the supranational integration towards a superstate that has been articulated by the others. Essentially, it may well be the EC's antagonists who may be most effective in pushing the EC towards a superstate formation, for as they organize and transnationalize, EC authorities will also re-group on a firmer and more transnational basis. The day there is a massive demonstration of say, youth and workers from all member states rallying at Commission headquarters in Brussels, in front of the Berlaymount building at the Place Schuman, *and* this demonstration confronts a transnational European Community police force, for instance organized with that particular French CRS expertise – that day the European Community superstate will be a reality.

However, since our concern in this essay is mainly with the impact of the European Community on the outside world, the internal structure is not our major focus. The proposition 'the European Community is becoming a superstate' cannot be proven wrong by referring to some of the cumbersome mechanisms of decision-making and a high level of decentralization that is a part of the reality of the Brussels Eurocracy, as well as for the 188 million citizens found as of 1969 in the member states. It is in the relationship to the outside that the superstate aspect, and possibly also the superpower aspect, will become evident; for instance as the fourth corner in a square or rectangle that Brandt pointed to. A more adequate geometrical figure would actually be a *pentagon*, with Japan as the fifth corner – already alluded to by President Nixon in a speech July 1971, and worked into the plans for the reorganization of the British foreign service.

That brings us to the other axis: what will happen to *extension* in the future? This is not a question of whether the Six will become the Ten; we are thinking beyond that debate. For the sake of the argument let us imagine that as of 1 January 1973 the European Community has ten members; for even if it has only eight or nine the other remaining two or one will probably be so strongly tied to the EC that for all practical purposes they can be considered members. Whether it is an advantage to be only on the receiving side of Brussels decision-making or also on the sending side will depend on whether one views full membership as sharing of decisions that mainly are good, or decisions that also can be bad. In the latter case sharing decision-making may also become sharing guilt. This seems to be the Swedish position.

The Treaty of Rome clearly states that only European states can become members. This gives a potential membership of 30 European states, leaving out the rest of the world. However, at least two simple principles cut down the number of potential future members to far below 20.

First, there is the underlying principle of basic *structural similarity* in the economic and political sphere. The European Community has a number of institutions, and it would be meaningless for a state to join unless it would have a structure where these institutions could plug in. A continental European plug for electrical apparatus does not fit a British socket, as any traveller will know, nor will it fit in a country where there is no electricity at all. In short, the *level of technical-economic development* must not be too dissimilar, and the *institutional political framework* must exhibit basically the same structure. There must be 'opposite numbers', institutions to at least most of the things organized by the Community so far; otherwise membership would be meaningless. Since the Community has not yet come quite so far in its integration process, this means one out of two: either an applicant country must be relatively similar in advance, or it has to adjust. The EC cannot be expected to adjust in any significant respect – not only because of its size, but also because of the complexity of its confederate structure.

The second principle for limiting the number of potential members is, of course, *ideological* (as opposed to structural) *similarity*. Thus, of the two founding members, France and Germany, both were NATO countries and ex-colonial powers; of the Six, all are NATO countries, and five (the exception being the smallest member, Luxembourg) ex-colonial powers; of the Ten, nine are NATO countries (Ireland being the only exception), and six are ex-colonial powers (Ireland and Norway being clear exceptions from this, Denmark somewhat less clear).

This certainly indicates the political profile, but if the EC were mainly concerned with economic affairs one might say that NATO is an outside activity of most of the member states, and that the status as *ex*-colonial power is exactly that, something belonging to the past. The difficulty is that the EC is more than an economic organization. In the field of foreign policy this becomes particularly clear in the Davignon Report with its drive for foreign policy harmonization.

Even if this had not been the case it is quite clear that the EC cannot be said to be politically neutral. It is based on a certain type of economic relationship to the rest of the world, to be explored in chapter 3, that induces a structure with very particular political consequences. Since it

27

produces dependency relations, reactions in other countries are bound to occur, to accumulate, and sooner or later to taken on sharper and sharper political consequences. Nothing social is neutral in its consequences, and at the giant level even less so – for which reason membership is clearly not an act of political innocence.

The consequence of these two principles of structural (economic and political) similarity and non-neutralitiy (to use an understatement) are easily found by anyone wanting to scan the European scene for potential members of the Community.

First, the Warsaw Treaty Organization countries, and Albania, are of course excluded, for both reasons. The absence of structural similarity is clear enough: there is neither a mildly centralized market economy, nor a parliamentary democracy. Political alignment there is, but with the opposite side. That excludes eight countries; the number of potential candidates is now down to twelve.

Second, there are the non-aligned countries in the middle of Europe: Sweden and Finland in the North, Switzerland and Austria in the Center, Yugoslavia to the South. With the exception of Yugoslavia, all four could fit from the point of view of structural similarity, since both economic and political institutions are largely the same – as evidenced by the fact that they are together with the Six, or with the Ten for that matter, in the Council of Europe. But non-alignment is incompatible with non-neutrality, whether that non-alignment is voluntarily self-imposed or imposed from the outside. That excludes five more countries, and the number of possible candidates for full membership is now down to seven. But it should be added that so close forms of association may develop (with Sweden, Switzerland, Austria) that any political virginity becomes purely technical.

Third, the three island countries in Europe: Iceland to the North, and Malta and Cyprus in the Mediterranean. All might offer some difficulties from the point of view of economic similarity. Iceland, for instance, has a high standard of living, but its economy is so much based on fishing that it has relatively few of the institutions of a modern industrialized society. The political similarity should offer no particular problem, however. But all three of them seem increasingly to adapt a non-aligned stand with a certain anti-Western admixture, and however close their association with the EC may become in the future we doubt that they will become full members. So, if this excludes three more, the number of possible candidates is now down to four.

These are the four countries that we would see as candidates for ex-

tension of the European Community: Turkey, Greece, Spain, Portugal. With these countries entering, the Ten will become the Fourteen. Although there is a marginal chance that some countries in the second and third categories above might join sooner or later, we think this is likely to be the maximum number in the foreseeable future *because at that time the European Community will start producing a polarization that will sharpen the cleavage between it and the rest of the world.*

Concretely, what would be the circumstances accompanying membership for these four Southern European countries?

Ideological alignment presents no essential problem in this connection: three are already NATO members, and the only exception, Spain, is for all practical purposes a member of the Western alliance. Three are ex-colonial powers, Greece being the only exception. In fact, if they were to become members, the political configuration so clear in the EC from the very beginning would merely be completed: of the thirteen European NATO members, twelve would be in (Iceland being the only exception, and by that time Iceland would probably already have a long history of non-NATO membership) with Ireland and Spain being the only non-members. Moreover, all countries with a colonial tradition in Europe outside Russia would be included, nine altogether. The latter is rather important, for if we add together the territories once included in the British Empire, the French Communauté, the Spanish, Portuguese and Italian empires, the Belgian and Dutch colonial possessions, the Turkish Ottoman empire and the impact of German colonialism (in Eastern Europe more than in Africa, Asia, and Oceania) very few parts of the world are untouched. In fact, the rest of the world would include almost only China and Japan. With some very minor exceptions Western Europe was spinning its net of dependency relations and extending its bloody paths of colonization all over the world. The world was, indeed, Eurocentric; and Europe did, indeed, have its center in the West!

Thus, the major reason why we believe that the Ten will become the Fourteen derives from the assumption that the European Community is born out of social inertia, as an effort to turn history backwards and give rebirth to the old world structure, although in the trappings of the last third of the twentieth century.

Even if there is no difficulty with political alignment, the factor of similarity rules out immediate membership for the four. With the criteria currently employed by the Community Turkey would appear ruled out because of low level of technical-economic development, whereas Spain would be ruled out because of the absence of parliamentary democracy and certain human rights. Portugal and Greece may be ruled out for both reasons.

Although Turkey and Greece are only in the § 238 waiting room (Greece with its permission to stay there temporarily suspended), and although Spain and Portugal at the moment can only aspire to the ante-room of the waiting room (trade agreement according to § 113), we nevertheless believe this process may become a relatively quick one.[14] There is no doubt that all four would very much like to become members. This is, for instance, a major platform in the policy of the present Portuguese leadership, partly dictated by economic weakness, but certainly also by a feeling of political insecurity. In all four countries regimes are challenged in a very basic way; in all four countries some type of revolution is a possibility that cannot be ruled out.

To be linked to the European Community and be gradually absorbed into it is not a guarantee against political upheaval, but it may serve as a protective mechanism. First of all, if a small country joins a big community this will serve as a drainage of political energy. The traditional sources of political ferment – exploited workers and frustrated intellectuals – will find refuge abroad, within the confines of the large community. This will work as a defense against extremism from the left, *and* from the right. Not only are the forces of opposition weakened: the forces in position are also strengthened because they become less vulnerable when resources can flow into them from the outside because of their strong ties to the Community.

Our thesis is therefore that the powers-that-be in these four countries, all occupying positions at various places on the fascist end of the political spectrum, will find it in their interest to trade some measures of parliamentary democracy, human rights, and individual liberties for EC membership. The dilemma all four are confronting might be formulated as follows: what is the minimum requirement that would make us acceptable to the European Community, and what is the maximum relaxation in the direction of more liberal regimes we can permit before a chain-reaction ending in some kind of revolution may be unleashed? These minima and maxima are highly subjective estimates, and the condition for a clear 'go ahead' is that the maximum be located above the minimum. But is it? That depends on the requirements of the EC. To take only one variable, censorship: there is considerable difference between the Ten and the other Four. It will take time for these regimes to sort this out, to smoothen a transition towards some type of political pluralism –

and it would be strange if the regimes should survive in all four. For those who see liberal, parliamentary democracy as the highest achievement human society has reached so far, this will be taken as a sign of the healthy impact of the European Community. Most might agree that the regimes in the Four are inferior to the typical European Community society; but it is also highly likely that once these Four are inside, there will be a locking-in effect: the EC giant will extend its pattern to the most remote corner and be extremely hard to change anywhere.

For Portugal this is particularly dramatic, since there will be one more condition under the general heading of similarity: *Portugal has to shed her colonies.* The colonial war has to be brought to an end, and our hypothesis is that this is a low price to pay for EC membership. In what Portuguese authorities have so far said concerning contact with the European Community there is no longer any talk of Portugal overseas; it is only European Portugal. The whole rationale for Portugal's stand in connection with the three possessions in Africa may disappear like mist before the sun, when Lisbon turns towards Brussels.

On the other hand, just as a colonial power becomes an ex-colonial power, colonialism becomes neo-colonialism. But the pattern, once Portugal is inside the Community, would have to be *shared* neo-colonialism: a status for Angola/Moçambique/Guinea-Bissau similar to that obtained for the Yaoundé states. It is therefore highly likely that trilateral negotiations will be started (or have already gone on for some time) between the EC, Portugal, and the liberation movements as to whether the liberation movements would be willing to accept some kind of Yaoundé status for their territories. In that case the EC might be willing to grant membership to Portugal, and Portugal on her side would withdraw political and military control and just become one of the EC countries. There are some indications that this trilateral deal might not work, for the liberation movements in the Portuguese territories are of an older generation than those who fought in the 1950s and early 1960s against the British and the French. They know more as to what may happen afterwards, they have lived in exile in those countries and may have drawn the conclusion. For this reason the Portuguese case for full membership may be a more dubious one than the other three, but not at all excluded.[15]

So this is the picture we consider likely by 1980: up to Fourteen member states, almost all of European NATO and colonial Europe inside. These will be so well integrated that *superstate* is the correct term, although of a slightly new kind.

But will it be a *superpower?* For that we have to turn to an analysis of the concept of power. The reader who finds that too abstract is recommended to proceed straight to chapters 4 and 5, where the general ideas of chapter 3 will be applied to the EC in a more general way; and to chapters 6 and 7, where they will be applied to Third World countries and to the socialist countries in a more specific manner. After that the reader might like to return to chapter 3 for a more theoretical perspective.

Chapter 3.
On power in general

'Power' is the most basic and richest concept in political science. It can be sliced, sub-divided almost any number of ways. When social scientists do this it may look like unnecessary hairsplitting. But it is more like cutting a many-faceted diamond: each cut brings out a new facet, a new insight. So let us try, even if power has to be cut and sliced several ways. The European Community is a complex as well as big entity, and simply saying that it is 'powerful', and in all probability is becoming more so, is not very helpful. For a complex entity on the world scene, a complex power concept is needed — particularly if we are to show that the power of the European Community may rapidly exceed that of the Soviet Union and even of the United States with regard to many facets of the power-diamond currently being cut in Brussels.

The *first* distinction[1] is between power-over-others and power-over-oneself. Usually people mean the former when they say 'power': the idea being that the more power X has over Y, the less does Y have over X, the sum being constant. 'Balance of power' is what obtains when that sum is divided equally. However, balance of power is not the only approach to countervailing power. There is also 'autonomy', which can be seen as power-over-oneself, the ability to set goals that are one's own, not goals one has been brainwashed into by others, *and* to pursue them. A person, or a nation, may be lacking in power-over-itself not only because it is the object of the power-over-others — but also for lack of internal development, of maturation into autonomy.

This is extremely important, because one way Y may counteract the power coming from X is by having more power over himself — more autonomy. To see this, it is fruitful to follow many political scientists in making a *second* distinction:[2] between three *power channels,* three *types* of power over others: ideological, remunerative, and punitive.

Ideological power is the power of ideas. Remunerative power is the power of having goods to offer, a 'quid' in return for a 'quo'. Punitive power is the power of having 'bads' to offer, destruction; also called force, violence. In the first case, one is powerful because the power-sender's ideas penetrate and shape the will of the power-recipient. In the second case, one is powerful because one has a carrot to offer in return for a

33

service; salary for work, beads for a signature on a scrap of paper, giving away a country or two, tractors for oil. In the third case, one is powerful because one has a big stick ready if the object does not comply so that one can destroy him or his property.

In the power game of nations, ideological power comes through Culture, remunerative power through trade and the Economy in general, while punitive power is the professional domain of the Military. The co-ordination of all this is called Politics, whether among men or among nations. Some nations specialize in persuasion through the normative force of their ideology, other nations in bargains through the goods they can offer, still others deal only in force or the threat of force. Many try all three, or would like to be able to use all three. To this, how-ever, we should add Communication: ideas, goods, and bads have to be communicated or transported. There have to be carriers of all kinds, not only for weapons. A radio-sender and a tele-satellite are for Culture what super-bombers and ICBMs are for the Military.

How, then, is it possible for a country or a person to resist the power pressure to which we are all exposed every day, for instance by complying in the principles and the details of our daily work lest we lose our salary? There are, as indicated above, two alternatives open.

First, our actor can try to balance the power pressure impinging upon him by directing at least equal power in the opposite direction, in all three channels. He can also have strong ideas; he can also have goods that are indispensable for the other party; and he can have the same amount of, or even more, bads, means of destruction at his disposal. The latter is usually known as the *military balance,* but it is only one special case of a more general equation – the general balance of power. A *balance of dependence* is perhaps even more important, since exchange of goods is more typical of human affairs than exchange of bads, with trade union formation being one typical strategy. *Balance of ideas* in a pluralistic, competitive idea-market (like what parliamentary democracies try to approximate) is by no means unknown. When one party has monopoly on idea-propagation, has monopoly on the goods and on the bads, and in addition monopoly on means of communication, then this party is powerful indeed – at least it would appear so.

This is where the second alternative, the second way of opposing power, enters the picture. A person, a people, a nation, or a state may withstand the power directed from the outside not by directing counter-power in the opposite direction, but by developing more power-over-itself. This power can be compared to immunization against bacteria: one

34

does not try to destroy the bacteria, but makes oneself immune to their destructive impact. Similarly, one can try to make oneself immune to power from others so that this power does not reach its target. One refuses to be a power-*receiver*.

Thus, for ideological power to work, some kind of basic *submissiveness* to the power-wielder is presupposed – otherwise his ideas would find no resonance. Substitute for that type of submissiveness a basic identification with oneself, or *self-respect*, and it can no longer be taken for granted that the ideas of others are superior to one's own, regardless of how cleverly propaganda and manipulation are employed. Similarly, remunerative power presupposes an element of *dependence:* only if one *needs* the goods offered will one extend the *quid* in return for the other party's *quo*. Substitute for that dependency relation the ability to make do with one's own resources or *self-sufficiency,* and remunerative power can no longer reach its target. Finally: punitive power presupposes *fear,* of losing what one *has,* even losing what one *is*. Without fear, threats of force, even force itself, will not be effective. Substitute for that fear an element of *fearlessness* – and even punitive power, force and the threat of force, can largely be resisted.

Combining self-respect, self-sufficiency, and fearlessness, we get some insight in the anatomy of *autonomy,* or power over oneself. A truly autonomous person or nation is no longer a power-receiver, as power can no longer reach him. We mention this not so much because it contributes to understanding the European Community – the EC is already largely autonomous and ready to exercise various kinds of power over others – *but to understand why the EC can exercise so much power.* Power over others can only be exercised in a medium of submissiveness, dependence, and fear. We shall use these three as guides in understanding where and how the Community is operating.

So far we have said something about how power operates when it does work, and how it can be counteracted. Very often the stronger the power exercised, the stronger the immunization – which is why dictatorship and tyranny only work up to a certain point. Power has to be subtle to operate, so subtle that it does not stimulate counter-power of either kind. Counter-power in the sense of anti-power is what the oppressor prefers, because he can trace it and destroy it. But counter-power in the form of autonomy is more difficult to destroy because it is much more located inside the mind of the person and the culture of the nation.

What is the *source* of power? Even if it operates through those three channels, where does it come from? This leads to a *third* and final dis-

35

tinction, between three sources (as opposed to channels) of power, here in the sense of power-over-others:[3]

> power deriving from something one *is;*
> power deriving from something one *has;*
> power deriving from *position in a structure.*

For persons one often talks about 'a commanding personality' (something he 'is') as opposed to the person's buying power (something he 'has'). Both of these are properties of the person. Power derives from *differences* in their distribution: one has more than others. But when a switchboard operator has power because she has so much information, this is because she occupies a *position* in a structure. The structure is asymmetric with regard to power, and she occupies a position with high power potential. Differential power is built into the structure and through the structure accrues to the individuals.

Correspondingly for nations: a nation *is* rich in natural resources, it *has* much weaponry, and it is located centrally in the world trade structure. However, the distinction between what a nation is and what it has is not a very clearcut one, so we shall join the two together under the term 'resources' and speak of *resource power,* or *difference power.* The third category, the power that derives from position in a structure more than from what the nation is or has, we shall call *structural power* or *relation power.* This is fundamental, because it is on the latter that the European Community is particularly strong, even much more so than the United States. In general this is also the more important dimension.

We now need to spell out the components of resource power and structural power in more everyday terms – in terms of the things newspapers talk about every day. However, in doing so, an important difference between the two kinds of power will become apparent. Since the former belongs more to liberal power theory, and the latter more to marxist power theory (but not entirely so) – and the autonomy approach (the 'power-over-oneself') belongs more to gandhian power theory – societies and cultures will be biased in favor of one of these three. The typical Western newspaper reader is more accustomed to thinking in terms of resource power, in terms of what X has in excess of what Y has. The excess, or the 'balance' (as defined in book-keeping terms more than in the terms of mechanics) is the edge X has over Y.[4] To think in terms of structural power is to think in terms to which Western journalists are not attuned, and to which they, consequently, pay very little attention. This is even more true for the autonomy approach.

36

To start with *resource power:* its major types follow readily from what has already been developed in this mini-theory of power. It is a question of possessing the instruments of ideological, remunerative, and punitive power, in excess of what others have. More concretely, consider this list:

Ideological power:	Ideology
	Culture
	Language
Remunerative power:	Population (labor)
	Land (area)
	Capital (GNP)
Punitive power:	Military expenditure
	Military hardware
	Military software

Ideology and culture are abstract expressions of how things should be. Culture being the wider term, ideology can be defined as political culture, defining what social relations in general – and power relations in particular – should be. Thus, ideology is like a map of the political landscape, not only outlining the Promised Land, but also indicating the paths to that Land from present circumstances. Culture in general is broader than art: it also defines life-cycles, the things we use in daily life, and so on. And language, not only common, spoken and written language, but other forms of symbolic communication – pictograms, mathematics, technical languages – serves to shape images of things that are and things that might be. This comes in addition to communication.

Under *remunerative* power we have listed the three classical production factors – population, land, capital. All three should be seen as potentials. How much can really be used to produce goods, and how much of the goods can be used to entice others to behave in certain ways obviously depend on too many factors to be listed. But as potentials, with some specifications, they can never be ignored in any analysis.

Under *punitive* power we have distinguished between three aspects of 'bads': the investment in the military sector, and the traditional expressions of military readiness in terms of military hardware (arms) and military software (manpower). The list of goods is unsatisfactory: at most it gives some ideas about the potential of destructive power available. It does not tell to what extent the military hardware is *targeted,* deployed and ready for action. Nor does it say to what extent the military software is *mobilized* – equipped with a *consciousness* that serves as a motivation to destroy and defend (often called 'morale'), and *organized* such that individual readiness can be maximally utilized at the collective level, whether in the form of small commando/guerrilla groups or conventional army formations.

Unfortunately, the only precise way of knowing what the balance of power in the three channels is, is to unleash it. Only by making contact can the workings of electric energy through a potential difference (voltage) be studied concretely. If the channels can be compared with tubes and the power potentials with water reservoirs, then both powers will have to turn on the faucets and let the power flow through the channels to see which one is stronger. For punitive power, this process is called a war (or in softer expressions, an armed confrontation, even an open conflict); for remunerative power, it takes the form of economic competition, for instance with cross-investment or competitive investment in third countries; and for ideological power, it takes the form of competition for the minds of men. All these processes generate new forms of power and anti-power. They may also stimulate autonomy, in processes so complicated that it may be futile to try to predict the outcome. On the other hand, to unleash the power flow may be catastrophic, for which reason some comparisons are carried out at the more formal level of power stock-taking alone, letting statistics decide the competition.[5]

Let us then turn to *structural power* – a more difficult, but at least equally important subject for the analysis of the European Community. Again, we should emphasize that structural power is not something found inside the most powerful country, or not found inside the less powerful one. Structural power is more abstract – although highly concrete in its consequences! It is built into the structure in which the two countries are placed; and it would apply to all other countries placed in the same positions, in the same relation to each other, much the way a president has power deriving from his position in the national power structure, as his predecessor had before him and his successor will have after him. In addition to that structural power comes, then, the personal element.

We shall distinguish between three aspects of structural power: *exploitation, fragmentation,* and *penetration.*[6]

1) *Exploitation* has to do with the direct exchange relation between two countries. Broadly speaking, there is exploitation if one country gets much more out of the exchange than does the other. The simplest case is the one-sided 'exchange' such as theft or the unrequited gift (the normal gift is usually an exchange over time, I give you a birthday present today and you will give me when my birthday comes up). The next step

38

is cheating: A gives some beads to B in return for land, a highly un-equal exchange by most assumptions.

This must be seen in the light of a more general framework of analysis not to be spelt out in detail here. Such an analysis might use exchange of economic goods as a point of departure, and then proceed to political, military, and cultural exchanges. The economic field is most easily anal-ysed because both liberal and marxist thinking have been focussing on it, so that more conceptualization has been developed and more data exist, relatively readily available.

Basic would be the concept of an economic cycle. Any economic cycle may be seen as originating in Nature and terminating in Nature. It starts with the extraction of some kind of raw material from Nature (for instance oxygen for breathing), it ends with waste products being returned to Nature. But between Nature and Nature the economic cycle passes such points as processing and consumption. Administration, finance, and research are involved; transportation comes into the picture, and so on.[7]

Although an economic cycle can be set up in many different ways, it still makes sense to analyze its impact on Nature and Man. Its impact on the former is becoming more clear nowadays than perhaps ever be-fore: a combination of depletion (due to extraction) and pollution (partly due to the waste from processing, partly due to the waste from consump-tion). Nature is a losing party in this type of economic cycle, and since it cannot speak for itself (except with such occasional reactions as ero-sion, disruption of ecological balances, perhaps an earthquake now and then) its spokesmen have to be those who are engaged in processing and consumption etc. These are thus persons with vested interests in the *status quo* of the cycle.

The impact of the economic cycle on Man can be positive, as when man is adequately fed and clad and sheltered; it can be negative as when the result is alienation from oneself and from others, a feeling of power-lessness, weakened health due to pollution, etc. Furthermore, it can be positive as when participation in the cycle is stimulating, challenging, de-veloping; it can be negative as when participation is degrading, boring, routine activity with no challenge whatsoever.[8]

Exploitation is concerned with the total impact of participation in an economic cycle on the various groups of people participating in it. Gener-ally, exploitation takes place when the sum total of costs and benefits for the various groups differs so that some groups get much more out of it than others. That does not mean that those deriving least benefits actu-ally incur more costs than benefits: this was the case for slaves, but not necessarily the case in general for the most exploited groups in a modern economic cycle. But exploitation is defined in *relative* terms, rather than absolute ones. When discrepancies between those who get most and those who get least are growing or remain constant, we would talk about exploitation. We would also say that the groups between which the gap is found are coupled together such that there is disharmony between their interests.

Today this can take very many forms. A rich country can throw an economic cycle around the world, with Nature, labor-intensive Production and most of the Consumption located in poor countries, and administration, finance, and research in rich countries. All challenging tasks are thus monopolized by the rich countries, all the routine tasks by the poor countries – including the depletion and pollution of Nature. Since the organization most fit to organize an economic cycle this way will by definition be a multinational corporation, with built-in division of labor and with a clear geographical address, an analysis of exploitation today will necessarily have as one of its major foci the analysis of the multinational corporation. But we should also remember that this is only one of many forms. What all these forms have in common is that they are *interaction-induced differences*. The problem is not just that one happens to be strong and the other weak; one rich, the other poor; one full of initiative, the other apathetic. Such differences may always arise, and may or may not be exploited as resource power. But in structural power these differences arise from the way the structure, more particularly the division of labor in the economic cycle itself, is set up. *For this reason one cannot fight against exploitation simply by redistributing resources*. The fight against exploitation is a fight for the change of the total structure, and particularly of those economic cycles that induce exploitation. This can take two forms: restructuring them so that the costs and benefits are more equally distributed, or simply cutting them.

Vital to the theory of economic cycles and their differential impacts on the countries and groups of people they pass through is the theory of *spin-off effects* from production. The general idea is that participation in a production process in the sense of *processing* has many side effects in addition to the *form* given to the raw materials, the *value* added to them, and the *man-hours* that go into this work. There are *subsidiary economic effects*, because processing sidelines are established, feeding into the main processing channels. There can be *military benefits*, as when production technology for civilian purposes can easily be converted into production technology for means of destruction (the person who knows how to make

40

a tractor can also easily learn how to make a tank; the person who only participates in extracting oil will know neither). There can be *communication benefits*, because means of communication can come as important byproducts. In the modern world, the *quantity* of communication and transport is a technological question in the hands of those who dominate technology. *Quality* of communication has to do with culture and with less technically dominated forms of development – but it counts less in a quantity-oriented world.

Then, the most obvious of all spin-off effects: to process is to give form; to give form is to impart Culture on Nature: hence, to process *may* also be to develop new cultures. We emphasize the word 'may', for processing can be ritualized and standardized to a point where no development of new forms is ever included. This is immensely important today where factories are increasingly placed in the poor part of the world, reserving the knowledge and research development benefits portion of the economic cycles for the rich (read: autonomous) parts. To make transistors according to a blueprint developed elsewhere is not by itself more of a challenge than to extract oil.

This is closely related to the types of specialists called for at various points and sections in the economic cycles. Research calls for specialists in *making,* for scientists and engineers; extraction of raw material calls for specialists in *having,* for lawyers.[9] For this reason, engineers, technicians, and scientists will gravitate towards the research and advanced processing sections of the cycle; lawyers towards the extraction and distribution sections. This process is often referred to as brain-drain.

Obviously, more skill and education are needed to carry out processing than to carry out extraction. In fact extraction can often be carried out in a highly capital intensive way even obviating the need for specialized labor. In Chile, only 3 % of the labor stock is engaged in copper, in Venezuela only 5 % in oil – because of high levels of automation combined with low levels of processing.

Of the less tangible spin-off effects are the differential impact on social structure, the psychological effects and summarizing all of it: the effects on the political position in world structure. The essential dividing line here is not between processing and extraction, between producing manufactured goods and raw materials. It is between challenge, exploration and new discoveries on the one hand, and standardization, routinization on the other; between high and low uncertainty, to speak in information-theoretical terms. As mentioned: economic cycles can be made to circle the world in such a way that challenge is monopolized by the countries in

41

the Center and the routines handed out to the countries in the Periphery. *But this means that the Center gets the power to define Culture for the Periphery,* because only the Center is at the forefront of cultural events with this type of division of labor.

All these effects can be traced concretely in the structure of the world today, and more can certainly be added. The total picture makes exploitation much more than a question of expropriation and appropriation of monetizable surplus value. To discuss it solely in terms of capital flows from Center to Periphery and back again – for instance, concluding that for each $ 1 the US invests in the developing countries over a 20 year period, it gets back $ 2.7 (in recent years much more)[10] is extremely significant. However, it may also miss the point. Exploitation is a far more ramified concept, and for that reason too important to be left to economists alone – whether of the liberal or the marxist persuasion.

2) *Fragmentation* is the age-old adage of all empire-builders, *divide et impera,* divide and rule. It is also a many-sided idea practiced in various ways through the ages, and it merits spelling out. The general principle is clear: it is a method that one party can use to dominate several parties. One government can dominate sections of the population, or one country can dominate several other countries, by splitting them off from each other. There are several ways of obtaining this.

The *first* method is to make sure that the dominated countries do not have too much direct, *horizontal* contact among themselves, particularly not economic interaction, trade. This interaction void may be brought about by geographical distance (as with the British Empire) or by stimulating conflict among the dominated parties (as in India, before, under and after the Empire). According to this principle, contact with the outside world should be vertical, towards the Center, rather than horizontal, among the Periphery countries. More particularly, the dominated countries should not be given the chance to build any *organization* around a pattern of interaction; or any such organization should be by-passed. Contact from Center to Periphery should be direct. 'Trade unions' of any kind among the underdogs should not be respected. Deal with workers individually, not with the troublemakers!

The *second* method is to make sure that *multilateral* contact involving the dominant and more than one of the dominated is avoided. The dominated parties should be dealt with one at a time. More particularly, no egalitarian multilateral *organization* of dominator with dominated is compatible with fragmentation. Added to the first aspect, this means the dominating power is free to make one deal with one dominated person

42

or country and quite another deal with another – pitting them against each other, holding out small favors – because they have so little to do with each other that they cannot come together to compare, and because one of them is not witnessing how the other is dealt with by the Center – except, perhaps, on some ceremonial occasion. In practice this means once more that there is a Center which controls what goes on because the Periphery is split. There is no context in which they act in a fully egalitarian way and in full visibility of each other. Periphery parties are admitted only individually, never jointly, to be with the Center. In this sense the Center is first class, the Periphery second class.

There is a *third* method of fragmentation which involves the outside world. Here the principles are equally clear: as little direct contact for the dominated countries with the outside world as possible! Just as contact among them should ideally pass through the Center, contact with the outside world – whether with other dominated or other dominating powers – should also pass through the Center. Both types of direct contact may be dangerous: contact with other dominated countries may lay the basis for organization of the world proletariat; contact with other dominating countries may give to the latter the bridgeheads they need to change power relations. In fact, a gentleman's agreement, the 'sphere of influence' theory, exists to the effect that 'if you stay off my satellites, I'll stay off yours!' But dominating countries reserve for themselves the right to deal with each other that they deny their underdogs.

These three aspects of the fragmentation approach are very effective if really enacted. Their essential function in the total structure is to protect exploitation, essentially by making it impossible for the exploited to organize, to join together – even making it impossible for the exploited to see clearly the structure in which they are embedded. These aspects counteract even consciousness-formation. Together they form, in their nakedness, a *feudal structure:* this particular way of building up social relations was characteric of Europe, and most other parts of the world, in feudal times.

3) The last, perhaps most significant, aspect of structural power is *penetration*. By this we mean penetration of the dominant country *into* the countries to be dominated. So far nations have been treated like billiard balls in our approach to structural power. The one may exploit the other, one may split the others and even be successful in pitting them against each other; but in a sense this is still at the superficial level of inter-state relations. Structural power really becomes operational when one nation gets under the skin of the other so that it is able to form and

shape the inside of that nation. This is penetration, which can take on a number of forms. We may distinguish between subversion, which is some type of penetration from the bottom or periphery of the society; and 'superversion', which is penetration from the top. Our focus will be on the latter, and we shall distinguish between two aspects of this type of penetration.

The *first* aspect concerns the relationship between the elites in the dominating and the dominated country. The latter serves as a bridge-head for the elite in the Center nation: as a recipient of its ideas, its patterns, of the economic cycles that emanate from the Center, etc. For this to happen, there has to be a harmony of interest between them. The two have to have roughly the same standard of living, and they have to be coupled together such that they share good days and bad days; what is good for one will be good for the other, and so on. In the long run the elite in the Center cannot hand out to the elite in the Periphery a similar standard of living, while at the same time taxing them without giving them representation in the bodies of policy-making. Both London and Madrid learnt this around the turn of the 18th century. In fact, the system can be maintained only if the elites are equivalent on a great many dimensions. This is where international organizations enter as the great equalifiers, not of countries (as people who confuse governments with nations seem to think), but of governmental delegations, of elites. The highly formal equality at this level is what elites in the Periphery often ask for, and this is also where they often stop asking for more.

The *second* aspect of penetration is more subtle. In both countries, dominating and dominated alike, there is some basic inequality built into the structure – otherwise we could not speak of elites or centers. There is inequality built into both countries: and *this inequality is in itself distributed in an inegalitarian manner.*[11] There is much more inequality in the Periphery than in the Center. Statistically this is one of the basic factors about the world community of nations: the higher the GNP per capita, as one expression of how rich a country is, the lower the level of inequality. Resources of various kinds are better distributed in the rich countries than in the poor, to put it simply. If this were not the case, there would be no cheap labor to exploit in the poor countries, for the assumption is that the elites are by and large at the same level (with the possible exception that some of the richest people in the world seem to live in some of the poorest countries).

Combined, these two aspects make up 'penetration'. This is above all a way in which the elite in the dominating country penetrates the elite of the dominated country; but since there is less inequality in the Center, it often takes the form of the total country on the top penetrating the country at the bottom, at its very center, at its top elite level. In recent years we have seen US workers supporting the US wars in Indochina, French workers supporting the French wars in Indochina and Algeria, British workers supporting British colonialism, Dutch workers supporting the Dutch colonialism – and so on. In this sense, penetration also becomes a strategy of fragmentation: it keeps the two peripheries apart by tying one of them far more closely to the combined world upper class than the other. In everyday terms, and in politically highly meaningful language: where does the loyalty of the European working class lie – with the European upper classes, or with the world proletariat? Much of the immediate future of the European Community depends on the answer to that question, to be explored further in chapter 10.

Now let us take a look at this forceful combination: exploitation + fragmentation + penetration. One word for this combination is *imperialism:* a country rules over one or several others through a small elite which serves as a bridgehead for the politics of exploitation, protected by a policy of fragmentation. Another word that will also be used in the following is *dominance,* to focus attention on the power aspect.

How, then, does a structure of dominance serve as an instrument of power? Obviously this is some type of structural power, but how does it serve as a medium for the three channels of power? How does it build up identification, dependence, and fear – as opposed to self-respect, self-sufficiency, and fearlessness?

Few questions in power theory are more easily answered, because it looks as if a structure of dominance, more than anything else, is precisely *the* way of making other countries susceptible to one's own power. The basic point is to leave the dominated countries with no alternative, to leave them like lonely satellites hanging from the end of the ropes extended from the center in the Center to the center in the Periphery, trying to make this rope look like an umbilical cord. Along this line, goods are supplied that become essential – if not for the whole country at least for the elite, and more particularly essential if that elite is to maintain the living conditions that make them serve as a bridgehead. And 'bads' are delivered plentifully if the system is threatened.

The basic key to the structure of dominance and its operation is *dependency.* Dependency in this context means that the Center supplies something that the Periphery (1) thinks is indispensable, and (2) thinks it cannot obtain elsewhere. And this is highly related to identification:

45

the Periphery thinks these things are indispensable because it has been taught to think so, because it has adopted and adapted to the culture of the Center. Thus, once the gospel of technical-economic development according to the Western model is accepted, very much is immediately defined as indispensable.

There are in the world several Centers from which these things can be supplied, so the problem here is *on which terms*. The mechanisms are many: one particular Center nation can offer the necessities on the basis of grants, where the other only can offer them on the basis of (even very favorable) loans. One Center nation can offer them in such a way that the elite is guaranteed to remain in power, another Center nation can only offer them provided an anti-elite comes into power. One Center nation can throw in military and political advantages in the bargain, and so on. Perhaps more important than all of this is the cultural message which has preceded the supply of necessities and defined them as necessities according to a development model, and, possibly, and in addition the attractiveness of the Center nation on the elite in the Periphery. In this sense identification and dependency go hand-in-hand in maintaining the structure.

Structural power, or dominance as it is here called, serves in other words to erode autonomy. The dependent country can grow and grow – which usually means that its elite will grow and grow so as to keep up

Table I

	Dominance	Equality
Exploitation		
1. Division of labor	vertical, exploitative	horizontal, equitable – or no interaction
Fragmentation		
2. Horizontal links	absent	present
Horizontal organization	absent	present
3. Multilateral links	absent	present
Multilateral organization	absent	present
4. Extra-bloc links	absent for periphery	present for all
Penetration		
5. Elite-elite relation	harmony, dependence	interdependence, or independence
6. Elite-masses relation	differential inequality	equal inequality, or no inequality

with the elite in the Center countries, and still never be able to offer anti-power or sufficient power-over-itself to withstand the pressure. All these mechanisms are complex; they are not so easily described statistically: *but they work.*

To gain perspective, let us now contrast this theory of dominance with a theory of *equality.* Dominance and equality are structures and they are each other's contradiction. One is meaningful only in the light of the other – not in any mystical hegelian sense, but concretely, that one is set up in response to the other, to avoid the other. Dominance is certainly not a step on the road to equality as the (neo)colonialist philosophy of paternalism and tutelage will have it. But equality may arise as a reaction to dominance.

Table I is one effort to define the two opposites, in terms of the three aspects of structural power (with sub-dimensions discussed above). On the left hand side of the Table the dominance structure described above is summarized, in its extreme form. In practice one could of course talk about degrees: horizontal links and organization, and multilateral links and organization, and extra-bloc links are almost never totally absent, but they can be present to a very low degree.

In the right-hand column is a structure of equality. Item for item, this is a negation of the corresponding link in the dominance structure. For vertical division of labor there is either horizontal division of labor with costs and benefits equally distributed, or no interaction at all. Links and organizations have been introduced to the point of saturating the total structure. As to the relationship between the elites there are, just as for division of labor, two models: one based on symmetric interdependence, the other based on total independence. And as for the elite-masses relations there are also two possibilities: inequality is equally distributed so there is no edge the Center nation can build on to split peripheries apart, or both nations have undergone some basic social change so there is no inequality at all. In this analysis, the last alternative will not be explored, however. Our focus is on international relations within the context of the nations found in the world today, and some measure of inequality seems to be present in all of them.

That concludes this mini-theory of power. Let us now turn to the European Community again, its resource power (chapter 4) and structural power (chapter 5).

Chapter 4.
The resource power of the
European Community

The time has now come to bring some data into the picture. Let us compare the European Community of Ten members, not only Six, relative to the other superpowers, particularly relative to the United States and the Soviet Union, to see if the EC is in the same class. The advantage is that we can now draw on the theory of power as a guide when it comes to know where to look, for what kind of data. Data are wanted that are relevant to politics, and the essence of politics is power. In short, we want data that will enable us to discuss the power at the disposal of the EC relative to the other big. In this chapter we shall deal with the concrete resources available to the Six and to the Ten; and in the next chapter, with structural power.

As usual we base ourselves on data given by the European Community,[1] and they are experts at producing tables and profiles comparing Europe at Six and Ten with the other big in the world. Unfortunately, statistics for China are missing, but there is sufficient basis for comparison with the US, the USSR, and Japan.

We start with the comparison given in the Fig. 2. The Ten are higher than the other three in population, second to the US in Gross National Product, behind in energy production (the imports of oil being the major dependency on the outside world), on top of all of them in steel output, but behind when it comes to computers.[2] All this is today fairly well-known; such comparisons are made very frequently.

Two of these variables are so important that more specific information should be given: *external trade,* and *computers in use.*

As to external trade, the EC has today 20 % of world trade, with the US as a good no. 2 with 18.5 %, whereas the UK has only 8.5 % and Japan 8 %. Extended to the Ten, the EC would command about one third of world trade, all the time excluding internal trade.[3] This means that the Ten together with the US and Japan would come not too far from two-thirds of the world trade, which would make for a very likely prediction: the OECD will increasingly become an economic triumvirate, practically speaking controlling world trade to the extent that the Big Three can agree.[4] In this case it is a triangle, for neither the USSR nor the People's Republic of China comes anywhere close to this order of magnitude. China's foreign trade is actually less than Norway's, and less than the foreign trade of Taiwan.

When it comes to computers, recent information seems to indicate that the US has 72,000, followed by the Federal Republic of Germany which has one-ninth of that, 8,000 computers. Then comes Japan with 5,000 and the USSR with 3,000.[5] Thus, in this field even the Ten still lag far behind, for which reason computer industry is given high priority within the Community. We should notice that these estimates of computers in use differ somewhat, but when it comes to the order of magnitude of the gap and the ranking of the nations they agree.

Let us then turn to the international comparisons given in Table II.

First come the three classical production factors: land in the form of area, labor in the form of population, and capital in the form of GNP. Actually, the only variable of much interest in that comparison is the very small area occupied by the Ten, and the even smaller area occupied by Japan. The prediction is almost inevitable: both the Ten and Japan will try to expand. How can they do this in an age where territorial conquest, in other words territorial growth, and far more than 5–10 %, is by and large not only outlawed (that was never so serious), but even outdated? What can Western Europe do today, when it has a surplus of population and capital, relative to its area?

There are several ways in which some compensation can be obtained for limited territory, even when the classical method is out.

For one thing, there is the typical 1950-and-onwards formula of *dependent territories*. These territories are not colonies: there is juridical, legal autonomy, but apart from that the colonial situation is more or less intact. These are areas of expansion, peripheries to which the center can look for new tasks, new investment, even for emigration possibilities. The associated states of the European Community are, of course, examples of what we have in mind. Each former colonial power has to operate jointly with other members of the Community, and they have to refrain from the use of military power and overt political power. But the other possibilities, economic and cultural power, and the skillful use of communication, are open to them. We have indicated above that the potential expansion area for a fully extended European Community with fourteen members will be practically speaking the whole world, with the

49

exception of the other Big – the US, the USSR, China, Japan – and possibly the areas that they control. We shall look more into this in chapters 5 and 6.

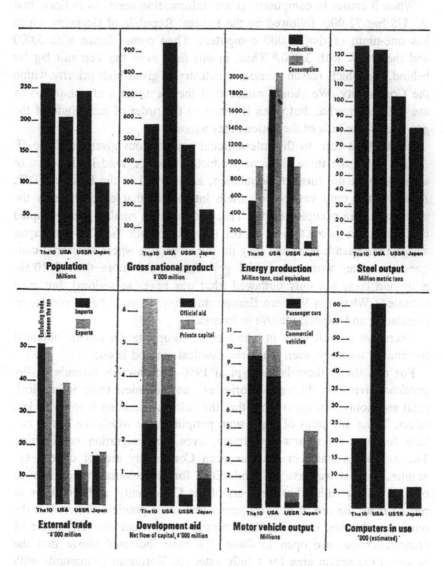

Fig. 2. *The resources of the EC (Ten), US, USSR & Japan*

Table II. *The resources of EC (Six and Ten), US, USSR and Japan*

	Six	Ten	US	USSR	Japan
Area (10^3 km^2)	1167.5	1847.3	9363.4	22,402.2	369.7
Pop. density per km^2	163	139	22	11	280
Population (1000)	189,787	257,242	205,395	244,000	103,540
G.N.P. ($1000 mio)	485.2	637.4	933.3	288	196.2
Reserves (10^6 $)	21,522	25,676	12,306	–	3,072
Imports (% World total)	30.3	41.0	13.7	4.0	6.5
Imports (% of GNP)	18.3	18.9	4.0	–	9.6
Exports (% World total)	31.8	41.2	15.5	4.6	6.9
Exports (% of GNP)	18.3	18.0	4.4	–	9.8
Primary energy total produc. (mill. metric tons, coal equivalent)	330,828	520,356	2,151,297	1,386,090	71,392
Sources of GDP (%)					
Agriculture	6.1	5.8	2.9	–	8.7
Industry (mining)	47.5	46.3	35.8	–	39.1
Other activities	46.4	47.9	61.3	–	52.2
Total gross production of electrical energy GWh	580,393	909,165	1,738,142	740,926	350,590
Crude steel production 10^3 t.	109,191	138,943	122,120	116,000	92,322
Merchant fleet 1.7.1970 10^3 tons gross	28,656	77,317	18,463	14,832	27,004
Rail transport Passenger/Kms (Mio)	120,711	155,748	10,568	266,300	181,921
Passenger cars per 10^3 pop.	220	218	432	7	85
TV sets per 10^3 pop.	216	231	299	127	214
Telephones per 10^3 pop.	185	203	567	50	194

There is also a second possibility, *the ocean floor*. The Geneva Convention of 1958 concerning the ocean floor defines the continental shelf as that part of the ocean floor adjacent to a coastal state and down to 200 meters, or beyond that, as far as exploration and exploitation are possible, only limited by the mid-line principle that forms the basis for the ocean floor borderline between two coastal states. So far the major practical test has been the case of the North Sea. *This case is interesting, for with the extension to the Ten, the North Sea will become an EC lake.* As is well known, most of the North Sea is very shallow, and the borderlines between the coastal states have by now been laid down firmly, especially after one problematic case was settled before the International

Court of Justice.[6] Right now it looks as if the oil from the North Sea is sufficient to cover the annual increase in demand within the Community.[7]

When it comes to the oceans in general, the interesting point is that the mid-line principle will give tremendous advantages to the former colonial powes, because several of them have left behind some tiny island possessions that may be highly useful in defining ocean floor territory. Thus, according to some calculations,[8] most of the South Atlantic will belong to England, the Central Atlantic to Portugal; to the North of that, Norway would be a major ocean floor master, whereas the Indian Ocean floor would largely go to France. In the Pacific, the US would lay claim to most, but there would also be some left for EC members. Since the pooling of EC member resources also largely means the pooling of their dependencies, this gives room, literally speaking, for enormous expansion unless some other international legal formula can be found and made to prevail, ruling out the use of such small islands to define ocean floor borderlines. The principle of the ocean floor as the common heritage of man must become the basic principle![9]

We mention all this because a rather safe hypothesis is that the Ten will be relentlessly looking for some compensatory mechanism for their smallness. The two possibilities mentioned are both very close at hand and at the same time compatible with current principles of non-aggression – abstention from the use of open force.

Proceeding down the list in the Table we see the Ten are a bit behind, relative to the US and Japan, on 'tertiarization': the tertiary sector ('other activities') as a source of GDP does not overshadow the secondary sector as in the US and Japan. But that will come, particularly since it is safe to predict that the EC will set up economic cycles around the world so as to put classical secondary sector activities in the dependencies, reserving for the Center research, finance and administration – as we indicated in the preceding chapter.

As to the rest of the Table it is interesting to note the highly leading position given to the Ten when it comes to merchant marine.[10] The Six are at the same level as Japan, and four times the US. The reason for this is simple: the UK contributes a merchant fleet of 26 million tons, and Norway 19 million tons.

Even if the Ten become a merchant fleet giant, they are somewhat behind in aviation, as in computers. In 1969, US airlines were responsible for 202 billion passenger kms, USSR is estimated at something between 50 and 100 billion (a somewhat rough estimate), whereas the Six had only 34 billion passenger kms and the Ten 55 billion.[11] With populations of the same magnitude, the reason is simple: the much shorter distances within the European Community. Small area pays off in terms of cheaper communication, but then there is also less challenge to develop really big capacity. Nor is it strange that the superpowers have bigger capacity for civil aviation, since the possibility of rapid convertibility for military transportation purposes is rather obvious. For the lesser powers this is less urgent. But that only leads to one more hypothesis: as the EC develops a military profile (not *qua* community, but as a European Defense Community inside NATO, as will be argued in chapter 8), it is reasonable to predict that civil aviation will suddenly undergo a rapid increase.

Thus, we have seen that the EC's capacity to disburse goods, in other words remunerative powers, is considerable. It is indeed of the same magnitude as the other big – more than sufficient to gain for the Ten a position on the top of the world power pyramid, whether that top is seen as a triangle, a rectangle, or a pentagon. What about the other two kinds of power: ideological power and punitive power?

As to the latter, the ability to distribute 'bads' around the world will be treated in chapter 8 because of its significance for the basic problem: will the Community not only become a superstate, but also a superpower? At this point we shall only say, in simple terms, regardless of how one adds up the military budget figures, the hardware figures and the software figures for the Ten, they come nowhere near the superpowers. The superpowers known so far, the US and the USSR, are just of a different order of magnitude. We shall argue later that this conclusion is arrived at because power is analyzed too simple-mindedly, in terms in resources and differences, too little in terms of structures and relations.

As to ideological power, the picture is more clear. Whether seen in terms of language, culture, or ideology, Western Europe has always remained the center of the world, the seat of three of the world's five 'world languages'; by definition the origin of the major cultures since these were the cultures of the imperialistic powers; and the cradle of the major ideologies of conservatism, liberalism, and marxism. If the leading culture is the culture of the leading powers this is by no means strange. That cultural hegemony has survived the decline of the European powers after World War II, and paves the way for the emerging EC superstate.

The only country seriously challenging this European cultural dominance is China. But China has been kept within bounds; unlike Western Europe it has not brought its culture around the world at swordpoint and together with its merchandise, nor did it ever really succumb to the Western ideological onslaught.

The political fission of the world after 1945, with new centers established in Washington and Moscow, was a political fission, with heavy economic and military components, but this was never really a cultural fission. The US has never been culturally attractive to Western Europe, nor has the USSR to Eastern Europe. Eastern Europeans have been looking to Western Europe as a source of culture, and Western Europe has all the time been looking to itself, except for technology and pop. It has been self-confident as the world's cultural center; that self-confidence has long had its apex in France, who seems to conceive of herself as the primordial source of cultural inspiration, as *la nation universelle*.

So far this tremendous cultural power has not been utilized by the European Community. But sooner or later it will. Sooner or later the cultural foreign agencies of the member states – the British Council, l'Alliance Française, the Goethe Institut, the Dante Alighieri institutions – will merge to constitute a cultural force that will make US and Soviet efforts look dwarfish and puny indeed. On the other hand, the more culture becomes institutionalized, the more does it look like an institution and the less like culture. For this reason the European Community may well just leave the cultural situation as it is, relying on its inner strength. However, that strength has to be communicated, either by importing people from the Community periphery on scholarships etc. and imbibing them with a cultural offer; or by sending it at very low prices to the extreme periphery – as through the satellite network Symphonie.

We stop here: from the outside, the Ten is a giant in everything except computers, energy supply, area, and military affairs. Computers: that will be taken care of, although it will not be easy. Energy: North Sea oil and nuclear energy will reduce the dependency on increasingly problematic Arab countries. Area: two expansion possibilities have been indicated, both already in a process of implementation. And military affairs: we shall see in chapter 8.

Chapter 5.
The structural power of the European Community

Let us then have a look at how the instruments of structural power are forged and put to use through the European Community. What international structure or structures is the EC promoting? This is the basic question, for the inter- and intra-national structure is also the medium in which the resource power will have to flow. If we can know the structure, then we also know how the more tangible instruments of power can be put to use. So, is the EC promoting a structure of equality or a structure of dominance in the world?

There can be no clear-cut answer to such a simple-minded question. It depends on *where* and *when* – possibly more on where than on when; such structures tend to be relatively stable. To analyse this we have to differentiate between the parts of the world, and in the way the EC does it. We have to view the world from Brussels – not from a geography book talking in terms of five or six continents. A political instrument does not respect physical geography too much, but it will show tremendous sensitivity to the political divisions of the world, and will follow economic divisions faithfully.

On the other hand, it would be wrong to assume that EC politics are equally crystallized in all corners of the world. Hence, the following list, found useful in discussing the EC, is not only a division of the world into six parts (with some subdivisions); it is also by and large a listing of these parts in order of decreasing crystallization as to EC policy:

1. EUROPEAN COMMUNITY MEMBERS
   a. Six original countries
   b. Four candidate countries
2. UNITED STATES OF AMERICA
3. THIRD WORLD COUNTRIES
   a. Former dependencies of members
   b. Other associated countries
   c. The rest

4. OTHER WEST EUROPEAN COUNTRIES
   a. Sweden–Switzerland–Austria
   b. Finland–Yugoslavia
   c. Malta–Cyprus–Iceland
   d. Turkey–Greece
   e. Spain–Portugal
5. THE SOCIALIST COUNTRIES
   a. Soviet Union
   b. DDR
   c. Other five Warsaw Pact countries (not Albania)
   d. Albania
6. THE REST OF THE WORLD
   a. Japan
   b. China (and associates)
   c. The rest

With the exception that the Mediterranean basin has recently become a category, this is the world as seen from Brussels, which is the perspective of interest here. In the center stand the signatories of the Treaty of Rome (category 1a). Then comes the giant to the West, the US; and then the developing countries, starting with the former colonial dependencies of the signatories. It may be discussed whether they or the US were foremost in the minds of some of the signatories when the Treaty of Rome was signed. Both were, perhaps, behind their immediate consideration with themselves. We have then chosen the hypothesis that the concern with the dependencies was largely an expression of fear of US penetration. This view is particularly reasonable as a consequence of the role the US had played as a champion of independence for all European colonies in Africa.

Then follows the rest of Europe with the Western part first and then the Eastern part. At the end comes 'the rest of the world', a residual category consisting of Japan and China, and again 'the rest' ('white' Commonwealth members).

A division of the world into only six parts (with some obvious subdivisions) and only two policy options (dominance and equality) is obviously far from sensitive enough as an analytical instrument to express the variety of EC politics. But as a point of departure this highly synoptic sketch may be useful:

	POLICY PURSUED	POLICY AVOIDED
1. European Community Members	Equality	Dominance
2. United States of America	Equality	Dominance
3. Developing countries	Dominance	Equality
4. Western European countries	Dominance	Equality
5. Eastern European countries	Dominance	Equality
6. The Rest of the World		
a. Japan	Equality	Dominance
b. China	?	
c. The rest	?	

We shall now comment briefly on the policy the EC seems to be pursuing in the six fields. More details will be given in later chapters.

First: in the relationship between the members of the EC, there can be no doubt that the policy *pursued* is equality, exactly as this is defined in chapter 3. This is indicated by the tremendous concern with equality in the EC. Not only is there fear that one or the other should dominate, singly or combined: open expression is given to this fear. This is a good indication that the norm of equality is really internalized. The EC is more than the traditional structure of dominance (for instance, found within the Soviet-dominated Eastern European system or the US-dominated Western Hemisphere system), with a thin layer of egalitarian ideology and some formally egalitarian structures on top of it. On the contrary, much seems to have been done to avoid vertical division of labor which could easily have taken place on a large scale with such relatively unequal partners as the Federal Republic of Germany and Italy with its very heavy *Mezzogiorno* component. The EC cannot be said to be a hierarchy of countries, exploited by Germany, fragmented her and penetrated by her. On the contrary, if there is exploitation, fragmentation, and penetration, then it is mutual, with cross-investment.[1]

This means that the EC member states have been building for themselves a *peace structure*.[2] What they have built is more than merely equality. Equality is easily obtained if trade and other forms of interaction and communication are kept at a minimum: yet these are certainly not at a minimum in the EC. On the contrary, relations are highly symbiotic, covering a broad spectrum of issues (deepening!) and certainly more than two members that could easily get into a polarized conflict situation (extension!). And the superstructure is more than strong enough, with its central organs and its numerous and competent staff.

The European Community has transcended the traditional, international system.

Thus, from a peace theoretical viewpoint, the EC is almost ideal where relations among states are concerned. Those who say that this is a structure for peace, because war among the members in general – and between France and Germany in particular – is rendered impossible, are probably right.[3] *It is peace built by associative means,* and certainly on a stronger foundation than attempts earlier this century to base peace on dissociation, balance of power, on Maginot and Siegfried lines, etc. But we should also remember that peace has an equally or more important domestic component, between regions, between classes. This aspect will be developed later; let us here only say that it looks as if the EC may have bought external peace among its members at the heavy price of increased internal peacelessness.[4] What manifestations that peacelessness will take, only the future will show, but a very one-sided and traditional concept of 'peace' is needed to see the EC as an unmitigated agent of peace within its own confines.

Second: With the relationship to the US, our major thesis is that *the EC is an alliance for economic defense,* striving for equality in its relationship to the US, trying to avoid dominance by the US over Western Europe. *Partnership,* on an egalitarian basis, is probably the sincerely pursued goal; for this to take place, the EC will partly try to make it more difficult for US business to establish herself in Western Europe, partly try to obtain balance through cross-investment.

But the goal is not European dominance over the US: the goal is parity. The division of labor should be horizontal, with spin-off effects equalized; the US should not be permitted to engage in any fragmentation strategies by encountering a united Western Europe; and if there is penetration of the US into European business elites, then there should also be penetration of the EC into US business elites – mutual penetration, in other words.[5] This is a clearly defined program, well executed, and it can also be seen as an instrument of peace.

For just as for relations within the EC there is no doubt that trade and other forms of interaction across the Atlantic will remain at such a high level that relations will be symbiotic. The exchange takes place over a broad spectrum: economic, political, military, cultural. On the other hand, from the viewpoint of peace theory: where there are only two parties (here, the US and the EC), relations tend to become rigid and polarize easily. This may be precisely where Japan can enter as a third party permitting trilateral deals within the triangle of capitalist economic superpowers. There is no doubt as to where that super-organization is found: it is the OECD which, as already indicated, will increasingly develop into an executive organization for this economic triumvirate.

In short, even though there will be tariff wars and periods of tension and mutual antagonism, by and large this is a structure for peace, much more so than the US economic domination of Western Europe that preceded it. Also, it is a structure that Third World countries, what remains of Western Europe, and socialist countries might look at to get ideas as to how a group of countries can defend itself effectively against economic aggression from a giant. What the EC has done relative to the US may well turn out to be what other countries will have to do relative to the EC – but are prevented from doing by EC divisive tactics.

Third: as to the relations to the Third World countries, let us here only state that these relations are characterized in extreme degree by all three aspects of dominance.

There is *vertical division of labor,* both in the classical sense that Third World countries serve as the provider of raw materials, of raw labor and of markets; *and* in the modern form that multinational corporations are set up involving Third World countries, reserving for the EC part of the cycle 'only' research, finance, and administration.

The *fragmentation* of the Third World takes place at two levels. First, where the UN is sytematically trying to treat all developing countries as one group (with UNCTAD the expression of this), the EC is splitting them into at least three groups. First come the Yaoundé states with the tight form of association referred to in chapter 2 as 'second class membership'. Then there are the looser types of association and stronger types of trade agreements entered into with some developing nations; and finally there are the Third World nations with little or almost no relation to the EC, such as India and (at least still for some time to come) Latin America. Fragmentation is to deal separately and in a particularistic manner with other countries, and this has indeed been done. However, there are limitations to this procedure, since simple principles of administrative expediency will discourage too much fragmentation.

In addition to this there is the fragmentation found most clearly in the first Yaoundé agreement: an agreement between the EC on the one hand, and the 18 associated states separately on the other. The second Yaoundé convention is based on more equality between the 24 signatory states, with an Association Council consisting of a minister from each (but also of the members of the Commission!), an Association Committee with one representative from each country, and an annual Parliamentary Conference where half of the 108 parliamentarians are from the EC and the other half from the associated states.

Thus, there is an effort to bring about some type of formal, elite level, equality. However, when the integration level among the EC members is so high and the total entity so strong, relative to the very low level of integration and the powerlessness at the bottom, equality will always be formal rather than real.

When it comes to *penetration*, the major instrument is probably shared economic interest and shared cultural outlook. If the people representing Third World countries in negotiations with the EC have had their total social cosmology, including their outlook on 'development', formed in complete agreement with the thinking in the center of the world, then in these negotiations the EC is really sitting on both sides of the table.[6] A basic aspect of this is the extent to which representatives from Third World countries accept the entire Western formula of what constitutes development, accepting not only the means (such as cars), but also the goal (such as individualized transportation) without much hesitation. A high level of autonomy is required to set one's own goals as opposed to having them handed over from the master, to develop one's own strategy and pursue them oneself. And, to return to chapter 3 on power, this can be done only on the basis of a high level of self-respect, self-sufficiency, and fearlessness. But immunization against the strong power emanating from the center is exactly what the whole dependency relation militates against – and this is where the major problem is located.

Fourth: the relation to the Western European countries. As indicated above, Western Europe has never been so split after World War II as today: there are the original six EC countries, the four applicant countries, and the remaining twelve are split into five groups, with different relations to the EC. In chapter 2 we made use of this grouping (only with a and b combined) in connection with the discussion of possible future extension of the EC. Again the EC is divisive at two levels: by handing out different treatment in different directions (as opposed to what the UN is trying to do as a universal organization), and also by having differential treatment within groups. Thus, except for the last stages of negotiations, the applicant countries have been treated individually rather than collectively, often according to their own wishes and desires, contributing further to the fragmentation process that goes on.

There is no doubt that applicant countries who become members will be accorded full equality. However, this will be an equality according to a pattern defined and developed by the original members, according to the principle that deepening has to precede extension. Thus a giant is growing up in the midst of Western Europe, imprinting its pattern on its surroundings, since the surroundings are more or less forced to adjust to it. If we are correct in our guess that the process will stop with the Fourteen, what remains are three small islands and the five non-aligned countries in the middle. If they acted as a bloc they might to some extent be a capitalist counterweight to the EC. But even so, the EC has had a highly divisive effect on them.

Fifth, there is the relationship to the socialist countries in Europe. A detailed analysis will be attempted in chapter 7. Much of what has been said concerning the developing countries and Western Europe also applies here: fragmentation on two levels. Different policies are administered in the direction of the USSR, of the DDR, and of the other five Warsaw Treaty Organization countries. Here there has been a division of labor among the EC countries, for some obvious reasons; the Federal Republic of Germany has had a major responsibility for *Ostpolitik* in general, and with regard to the USSR and the DDR in particular. The EC constitutes a major problem in connection with divided countries, because of the tight borderline it draws around itself. This is the major reason why Ireland is applying: it cannot afford to let England enter together with the six counties in Northern Ireland referred to as Ulster, itself remaining outside with the 26 counties of Southern Ireland. Correspondingly with the DDR: to practice the policies of the European Community with the DDR as an outsider would be tantamount to recognition of the DDR as a separate state. This recognition may come, sooner rather than later, but in the meantime there was obviously a problem here which was not inelegantly solved.

It is now probably correct to distinguish between two phases in the relationship between EC and Eastern Europe. In the first phase efforts were made to establish relations with Eastern European countries individually, with the more or less clear aim of entering into bilateral agreements with the EC on the one hand and Eastern European countries singly, never combined, on the other. Intended or not, this was clearly seen as a divisive strategy, splitting them off (1) from each other, (2) from the USSR (and the DDR because of the special policy adopted in that direction), and (3) internally by playing up to internal divisions. At the same time there was and still is vertical division of labor, with processed goods in one direction and raw materials in the other, with joint ventures set up according to the economic cycle formula described above, and so on. What was missing in this general setup was penetration, the effective control of the minds of the people in power in the Eastern European countries, as well as the simple (but highly effective) appeal to their economic self-interest.

For that reason, the second phase came very early in Eastern Europe: the countries rallied together in self-defense. This took a form not too different from what the EC had done relative to the US: deepening of the integration formula for the Eastern European countries as found in CMEA (Comecon). This will be described in more detail in chapter 7; but the net result seems to have been an *integration race* where both Capitalist Europe and Eastern Europe feel they must stand united before they can enter into serious negotiations with each other about the future shape of all of Europe. Unlike the arms race, the integration race does not have well defined plateaus. Like the arms race, it is only partly stimulated by what the other party does; most of the energy comes from *Eigendynamik*.

Sixth, we have the rest of the world. This division includes also the developed, 'white' Commonwealth members (Australia and New Zealand, Canada and South Africa – the ruling class of which is no doubt both white and 'developed'). With all these countries separate agreements with the EC will surely be established. But a joint firm stand, e.g. together with non-EC Western European countries, is certainly not encouraged by EC policies.[7]

But then there is *Japan*. Relative to her, we would hypothesize that the European Community will try to establish something similar to what it is working towards in relation with the US: *parity*. The Japanese expansion not only into the traditional markets of Western Europe but into Western Europe itself has led to the collapse of several Western European firms. Whether protection takes the form of cross-investment (which the Japanese would resist) or barriers against Japanese expansion into the EC, remains to be seen.[8] Most likely, in our mind, is the OECD directorate hypothesis, together with the other regulating mechanisms of the capitalist world.

As to *China*, the EC is for the first time encountering a power capable of herself defining the relationship, rather than waiting for the EC to define it for her. China has probably been for the US and Japan what Eastern Europe and the USSR have become for the EC: an enormous potential market, much more reliable than the Third World countries because of the presence of what Gunnar Myrdal would call hard as opposed to soft states,[9] but also much more self-sufficient. This does not mean that the US, the EC, and Japan will switch their economic expan-

trary: precisely because the socialist countries are at an intermediate
sionism from Third World countries to socialist countries. On the con-
level of technical-economic development, they may be seen as the potential consumers of products one production cycle behind, whereas Third
World countries might only be able to absorb products two or more production cycles behind. It is unnecessary to point out how well this would
tie in with the general philosophy of international division of labor: the
three at the top defining what should be produced with tremendous
emphasis on research and development, setting up production cycles with
planned obsolescence but at the same time guaranteeing themselves
against wasting productive forces, and against unemployment by having
markets that can absorb products left behind by the development in the
three centers themselves.

*The general picture, in other words, is one of a highly differentiated
policy pursued by the EC in the various directions of the political compass.*
In one formula: *equality at the top, towards the US and Japan, efforts
to dominate in all other directions.* The latter takes its clearest form in
relationship to the Third World countries, where all three strategies can
be pursued simultaneously: exploitation, fragmentation, penetration.
Towards Western Europe only fragmentation can be made effective use
of, although there will also be some vertical division of labor.[10] And when
it comes to the socialist countries, because of the integration race, only
vertical division of labor can be used – and only so long as Eastern
Europe accepts this type of game.

That concludes our survey of the structural power of the European
Community. It remains only to give more precise data. When the UK
becomes a member of the European Community, as of 1 January, 1973,
she will bring into this all British dependent territories (and the Anglo-
French Condominium of the New Hebrides), who will be offered association under part IV of the Treaty of Rome. These 'dependent territories'
are 19 in number. Similarly, Norway will bring with her, if she becomes
a member, three dependent territories.

In addition to this (British White Paper, section 117) the independent
Commonwealth countries in Africa, the Caribbean, the Indian Ocean
and the Pacific will be able to choose between three options: association
under a renewed Yaoundé convention (the present one is valid till 31
January 1975), some other form of association of the kind exemplified
by the Arusha convention, or a commercial agreement to facilitate and
expand trade with the EC. This situation applies to 20 countries, including Nigeria and the three East African countries already covered by the

Arusha convention. Imagine that they all opt for association. In that case the total system will lokk something like this:[11]

	No. of units	Population
The European Community	10	257.2
Their former dependencies		
of the Six	18	70
of UK	20	118.7
Their dependent territories		
of the Six	13	2.4
of UK	19	5.1
of Norway	3	0
Total	83	453.4

Nothing like this has ever before been seen in world history. It is about one third of the territories of the world, perhaps one eighth of the world population: and it includes 48 out of the about 140 independent states currently found in the world – more than one third of them. To object that many of the units listed above are small, some of them even unpopulated, is in part to miss the point. Fundamental here is their excellent geographical dispersion, their potential as supply bases for obvious economic and military purposes, as sources of raw materials, and their possible use in defining midlines for dividing the ocean floor is equally obvious. Besides, some are not so small in territory and may offer settlement opportunities with improved technology – for instance the Antarctic territory Norway brings into the picture. Thus the old powers in Western Europe are able to encompass the world partly because of a major loophole in the whole theory of anti-colonialism: the idea that independence from colonial rule has as a necessary condition the presence of an active independence movement. Where there is no local population, there cannot be any kind of independence movement – hence nobody to grant independence to, hence no need to give up the possession. That perpetuates the grip of the old colonial powers over the world.[12]

Still what has been said so far suffers from one important weakness: it has touched only the visible continents of the world. Our figures have said nothing about the invisible continent, the continent of non-territorial actors, of the intergovernmental and inter-nongovernmental organizations, of the so-called multinational corporations, and their like. What about that continent, since this is the medium through which structural power can most easily be exercised?

Two Finnish researchers, Uolevi Arosalo and Raimo Väyrynen, have recently done a painstaking job in collecting data about this. Some of their findings can be recalculated and summarized for our purposes as a comparison with the other big in the capitalist world: the US and Japan. In this, comparisons with the USSR and China make no sense since they are playing a different game, even a countergame. Their state enterprises also operate abroad (USSR in India, China in Tanzania); but we have no data.

We start with the multinational corporations[13] (Tables III and IV).

Table III. *Distribution of the 300 biggest industrial corporations, %*

	1965	1969	1970
United States	59	61	61
EC of Ten	29	27	28
Japan	7	9	9
Others	5	3	1
Sum	100	100	100
(N)	(300)	(300)	(300)

Table IV. *Distribution of parent companies of multinational corporations, %*

	Total 1968	Operating in ten or more countries 1968	1970
United States	40.0	45.5	41.9
EC of Ten	48.9	44.5	48.4
Others	11.1	10.0	9.7
Sum	100.0	100.0	100.0
(N)	(7046)	(595)	(673)

Many conclusions can be drawn from Tables III and IV. Thus the major conclusion is how *three* big powers in the capitalist world together dominate the total scene, whether we look at all multinational corporations, those operating in ten or more countries, or the top 300. Second, if we leave Japan out, the same applies to the top *two* powers: the US and the EC. Third, when it comes to relations between the top two, it is changing: the US is declining. But, and that is our fourth conclusion: the US still holds its leading position among the biggest corporations.

A similar picture can be obtained from the distribution of the leading banks (Table V).[14]

65

Table V. *Distribution of the 300 biggest banks, %*

	No. of banks		Assets	
	1969	1970	1969	1970
United States	32	33	36	35
EC of Ten	27	28	30	32
Japan	15	15	16	16
Others	26	24	18	17
Sum	100	100	100	100
(N)	(300)	(300)		

As above, one important losing category is 'Others': the concentration on the big capitalist three increases. But the EC is closing in on the US, contrary to what many seem to believe.

Let us then give a Table which once more changes the picture in the favor of the EC: some information about the headquarters of organizations that are international, but not concerned primarily with business: the intergovernmental (IGO) and inter-nongovernmental organizations (INGO). The distribution is as shown in Table VI.[15]

Table VI. *Distribution of the headquarters of IGOs and INGOs, 1968, %*

United States	12
EC + GB	74
Japan	1
Others	13
Sum	100

When it comes to hosting the headquarters of the more traditional international organizations, governmental and nongovernmental, the Third World is once more kept outside – but so is the Second World, the New World, the US. It is Western Europe that is used as a center for the political, ideological and cultural organizations[16] – even though the US has a certain lead when it comes to economic organizations.

It remains only to be said that if and when this lead is changed into a lead for the EC, the total picture becomes even more clear: the EC on top when it comes to controlling territories around the world, and the EC on top when it comes to controlling the non-territorial continent, the invisible continent of international organizations. In short, there is no doubt that the European Community, when it comes to these indicators of power today, is in a group where there is only one other country, the United States.

Of course, an international organization with its headquarter in the EC is not for that reason controlled by the EC. But the business organizations will hardly turn against their parent countries – the only problem is whether they will on the whole favor the US or the EC more. Like the other international organizations they are transmitters not only of capital, labor and products – but of European languages, forms of organizations, modes of thought. Even if these international organizations exist in order to work against, to counteract the resource power and the structural power of the European Community, they are still profoundly Western. There is little new in this pattern: Western Europe is like that man cooperating with Chaplin in knocking out window panes so that Chaplin can offer his services in putting in new panes. Western Europe creates problems all over the world through its capitalism and liberal ideology, and then exports other organizations and a marxist ideology as a possible remedy – all the time remaining a center of world activity. In the center itself this may look like the very opposite of coordination. It is from the outside that this unity of opposites becomes clear, and may become something to protect oneself against.

Chapter 6.
The European Community and the
Third World countries

The relationship between the European Community and the less developed countries of the Third World (TW) can only be described and evaluated relative to a theoretical model that gives a baseline for whether the policy is good or bad. Our model will be the one that unfortunately seems to come closest to the reality of the EC–TW relationship: the model developed in chapter 3 of dominance, or imperialism, based on the three major components: *exploitation* defined as vertical division of labor, *fragmentation,* and *penetration.* Since the only extensive experience over time as to how the European Community works in its relationship to developing countries comes from Africa, and more particularly from the relations with the 18 Yaoundé states, our discussion will largely refer to Africa.

1) *Exploitation: the vertical division of labor*

Our criterion for exploitation cannot be expressed in terms of trade flows alone. It is well known that the OPEC countries have recently obtained better prices for the raw material, the crude oil, they export to the rich countries in general and to the EC in particular. But this is only bargaining within an old pattern, not a change of international structure. The crude oil that reaches European countries is still so cheap that it is possible for, e.g., the Norwegian government to impose a price structure on gasoline so that when the Norwegian consumer pays N. kr. 1.54 for one liter, only 7 % is to the supplier (a multinational corporation, one can imagine how little of this accrues to workers in the periphery country!) and 71 % to the Norwegian government. This is a basic source of revenue, supporting among other things the Norwegian welfare state; this in turn will tend to make Norwegian masses allies of their own elites rather than of the masses in the periphery countries. With the current power structure in the world, out of which vertical division of labor is one element, this is possible. The reverse, 7 % to the government of Norway,

71 % to the workers producing the oil, would be impossible in the present world.

Imagine the OPEC countries took a *radical* step (which will have to come, sooner rather than later) and simply said: 'from now on, we shall process our crude ourselves and enjoy both the profits and the economic, research, educational, military, psychological etc. spin-off effects that accrue to the country where the processing takes place'. Something fundamentally new would have happened. To see clearly that it is fundamental let us imagine that Norway were at the same time encouraged to try a century or two as exporter of dried fish and neatly bottled bacteria-free and unpolluted water – profits from the latter accruing to the owners of the waterfalls, spin-off effects being nil. A couple of centuries with this pattern might be instructive and increase both empathy and sympathy with say, the OPEC countries who still are in this position. It is likely that research and education in Norway would dwindle. Norwegians would become 'lazy' and 'traditional' – except for the energies displayed by the owners of the waterfalls when they come as delegates to international organizations, functional and/or regional, asking for technical assistance, for lower tariffs and higher quotas for their water export, and for higher and more stable prices for water. Autonomy, as defined in chapter 3, would be close to zero.

Yet this is no caricature of relations between EC and the TW countries in general, and the associated states in particular. It is *not* a relation aiming at even encouragement of a diversified spectrum of extraction and manufacturing, leading to *horizontal* exchange between rich and poor countries, raw materials against raw materials, foodstuffs against foodstuffs, semi-processed and processed against semi-processed and processed. If this were the goal, if the parties to the association agreement were anything like equal, there would be a central authority, distributing important processing industries more evenly between member and associated countries, with special attention exactly to the spin-off effects, to the amount of challenge and stimulus, to the inspiration given to local research and education: in order to avoid having patterns developed in rich countries just slavishly copied or adapted by an expert team from the center. This would be the pattern *inside* any modern state, encouraging its periphery through policies that are often *not* short-term economically rational. We must recall that a factory in a remote district serves other purposes than merely economic ones.

Three factors work against such a structure, based on solidarity and equity, in the relation between EC and the associated states:

First, the 18 states so far associated with the EC in the Yaoundé agreements count among their number some of the poorest, least developed, least viable countries in the world.[1] It will take time by any development strategy before they have an industry of significance, even for the local market. They can be fitted into the role as deliverer of raw materials without too much difficulty, since on a short-term basis there is little else they could deliver. The present arrangement looks 'natural'. If association had started with more industrialized countries – say Tunisia, India, some of the Latin American countries – this role allocation would have been considerably more problematic. But by now a pattern has been set from the very beginning: the European Community picked her preferred trade partners from the weakest, least developed, most vulnerable and submissive countries of the Third World.

Second, the arrangement is highly protective for the EC countries, since the association agreement by no means constitutes a real free trade area. There are tariff and quota barriers for products that are 'homologues et concurrentiels', i.e. products that would compete with products in EC countries. This also applies to foodstuffs. The agreement is made such that the EC can import just what *it* wants and needs on the basis of the rules of a market economy, not according to the needs of the associated states. This we see clearly from trade figures: whereas over a ten-year period the average increase in import from non-associated developing countries on the EC was 8 % p.a., it was only 5 % p.a. from the associated states.[2] This means that not even in the traditional role as supplier of raw material do they get the traditional benefits of increased trade and improved prices. And this is also reflected in the failure to 'grow' from $ 86 to $ 89 per capita in ten years.[3]

Third, highly significant is the increase in the EC *export* to these countries.[4] Partly this must be seen in the light of the two institutions, the *European Development Fund* and the *European Investment Bank*. Through these institutions West European governments can continue doing what they have always done: subsidize their own industry in two ways, by paying for the infrastructure in the TW (roads, telecommunication, sewage, etc.), and by giving grants tied to procurement of manufactured goods from EC countries. During the first EDF only 0.7 % of the funds disbursed were used by these states themselves to build local industry (for the local markets); during the second EDF it was 1.3 %. The total amount of aid through the European Development Fund has increased from $ 581 million in the first period to $ 730 million in the second, but the level of tying is as high as 80 % (82 % of all French aid, for instance) – i.e. capital goods are to be procured in EC countries.[5] In this way European governments subsidize not only their own industry but ultimately also themselves, because of what they get back in the form of taxes. This is also an old pattern: governments paying industry located in the center (of the country) so that they can build an infra-structure in the periphery, so that industry from the center can move into the periphery – all under the heading of 'development'. These grants that look highly attractive on a short-term basis will only be made available to countries willing to enter into an association agreement. Of course such grants will be a major argument used by local elites arguing in favor of association.[6]

But in the *long* run the net result will be a surplus of semi-processed and processed goods for export even from the poor Yaoundé states. It is not at all unlikely that some of this under the Generalized Preferences System (GPS) that involved 91 developing countries from 1 July 1971[7] (but has not really been put into practice so far), and particularly the reduction of tariffs for processed goods, often down to zero, will eventually find its way into the EC countries. It will take time, because the system is based on the trade structure during the last years and will therefore have a tendency to freeze the past: there is a low limit to how much the 91 countries can increase their export under GPS relative to what it was before. However, in the longer run this will happen. But under the logic of the total system, large-scale export of processed goods into EC from associated states will surely take place only under three fundamental assumptions, all related to vertical division of labor in its more modern form:

a) *That the processed goods do not compete with EC industry because they are no longer produced inside the EC,* hence that they are not 'homologues et concurrentiels'. It is easily foreseen what kind of goods they would be: predominantly goods produced in the early period of industrial development, e.g. textiles and not-too-processed iron, and/or goods produced by highly polluting industries that EC (and other industrialized countries) would prefer to have outside its own borders. Theoretical rationales for this *new* type of division of labor, higher up on the degree of processing scale, are already being produced in the center countries (e.g. in the form of Tinbergen's plan[8] for divison of labor, based on the Heckscher-Ohlin principle).[9]

b) *That the processed goods are produced within multinational corporations with headquarters in the EC countries.* Thus, there will be economic cycles tying center to periphery in such a way that finance, administration and research will be located in the center; and extraction of raw materials, cheap labor and factories working according to old blueprints elaborated in the center will be located in the periphery. This may easily become competitive with center-located industry on the center market, for periphery labor is much cheaper whereas the costs involved in transporting processed goods for consumption in the center may be of the same order of magnitude as the costs involved in transporting raw materials for processing in the center. *In addition, since all this takes place within a multinational corporation, a number of financial manipulations are available.* Thus the corporation can fix internal prices such that the profit shows up where taxes are lowest. If taxes should become inconveniently high in a periphery country – the 'climate' becomes less 'friendly to investment' – one obvious method would be for the mother company to deliver capital goods produced by herself to the daughter company at so high prices that profits become negligible (but they would show up as earnings on capital goods made by the mother company in the more friendly mother country). Obviously, a high level of insight and direct access are needed for the periphery country to control effectively a multinational corporation that often turns out to be a trans-national juridical entity with its own internal jurisdiction.[10]

Simply stated: the vertical division of labor survives, but it is now placed inside the corporation. Hence a certificate of origin for the goods produced becomes almost meaningless when the factory is only geographically placed in the developing country. In all probability this is the pattern the EC system will be heading towards, reserving the most challenging segments of the economic cycle for herself, pushing factories etc. into the Third World, and turning to the pursuit of 'quality of life' for herself.[11] The egotism of this is nothing new; it is an old European tradition.

c) *That the EC countries will still be free to export goods at a higher level of processing than what they import from the TW countries.* When EC imports cars and black-&-white TV's they will export computers and color TV's to the obvious consumers: themselves, other Western countries, Eastern European countries (which have a more 'advanced' demand structure, a more predictable market because it is centrally planned, and are generally more reliable customers than developing countries) and to elites in developing countries – associated or not. This would be a direct extrapolation from the current trade policies of the EC.

When export from the associated states does not increase, when terms of trade do not improve, when very little diversification takes place, when the old international division of labor is practically speaking unchanged or reappears in some new forms: *what, then, has changed?* essentially, that European countries now do collectively what they used to do singly and in competition regulated by the division of the world into empires, or 'spheres of influence'. As Nkrumah has pointed out, this is 'collective colonialism'. This pattern was brought into the Treaty of Rome at the instigation of the French, who became highly frightened at the thought that other members, particularly Germans, should benefit from the infrastructure investment the French had made in the colonial period and move with investments into markets that had been prepared by the French. What the Germans, and others, should do would be at least to share the infrastructure costs, and this sharing became the European Development Fund. Nevertheless the old trade pattern prevailed: data show that the old dependencies tend to maintain their ties with their old mother countries – for obvious reasons, one being the factor of penetration to be discussed below.

To conclude: vertical division of labor is maintained, both in the field of *capital* (center provides investment, periphery provides market); in the field of *labor* (center provides know-how, research, periphery provides unskilled labor) some of it locally, in the periphery, some of it as Fremdarbeiter in the center; and in the *'land'* factor (periphery providing goods at a much lower level of processing than the center).

After this general overview let us look in more detail at the problem of vertical division of labor. First, a warning against this reasoning. It is easy to criticize vertical division of labor, but from that criticism does not follow that horizontal division of labor is the alternative. Both patterns have one thing in common: exchange of products, economic transactions, trade. But is it so obvious that trade is to the good? Or, could it be that trade also is a part of the capitalist system, creating a class of traders who will benefit from any kind of trade, vertical or horizontal, and in either case be a caste to themselves, removed from the rest of the population? Could it be that trading is the opposite of a self-reliance that in the short or long run may lead to self-sufficiency? Could it be that such self-reliance would help the masses in the poor countries, the real world proletariat, more than exchange of goods over their heads? And, could it be that a focus on trade, also within UNCTAD, essentially plays into the hands of the traders? We simply raise the questions,[12] and shall return to them later.

One point of departure for a more detailed study of the EC and the Third World would be the tariffs agreed upon as the Common External Tariffs of the EC in 1966. Let us look at these tariffs for six typical TW export products: coffee, cocoa, groundnuts, soya, cotton and jute; and at three different levels of 'processing'.[13] (Table VII.)

Table VII. *Tariffs (CET) in 1966 for major Third World products, %*

| | Degree of processing | | |
	I (none 'raw')	II (a little bit)	III (a little more)
Coffee		9.6 (beans)	15 (roasted)
Cocoa		5.4 (beans)	12 (butter)
			16 (powder)
Groundnuts	0	10 (raw oil)	15 (refined oil)
Soya	0	10 (raw oil)	15 (refined oil)
Cotton	0	6 (spun)	14 (woven)
Jute	0	8 (spun)	19 (woven)

The idea is simple enough: the product just picked off the ground or cut down from trees (like bananas) can be imported with no tariffs; as soon as some element of processing is involved, there is a protection of the same process in the EC country. Actually, 'degree of processing' for the three steps indicated in the Table is a misnomer: this is not processing in the 20th century sense, but very simple processes, even though they may be organized like big industries.

The effective protection of this type of processing, as Wagner[14] points out, is much higher than these percentages should indicate. The local producer in an EC country can import the raw materials without paying anything extra, and can then process under the protection of the increasing tariffs. *It is the steepness of the increase of tariffs with increasing degree of processing that matters,* so effective protection is higher, the more the tariffs for raw materials and processed goods differ. Thus a 0 % tariff for raw material adds to protection as long as there is a non-zero tariff on the processed goods. There is nothing gradiose in lowering tariffs for raw materials alone; this only helps to freeze the structure and increases effective protection.

Under this type of structure the colonial system worked for years, centuries – only that the 'customs tariffs' are an institutionalization, expressed in cool percentages, of the robbery and brutality of former times. The net result of that system is simple enough, as shown in Table VIII.[15]

74

Table VIII. *The participation in world export of processed goods,* %

	1960	1969
World	55	65
Industrial countries	83	83
Third World countries	5.5	6.5
Industrial countries, relative to their total export	68	75
Third World countries, relative to their total export	14	24

Thus, world export as a whole is moving towards more processed goods; this is also reflected in the composition of Third World export. But throughout this 'decade of development', the industrial countries maintain their position as suppliers of 83 % of the world export of processed goods, while the Third World countries remain at their low level (the balance is made up of socialist countries). Why? The simple factor they have in common, almost all of them, is that they were colonized, one way or the other – although we should add that this cannot explain 100 % of the difference.[16]

Obviously, lowering tariffs for raw materials does not help change the trade composition. But lowering tariffs on processed goods does not help much either, since in the first run only countries producing processed goods already will benefit from it. That in fact is the criticism of the Yaoundé agreements and the Kennedy round. What about the system of generalized preferences?

Our major point here is that new non-tariff restrictions in the form of a complex quota system replace the tariff restrictions. First, there are the famous 'sensitive products', i.e. products where TW countries might complete effectively with EC countries; but that is an old point. More important in this connection are the three restrictions placed on the quantity of processed goods from any TW country (under the agreement) to the EC countries in order to get reduced tariffs (or no tariffs):

- It applies only to an export quantity corresponding to the export of that country to the EC in 1968 (the basis year) + 5 % of all other TW countries export to the EC the year before. This makes for an increase, but a slow one since the export of industrial goods from the TW countries was already very low.
- It applies only to the percentage of the export to the EC that corresponds to a general distribution formula for trade on the EC countries, according to which Germany shall have

37.5 % of the export, France 27.1 %, and so on. Since many developing countries have a very high level of partner concentration in trade, e.g. former French colonies, they may have difficulties dispersing their trade.

- Any single less developed country can only get tariff exemption for a certain percentage, normally 50 %, of the total import of any given commodity (for textiles only 20 %). Since many developing countries have not only commodity concentration in trade, but also a high proportion of the total world trade, they may have difficulties dispersing the trade sufficiently.

The most vital aspect of all this is not how this apparent generosity is eaten up by quota restrictions of various and imaginative kinds – which, incidentally, all favor the strongest of the less TW developed countries in obvious ways. More important is that these rules are not only complex,[17] but often have to be applied *after* the duties have been paid, by paying back the excess. No one can know in advance what trade for a given year will be and how it will stand up statistically, relative to the three rules of 1968 + 5 %, distribution *to* EC countries and distribution *from* Third World countries. The rules must have a highly stimulating effect on bureaucracies (and computer sales), but then there is also the basic question: what happens to the excess duty paid back? If it is paid back to the importers in the EC countries[18] (who paid the duties in the first run), then it is too late to build it into the prices and make them more competitive. Nor is it likely that the money will end up in the developing countries. Of course, it remains to be seen how all this works out in practice, but right now it looks very much like the old game, the rich countries redistributing some money among themselves.

Who can benefit? A simple guess would be multinational corporations who have the capacity to understand fully and make use of the system. Thus, US multinational corporations may place some production facilities in Africa; the same will certainly be done increasingly by corporations with headquarters in the EC, whether controlled by EC or US capital (or both). This is clearly the precise opposite of the professed intention to create industries in developing countries which would be genuinely their own.

2) *Fragmentation*

Fragmentation means that whereas the center is well coordinated, even unified in the European Community, the periphery, the developing countries, are split in many ways. This is partly a question of absence of *links:* little or no trade,[19] indirect or very expensive communication and transportation. Both are typical left-overs from the colonial period, illustrated in the proverbial telephone connection between Kenya and the Central African Republic:[20] via London and Paris. But as a consequence of this (near) absence of interaction there is also an absence of effective horizontal *organizations* among the developing countries; organizations that could serve as an expression of solidarity between the developing countries, not only as irregular manifestations of the need for solidarity as in Beograd 1961, Cairo 1964, Lusaka 1970.

Fragmentation also extends to the multilateral level: the center tends to deal with the periphery countries one at a time, particularistically, not in the presence of the others. Trade tends to be bilateral, between the center and *one* of the periphery countries, without, for instance, institutions for multilateral clearing. Partly as a consequence of this, there is also a scarcity of multilateral organizations where all parties can deal with matters of common concern in full view of each other.

Finally, fragmentation has an aspect of monopoly: whereas the center has links in all direction, with other center countries and groups of countries, the periphery countries tend to direct their external activity solely in the direction of that center, 'their' center.[21] How this is all related to such trade phenomena as partner concentration and commodity concentration is obvious.[22]

This general pattern can now be explored at two levels: in relations between the European Community and the Third World countries in general, and in relations between the EC and the Yaoundé countries in particular. Let us start with the former.

(a) *Relations to Third World countries in general.* There is no doubt that the EC has a divisive effect, and was intended to. Against the whole trend in the world towards uniform treatment, and more particularly most favored nation (MFN) treatment to all nations[23] the European Community based itself on a system of *selective preferences* for the associated states, as opposed to other developing countries.

This must be seen as an extension in time of the 'particular relation' prevailing between colonial countries and their colonies, and not evaporating overnight with the disappearance of traditional colonialism. Fundamental here is the very concept of 'associated states'. The EC is not only about economics: it is as much or more about *politics*.

First, this concept institutionalizes a *second class membership* within EC itself – in an age of universalism, in an age where a basic, fundamental dictum has been that *all nations are first class nations,* as all

77

citizens of a country have the right to the same first class citizenship. Unfortunately this plays only too well into the age-old European complex of superiority.

Second, the EC is not open for all, it is exclusive: only for 'former dependencies'. However, although not explicitly stated, it is obvious that socialist nations cannot join even when they are former dependencies, for their entire theory and practice of economic relations are fundamentally opposed to the capitalism found inside the EC. As a consequence one finds that neither Guinea, nor Algeria can be associated states, and one also finds that states already in the system show little signs in the direction of nationalization (exceptions are Congo (Brazzaville) and Somalia). Thus, a wedge is driven between less developed countries that have chosen different directions when it comes to the basic pattern of economic development. The exception here is Tanzania – but then, the Arusha Convention is little more than a trade agreement.[24]

These consequences are serious and would remain even if all tariff barriers were evened out – even down to zero, which is *not* to be recommended. The less developed countries as a whole *need* protection for their infant industries. They also need export subsidies corresponding to negative tariffs for their export of processed goods to the more developed countries.[25] But with the EC system, such global problems are handled in different settings, for different groups of countries, where different and often contradictory interests are expressed. Less developed countries get their loyalties split because of the wedge driven between those that are former dependencies and those that are not, between socialist and those that are capitalist, and between continents. Most of the associated states will be African, making Africa to the EC what Latin America is to the US. So far the system has also had a fundamentally divisive impact *within* Africa, slowing down the move towards African unity, as well as the work of the UN Economic Commission for Africa. The same can be said for the Third World as a whole.[26]

(b) *Relations to the Yaoundé States in particular.* These relations should be seen in two stages, corresponding to the two Yaoundé conventions. The fragmentation aspect was most apparent in the first stage, Yaoundé I (22 July 1963), with Article 40 of the convention mentioning an annual meeting between the EEC *Council* and *Commission* on the one hand, and one representative from each *government* of the associated states on the other. This has now changed with Yaoundé II: there is a provision for a ministerial committee and a parliamentary assembly with 108 members (54 from the EC, and 54 from the 18) for the 6 plus 18 = 24. In other

78

words, there is a provision for a multilateral organization – although it will be a feeble one. It will meet infrequently, and only briefly, and since the 18 will not participate on anything like an equal footing in the much more important day-to-day work of the Commission (the center of power) because it is the EC organ taking initiatives (if not the final decisions). If partipation in all organs were equal, then some of our objections about fragmentation would wither away. *But in that case the EC would no longer be European* – which would be against the Treaty of Rome, where § 237 stipulates that members be European States.

However, multilateralization is not that significant, and not only because these organizations tend to be elitist. Experience from the UN, which is universal and multilateral and based on one class of membership for everybody but the big powers, indicates that multilateral organizations can also be very effective means to maintain, even reinforce, vertical control. What is missing can be clearly seen from the history of UNCTAD: the emergence of the Group of 77 as a forceful horizontal organization of the small and the poor where these can develop a common stand and build up solidarity ties without being impeded by the countries on top of the vertical division of labor. The Group of 77 is probably the most significant outcome of UNCTAD; it is not at all inconceivable that its meetings alone, problematic as they are, might lead to a new organization which might one day become an effective trade union of exploited countries.[27]

There is nothing explicit in the Yaoundé agreements to impede or facilitate this kind of development from taking place among the 18, or even among all developing countries. But horizontal trade being as low as it is (intra-African trade is only 5 % of African trade: African trade with other developing countries only 10 %)[28] it is obvious that very active 'uphill' steps must be taken for this to happen. An organization does not come about by itself. Since the Yaoundé agreement by and large tends to freeze the status quo, it gives no impetus in the direction of solidarity. On the contrary, it plays up to the short-term interest each developing nation, including the associated states, has in preserving *its* share of the export of raw materials, and in increasing it (even against a nation's own long-term interests in a more equitable deal), for fear that any change will impair the present position. For that reason the associated states have tended to be the allies of the *regionalists* in the EC, the old 'mother countries' France and Belgium (17 of the 18 Yaoundé States, no. 18 being 'Italian', Somalia), not of the so-called *globalists*, Germany and Netherlands, who have more evenly dispersed trade interests. Even if the globalists should win, the institutions would remain; and the total set-up would still weaken the UN as an organization involving *all* countries, less developed and more developed alike.

3) *Penetration*

Penetration into the elites of former colonial dependencies will usually be based on two factors: ideological *identification* with the elites of the European Community and *dependency* on a continued relation with them. These relations are very concrete. The identification comes from *education* in insitutions originally set up by these European elites. Dependency takes the form of *economic vested interest* in a high (and increasing) trade level between center and periphery countries. The third possibility from the real colonial period, basing the penetration on *fear,* concrete fear of some kind of punishment for non-compliance, disappeared with colonialism: European elites can no longer exercise punitive expeditions and other forms of direct jurisdiction; the countries are 'free'. But the other two power-channels are still open.

As to ideological identification, what really matters seems to be the kinds of things social scientists rather than men of letters talk about. That local elites speak perfectly the tongue of the former colonial country, and know its culture sometimes better than they know their own, is important: but it is not crucial. More significant is how they conceive of international relations in general, and the development process in particular – their global and domestic cosmologies, so to speak. More concretely: if one accepts the basic features of Western European society as the development *goal,* and heavy reliance on vertical division of labor (relative to Europe, but also inside one's own country, between city and village, between regions, between skilled and unskilled) as the *means,* then one's mind already provides fertile ground for penetration. When deals are suggested that are compatible with this type of development model, they are seen as natural, as realistic – and the only problems to negotiate would be some details to make the deal as profitable as possible within the limits given by the model.

If in addition there are solid material benefits to be derived from this, penetration will be even more profound. But in very many periphery countries, 'socialism' has been interpreted to mean a type of state control which has catapulted into power the man of the book (and the man of the party and the man of the gun) much more than the money-man. To derive private *monetary* benefits from deals with other countries has been frowned upon as detrimental to the country, and as immoral at the personal level. To derive private *intellectual* benefits – e.g. from conference participation, from study abroad, from missions – is not similarly frowned upon. It is assumed that the intellectual currency is invested in one's own society and put to work for the common good. Obviously, this very often is not the case: the benefits are used for the promotion of one's own career. And this opens for a new and wider concept of 'vested interest'.[29]

Penetration into local elites has to be well prepared. The old colonial method of using the local white settler working in administration, education or business is largely out, at least in the more autonomous of the periphery countries. An indigenous business elite is also insufficient. The target of penetration would have to be the local leadership, well educated and highly placed in administration. But many colonial countries did not prepare the ground: the number of university graduates in former Belgian Congo and former Italian Libya has been given as 16 and 18 respectively[30] – out of whom most worked in the mother country. Training elites, moulding their minds in the right direction, therefore becomes crucial. The means are well known: aid to local education programs, a flow of processed teachers in one direction and raw students in the other. The focus is on what is 'useful' for development. From both the teacher from the center and the student from the periphery comes the claim that there is no time to be wasted on, say, more critical explorations of the foundations of the educational message.

In what can be characterized as a typical egocentric Western European pattern much of this has been paid for by the Americans – by Ford and Rockefeller Foundations and others, for instance in Africa – but with Europeans hoping to reap the benefits.

The content of the educational message can be clearly seen by inspecting curricula in social sciences in periphery countries. In economics it is the theory of comparative advantages and its concomitants, much trade, vertical division of labor, free flow of production factors (modified by some Keynesian mechanisms). This theory should have been referred to as 'capitalistics' since it is only the theory of capitalism, and not be dignified with the term 'economics'. Its specialists, however, refer to themselves as 'economists'. Nobody will deny the significance of knowing how the different varieties of the capitalist system works: but to identify capitalism with economic relations in general is a violation of basic intellectual rules. An over-concentration on capital-intensive, research-intensive, elite-oriented production that inevitably leads to economic cycles

81

tying the periphery to the center, not least intellectually, is not identical with 'economics'.

This is not the place to spell out the alternative, but some of its broader features should be mentioned. First, however, two false approaches in the search for alternatives to the typical Western educational message in the fields of economics – and social science in general. Criticism of capitalism and of 'capitalistics' are not enough. This has been done for more than a century, largely within a marxist frame of reference. One cannot build an alternative economic system on criticism alone. Second, the alternative that long stood out as acceptable to many, a centrally planned economy (as opposed to a market economy) is today much less attractive. It has become clear in Eastern Europe that although socialism has meant an end to the Western imperialistic penetration of earlier periods, the system has not solved the problem of *general participation,* or the general problem of vertical division of labor. Planning has become the prerogative of a small elite, often self-encapsulated and self-recruiting. It is certainly not the population in general that plans the planners. Furthermore, the division of labor between a manager and a worker in an East European factory is more or less as in Western Europe. The manager has the challenges, the personality-expanding jobs; the worker is given a routine, a standard operating procedure, and although he may derive some satisfaction from not producing for the private profit of the owners, his work is no less boring and degrading because of its lack of challenge than in the capitalist West.

The theory of horizontal division of labor, or socialist division of labor, has yet to be developed. This is perhaps fortunate: the moment the search for equity, for a truly non-exploitative form of production within and between countries becomes a 'theory', it will also easily become a doctrine with *its* high priests with *its* experts – and that will introduce a new vertical relation. Yet some features can be seen: shorter, less alienating economic cycles;[31] more 'intermediate', 'soft', technology;[32] more self-reliance; more utilization of local, indigenous expertise; more rotation in jobs; a reconstruction of jobs so that people are less compartmentalized and specialized than in the present system; production for fundamental needs of the masses and with more attention paid to *equity* in production *relation* and *equality* in *distribution,* than to productivity and accumulation as goals in themselves.

This is bound to come, and relatively quickly with the increasing dissatisfaction with the capitalist system of production throughout the world. This dissatisfaction is certainly not new. What is new is that it has also reached well-to-do strata in the capitalist countries who militate against both productivity and accumulation because of the harmful impact of either on *relations among persons* (exploitation) on *inner* person (alienation) and on the *environment*. Typically it is the latter, the impersonal, technical, 'non-political' argument that has met with most acceptance.[33] Thus, forces in the periphery countries that want to escape from the vertical international division of labor for which they have been prepared will find new allies in these strata. These will probably be better allies than the workers of Western Europe, who have rarely been seen to revolt against participation in the imperialistic wars waged by their leaders, nor to have basic complaints about vertical division of labor with the Third World as long as they – as the British Labour Party argues – get a fair share of the profits.[34]

In this change the experience of countries like China, Cuba and Tanzania is crucial. This whole matter is so vitally important that one cannot afford to be dogmatic about it. Dogmatism about an alternative system is no better than the 'value-neutral' empirical science about the economic system that happens to prevail and hence to supply empirical data: some version of capitalism. Empirical methods will have to be modified; only on the basis *both* of data and of fundamental values, and theory to point beyond what is found empirically right on one's own doorstep can science become a tool of progress.[35]

This will all happen and is happening – sooner and more in some poor countries like Tanzania than in many rich like Norway. In the meantime there will still be ample opportunity to witness the sad show of local elites in periphery countries, well trained in the mode of thinking that provides a rationale for the entire system, demanding more of the same because this is the only thing they know how to demand. Their testimony will be well propagated by center elites who will tell the sceptics: 'they ask for it themselves, it would be cruel not to yield to their demands, they are sovereign states, it is not for us to tell them what they should demand'.

One obvious prediction is that aid from the European Community – in the form of scholarships, support to local universities etc. – will increase in the years to come, as a part of the penetration program, deliberately or not. And an equally obvious prescription: that the intellectual struggle for the content of university curricula in developing countries will be intensified considerably in the years to come.

In this comment on penetration we have focussed on relations between European elites and elites in the developing countries, particularly in the general field of ideas and identification, and more particularly in the field of social cosmology. In conclusion, we must emphasize the other major factor that enters into the chemistry of penetration: that the distance between elite and masses is so much greater in the periphery countries than in the center countries.

The ministry official, the professor, the businessman live about the same way in both type of countries. They understand each other, mix at parties and go to each other's homes with ease. There is an equality between the standard of living that both will easily mistake for political equality between their two countries. But whereas the European elite lives in a way not too dramatically different from the life-style enjoyed by those in the lower strata of *his* country, this is by no means the case for his less developed country counterpart. A gulf separates this man from the woman in the villages, from the man in the slums. This has a number of consequences. In terms of *identification:* the local, periphery country elite would have to be superhuman not to identify more strongly with his elite counterpart from the center nation than with his own pauperized and miserable countrymen – whereas the center elite can more easily identify in both directions, with other masses in his own country and with his counterpart. And in terms of *fear:* the local elite gets a vested interest in continued elite-elite relation; the fear of losing his elite position is much more real to him, since the distance he can fall is of a quite different order of magnitude. There will be tremendous variations from person to person as to such factors – but they cannot be disregarded. These factors are supported by the structure of dominance itself, and will only disappear together with dominance in general.

The conclusion? Essentially that the model used to describe and evaluate the European Community in its relation to the less developed countries *fits*. There are some nuances. *The vertical division of labor* takes on new forms; is placed increasingly inside EC-dominated multinational corporations, is moved up the processing ladder and takes gradually the form of an exchange between super-processed and semi-processed goods. But the *gap* is the same. *Fragmentation* is still the dominant aspect, although there exist some weak solidarity organizations among the TWs, and some very limited multilateral participation. As to *penetration:* it is more economical and cultural, less military and political than in the days of traditional colonialism.

The total impression is that these are old policies pursued with new means. The old policies left these countries exploited, fragmented, and penetrated. There is nothing in the new joint policy so diametrically different that the result should be qualitatively different from what today's EC member countries obtained separately during the last centuries. On the contrary, the giant size of the EC empire may make the struggle for equity even more difficult.[36] Conclusion: trade with the EC is unavoidable. But *close* participation in this system is not in the interest of the less developed countries and should be avoided.

Chapter 7.
The European Community and the socialist countries

A new approach is needed to analyze the relation between the EC and the socialist countries, although the approach used in the preceding chapter to study the relation to the Third World still has some validity. The point of departure would be that the EC is the largest capitalist association of countries the world has ever seen, and that capitalism is 'the system of production under which there is a very high mobility of the classical production factors; capital, land, labor'. Capital has always been mobile; land and labor depend more on rapid transportation – and that Western speciality, the multinational corporation, is a form of organization that facilitates tremendously the mobility of all three factors.

We have chosen this definition of capitalism rather than one in terms of 'ownership of means of production'. The latter is important, but it is quite possible to have a system of production with state ownership *and* high mobility of production factors. Capital, land, and labor then tend to end up at the same place: this place becomes the center, and the rest becomes the periphery. For certain definitions of efficiency, this seems logical and rational. But the *consequence* is that the periphery becomes dependent on the center, does not develop its own resources, and does not go in for autonomy in general and self-sufficiency in particular.

We mention this because the term 'socialist countries' above stands for at least two very different systems. Both have abolished private ownership of means of production, but only the Chinese (and perhaps the Albanian) systems are really strong on stimulating the type of local self-reliance that is also the goal of the African socialism, the *ujamaa*, of Nyerere.[1] 'State capitalism' or 'state monopoly' seems a good description for a system of state ownership combined with high mobility of production factors towards centers of production and away from a periphery that becomes a source of raw materials, foodstuffs and talent. Since by 'socialist countries' we are mainly thinking of Eastern European countries, 'socialism' often looks more like the latter than the former.

86

Let us start by seeing what an analysis in terms of exploitation, fragmentation and penetration can yield. The conclusion where the Third World as a whole is concerned was that EC power was based on a combination of all three factors. One could now imagine several types of less extreme combinations. For instance, in the case of Latin America there is only exploitation and penetration, since both the EC and the Latin American countries (except Cuba) seem to prefer to regard Latin America as a unit.[2] That unit has a highly penetrated elite that would not object too much to exploitation within a capitalist framework – and its joint stand in favor of unequal deal with the EC is by many misinterpreted as solidarity and strength.[3] Similarly, the strong point of the policies of the non-EC Western European countries is probably their insistence on the right to continue export of manufactures to the EC, but they are certainly also fragmented and their elites are heavily penetrated by the giant in Brussels. What about the socialist countries? Our conclusion is certainly vertical division of labor, but not so much fragmentation and penetration. After all: their revolution was above all a defense against capitalism, taking them out of the orbit of capitalism.

1) *Vertical division of labor between East and West in Europe*

Trade statistics between the two parts of Europe show convincingly the colonial structure[4] of the trade composition: raw materials one way, manufactured goods the other way; and also that the EC countries have an even more colonial structure in their trade composition with Eastern Europe than does the rest of Western Europe. The old formula of capitalism, to secure sources of raw materials (in this case particularly oil and gas), and markets for manufactured goods, is largely fulfilled. The structure is well known, but there are some additional aspects that do not apply so well in connection with Third World countries.

First, informed sources[5] insist that what the Eastern European countries try to obtain in their trade with the West is not so much short-term rationality, the best goods at the lowest price, but contracts with the firm with the biggest research capacity, the largest laboratories, etc. A contract is for technology rather than for goods; the products are then analyzed in Eastern Europe to gain maximum insight from them. If Eastern Europe were open to unlimited penetration by multinational corporations with headquarters in the West, that would take care of the 'transfer of technology'; 'joint venture' is another formula for such 'transfer'.[6] But either form has a distinct disadvantage: the technology transferred is often outdated, and carefully selected by the West so as to prevent competition in the development and marketing of new products. Hence the need for another arrangement: a more open contract where production takes place in the West in such a way that the newest is always available – for analysis. A more equitable production arrangement would reduce access to the most recent technology developed. Hence technology is bought at a high price in terms of raw materials.

Second, the whole machinery for trade with the West is still clumsy and bureaucratic. That would favor exports of raw materials which can be handled on a bulk basis, and without service people etc. to cause embarrassment by being politically unreliable, even to the point of seeking asylum in the West. A pipeline for gas or oil does not seek refuge in a local police station.

Third, as both parties would point out: East European goods do not have the same quality. Under the theory of capitalism presented here and in other chapters this is certainly not strange: some five hundred years of vertical division of labor with the rest of the world has given the West a lead in science and technology. What is strange is that Eastern Europe is improving its own quality and quantity of production so quickly relative to its past (with the exception of Czechoslovakia). Actually, Eastern Europe is 'behind' if one engages in a very unfair comparison of, say, Poland with France and Romania with Italy – not if one compares Bulgaria with Greece and perhaps also Hungary with Austria.[7]

More surprising, and also disappointing, is that Eastern Europe has not produced *other* types of goods than found in the West, but has insisted on 'catching up' and 'taking over' in exactly the same lines of products. It is hard to see any original product at all, except perhaps in the field of toys and arms. Unlike the other major competitor to the West, Japan, the socialist countries seem to be systematically trying to compete with the West where West is stronger. It is as if the socialism of Eastern Europe is unable to find socialist solutions. Example: where is the answer from socialist Europe to the problems posed by those dangerous, polluting, costly, short-lived, excessively individualistic modes of transportation referred to as cars? Nowhere – only unadulterated imitation is found: the Fiat 124 in Poland and the USSR, the Dacia (Renault 10) in Romania, etc.

On the other hand, the West is of course exaggerating the argument of the inferiority, the 'shoddiness', of Eastern European goods. The USSR has jet-liners, watches, cameras, pharmaceutica, hydrofoil boats, to mention some examples, that might compete well with Western products.

The reason why trade is not developed is hardly that these products are not competitive, but rather that they are too competitive, particularly under a socialist pricing system. Liberalization of trade between East and West would probably lead to considerable import of more industrial goods made in the East, not of less. But there are also elements of Western instinctive arrogance, 'only what we have made is really good, because we made it'.

The net result will probably be an even more 'colonial' trade composition in the years to come, and that seems also to be what the Soviet leadership wants.[8] Great flexibility in marxist thinking is mobilized to justify cooperation with capitalist firms.[9] Manufactured goods produced in the socialist countries are used for trade among themselves, with less embarrassment due to inferior quality or political difficulties. Considerable thinking goes into the nature of the deals with the West: how to obtain maximum technology with greatest ease and minimum commitment.

However, it is difficult to see how the net result can be anything but dependence, on Western technology. The socialist countries themselves will be able to produce as soon as factories have been set up on the basis of imported technology under the formulas mentioned above. But imagine a car is produced, even a more perfect version of some Western car.[10] Is there any reason at all to believe that the socialist countries would be immune to the spirals of increasing demands? Once the car has been mass produced there will be a demand for better roads and service facilities for cars (service stations) and people (motels). When that need has been satisfied there will be a demand for faster and bigger cars to make fuller and better use of the facilities – as witnessed by how the *Autobahnen* in Germany and the *autostrade* in Italy have stimulated the spread of much faster cars.

Can one really expect the population in the socialist countries will have a built-in ability to say 'enough is enough' when all the propaganda they have been exposed to after the 1917 revolution has been in terms of catching up in technology rather than in terms of developing an alternative technology? More particularly, since the car permits of privatism and familism – for instance on Sunday outings, denied to those without cars who will be referred to the trade union bus excursion – there is a distinct class mechanism at work here, even a strengthening of bourgeois life patterns. One may be in favor of or against such life styles, but production cannot stop when the needs of a small elite for private means of transportation have been satisfied. Hence, there will be an increasing demand for more cars, and for stronger, faster cars, once the process has really been started.

If one now assumes that the socialist countries will themselves be able to satisfy that spiralling demand as soon as the first big factories with Western technology are fully operative, then no dependency might be the consequence. But is that very likely? Is it not exactly the type of process the capitalist countries are specialists in? Capitalism has nothing to boast of when it comes to satisfying the primary needs of the world periphery, the real proletariat of the world – but capitalism does know how to generate and satisfy, and once more generate and satisfy demands, over and over again. Western firms will have their specialists on the spot; and whenever a new demand raises its head, it will just so happen that a new product has been turned out from the Renault, Fiat etc. factories, at least designed on the drawingboards, that will meet the demands and even yield a bit extra in the bargain. In this situation, Eastern European leadership will be in a squeeze: they can reject the offer and have to confront a mass of unsatisfied, demanding converts to car consumerism at ever increasing levels; or they can accept the offer, in which case they have moved one step further on a road which promises to be a cul-de-sac – but only after a long and complicated journey. At this point, moralism from recent converts to anti-consumerism in the West – and they are numerous – will not help. If Western Europeans admonish Eastern Europeans to take to bicycling, listing the evils that result from motorism, from pollution to heart attacks, this only sounds paternalistic. Any such conversion would have to come from people in the socialist countries themselves.

Conclusion: the total picture is complicated, but the net result has distinct features of an exploitation leading to increased dependency. The implications of this will be explored further in the next chapter.

2) *What about fragmentation and penetration?*

Fragmentation and penetration are almost equally important. Where these two are concerned, the picture is even more complicated. To start with fragmentation, imagine three contrasting images of the total European scene:[11]

a) *L'Europe des patries:* Europe as a collection of 30 countries with weak or even non-existing subregional[12] organizations, each country free to develop ties in all directions, bilaterally and multilaterally.

b) *A unicentric Europe:* a Europe dominated by one of the two parts, with vertical division of labor, with the countries of the other part attached one at a time to the stronger part, and with the elites thoroughly penetrated. This would be, inside Europe, more or less like the relation between the EC and the Third World countries.

c) *A bicentric Europe:* a Europe with two parts, neither dominating the other, with no effort towards exploitation, fragmentation or penetration. This would be, inside Europe, more or less like the relation that may develop between the EC and the US.[13]

Of course, these 'models' are all too simplistic to be images of concrete reality. But *one* thing is certain: the first alternative is out; the integration process in the European Community has come too far. Nothing is eternal in human and social affairs, but for the foreseeable future the disintegration of the EC in Europe seems unlikely (its power outside Europe may be seriously curtailed, but that is another matter). The reality of present-day Europe seems located somewhere between the other two alternatives: certainly not unicentric with its center in Brussels (including NATO in Casteau), nor bicentric in any really egalitarian sense because of the vertical division of labor.

There is no doubt that strong forces in the West would love to see (b) as a model for Europe.[14] This could even be spelt out in details which to many will sound very attractive, something like the following:

- the treaties of non-aggression are ratified, other issues coming out of World War II and its aftermath are also resolved
- substantial reduction of the military levels on either side is brought about; the savings are used to increase the level of living of the peoples of Europe – particularly of the poorest regions, East and West of the Mediterranean basin, and for the developing countries
- East and West agree, explicitly and/or implicitly, about a division of labor to the effect that West satisfies the needs for more sophisticated consumer and capital goods, East for the less sophisticated goods. The less developed East also becomes recreation area for the more developed West.
- Brussels becomes the center of Europe with the Eastern European countries tied to the EC by a new type of association, and by the high level of production factor mobility
- with more prosperity to the peoples of Europe, with freer exchange of people and ideas also comes more peace. The net result would be an all-European peace system.

Would this not be the best one could hope for in a difficult world? No, all this would mean would be a return to the past, to the Europe that was rejected in the Russian revolution – although certainly at a higher level of technological achievement and standard of living.[15] It would be a unicentric Europe in a very real sense, where exploitation would persist underneath a cover of consumer prosperity, bound sooner or later to result in new revolts, new searches for liberation and for new alternatives. These are the contradictions in a capitalist system, and they become particularly pronounced when nationalism adds to the forces generated by exploitation because the exploiters are of one nation (or group of nations) and the exploited of another.

Here we stand at the moment. There would be forces in the West jubilantly welcoming every little sign of one socialist country or the other 'recognizing' the European Community. Thus, even when Romania demands access to the GPS there is a cry of triumph as if total acceptance of EC principles were involved. At the same time the DDR has its special and highly profitable formula with the EC. Furthermore, all the big EC powers are hurrying to close deals of different kinds with the individual socialist countries before 1 January 1973, when such deals are supposed to be made on a European Community basis. Moreover, every sign of willingness to play the capitalist raw-material market game is hailed welcome as 'realism', 'pragmatism', 'decline of ideology', and the like – all of them different terms for successful ideological penetration of socialist elites whose state capitalism is often quite reconcilable with private capitalism.

There would be forces in the East who would favor this development, partly because of its promises in terms of consumer satifaction, and partly because domination by Western Europe may be preferred to domination by Moscow (we say Moscow and not the USSR, for such forces might also be found inside the USSR, say, in Ukraina or the Baltic states). The very existence of such forces would make it even more important for the socialist regimes to be on guard against this type of development. Their strategy would have to be based on four elements, all of them problematic: be on guard against exploitation, be on guard against fragmentation, be on guard against penetration and try not to recognize the European Community.

The latter is doomed to failure: the EC is too big not to be recognized sooner or later. What form this recognition will take is another question. It may not take the form of diplomatic missions in Brussels accredited to the EC,[16] but could take the form of increasing recognition of the EC in international organizations, such as the UN Economic Commission for Europe and UNCTAD, where the EC at present is accorded presence as an intergovernmental organization in consultative status, with right to circulate documentation. One might even imagine some kind of deal whereby the DDR and the EC both obtain full recognition at this multilateral level,[17] for the time being, at least, relieving NATO nations of the need to recognize the DDR directly, and the WTO nations of the need to recognize the EC directly. As to the latter: 1 January 1973 has been set as a deadline after which trade agreements must be accepted by the commission. It remains to be seen how firm this deadline, and that rule, will be in practice.

A far better strategy than this attempt towards non-recognition of the EC, it seems, would have been to support alternative Western European groupings, such as NORDEK, a Nordic Economic Cooperation Organization. But Soviet suspicion that for the Norwegian and Danish leadership EC membership was always the preferred solution, and that they might either leave NORDEK in case of a conflict, or try to use it a a way of getting Sweden and Finland more solidly tied to the EC, was certainly not unfounded.[18]

With this strategy largely speaking untried, with the non-recognition strategy headed for failure, with vertical division of labor increasing rather than decreasing, with elites going for many of the same social goals as the elites in the West and with severe splits between and within the socialist countries – the situation is not easy. But there is one alternative to a unicentric Europe: solidarity among the socialist countries. Any *l'Europe des patries* would be subject to the influence of the strongest, the USSR; this would in any case lead to the formation of some kind of European Community lest the US not offer sufficient protection. The EC then becomes the strongest party, and *this leads to the integration race.*

3) *From arms race to integration race*

Anyone who travelled around in Europe, East and West, some years ago would have no difficulty picking up the traditional rationalizations of the arms race: 'we (West, East) have to negotiate from a position of military strength; otherwise the other side (East, West) will not respect us but run us over'. Today the traveller can hear, with about the same frequency and more or less from the same people: 'we (West, East) have to negotiate from a position of unity, integration among ourselves; otherwise the other side (East, West) will not respect us but make use of the splits among us'. In the old day, images of tanks rolling westwards and missiles being fired eastwards were conjured up on the wall. Today

93

the images of separate deals such as the USSR concluding her own treaty with the German Federal Republic; the Federal Republic making her own deal with the DDR; Romania making a separate deal with who-knows-whom (China must be the major Soviet nightmare in that connection) are frequently used arguments. In the old days the manufacturers of arms and the military forces enjoyed such images; today manufacturers in general and integration politicians would market the second type of argumentation.

As for the arms race, it can be argued that the West was first, and that East dependency on West also shows up here: East has to some extent to be a mirror reflection of West. The result is seen in the plans for the deepening of CMEA, made public in the communiqué from the 25th meeting of the CMEA Council July 1971 in Bucharest.[19] It is an obvious consequence of EC policies in addition to internal growth: CMEA has to do something like that, it has to prove its ability to match the EC in some important respects, as increased internal trade, consumer satisfaction and international cooperation. The alternative would be the victory of the West, 'all-European' integration on the premises of the West: in other words a unicentric Europe.

So, CMEA integration takes place, and probably on an increasing scale in years to come. No one in the West can complain with any right, since this must be seen, to a considerable degree, as being caused by the West. There are also two extremely important side effects: the impact on the small Eastern European countries, and the impact on all-European integration.

4) *Consequences for the small Eastern European countries*

There are six of them, and they can conveniently be grouped in two groups: a Northern group consisting of Poland, the DDR, and Czechoslovakia; and a Southern group consisting of Hungary, Romania, and Bulgaria. Together they have a population of 103 million, in other words of considerable magnitude. It is well known that they are divided among themselves over age-old issues and new issues, for instance Hungary–Romania over Transylvania, and later on, possibly, DDR–Poland over the former German territories. There are four obvious alternatives for the future: continued dependence on the USSR, dependence on the EC, complete national independence, or integration of all six (or of some sub-grouping of them). We then assume that egalitarian integration of the present socialist countries, ranging from the giant USSR down to the smaller of the Six, is almost meaningless, even given the best intentions and efforts by the superpower involved.

Let us look at the possibility of forming an ESC, an *European Socialist Community,* on the basis of these Six. Let us assume that like the EC relative to the US its aim is unification to obtain sufficient size for independence *and* partnership with Big Brother. In this case, however, the independence would be political, and the partnership economic – with a horizontal division of labor according to socialist principles. It would not be economically competitive like the US–EC relationship. There are already very interesting trends, such as the present bilateral arrangements between the DDR on the one hand and Poland and Czechoslovakia on the other, whereby citizens of the countries can move freely to the other and exchange their currencies. The arrangement is likely to be extended very soon to Poland–Czechoslovakia,[20] making out of the Northern group an area with much higher mobility than before, and possible extensions so as to involve Hungary are explored. Whether this can be expanded to comprise all Six is an open question, but it is at least a question, and discussed all over Eastern Europe.

If this took place, and other steps followed, what would be the attitude of the USSR? The USSR should not be seen as completely monolithic in this connection, for it seem obvious that Ukraine would have special interests in contacts with Czechoslovakia and Poland, Lithuania with Poland, and Moldavia (Bessarabia) with Romania. These contacts would in some contexts have a highly nationalistic and political connotation, in other contexts they might be more economic, touristic, cultural, and personal – a question of relatives who want to meet.

The list of speculations as to how the regimes in the countries and republics concerned might respond to demands from the peoples can easily be made very long – because these are very real, if so far rather weak, forces. They may show up at many levels, for instance as an increasingly consistent cooperation among the Six before a CMEA or WTO meeting to prepare a joint position. Today this is unlikely because the USSR, like any other big power, has special relations with all its underlings – but that may change. Thus, it might change with internal cleavages coming more out in the open inside the USSR – from the minorities, the peasants, the intelligentsia, particularly if these three should ever find each other and be able to develop a common platform. But it may certainly also be argued that a more relaxed attitude by the USSR relative to the Six is more likely to come when the Soviet leadership senses it has internal affairs well under control than when it is exposed to internal pressure and feels it also has to be on guard against external enemies. However this may be, it is unlikely that the situation will remain static; there are forces of change in all seven countries.

That brings up another issue: what kind of community would the ESC make?[21] Imagine it would stay socialist, but become much more pluralist, permitting, even encouraging, 'several roads to socialism', not only among the Six but also inside some of them – e.g. as to the problem of how factories should be organized, how country and town should relate to each other, how much self-reliance and how much factor-mobility at the local level, etc. The conclusion is relatively clear: it would be in the joint EC–USSR interest to discourage this type of development, for it might challenge either regime. Probably nothing has stopped the spread of socialist organization of economic life to more European countries so effectively as the image of totalitarian and authoritarian Soviet society. The existence in Europe of socialist countries that are innovative and permit a great deal of individual self-expression might have considerable influence on such border states as Finland, Austria, perhaps even Switzerland (or at least some cantons in Switzerland). They might in the future simply like to associate themselves closely with this kind of community – perhaps even to the point of modifying the economic system. In that case something different from both the EC and the USSR would have taken shape in the midst of Europe – and precisely for that reason, the short-term likelihood is rather low.

However, if it should happen, the mirror process referred to above would have been completed. The whole system that once made up the cold war would look something like Figure 3.

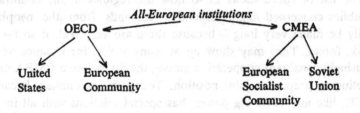

Fig. 3.

A structure of this kind may some day come into being, and its symmetry is quite attractive from a peace-theoretical perspective.[22] It would be more flexible, and one major problem would have been solved: independence of Big Brother on either side.

96

But this is not what is taking place at present in Europe: there is no such structure in view. On the contrary, exactly because of the integration race between East and West the small Eastern European countries are being squeezed into much closer integration with the Soviet Union than they may have wanted. If one goal of Western policy was to make the Six in the East less dependent on the USSR, the result seems to have been the exact opposite.

5) *Consequences for all-European integration*

The net result of the integration race is not only that the small Eastern European states come into a squeeze, but that Europe becomes split in a much more fundamental manner than by the cold war. The cold war was based on anxiety, hatred, willingness to kill – partly due to real issues, partly due to imagined ones. The present situation is based on a rapidly increasing level of integration on either side, a self-centeredness at the same time as the level of all-European cooperation of various kinds remains more or less constant. All-European cooperation will increase in years to come, but not nearly so fast as the subregional activities. The net result is as follows: the two parts of Europe postpone and postpone any really integrating work on all-European cooperation till they are both so well integrated that almost all resources – capital, manpower, ideas, energy, political will – are channeled inwards and what is left for the all-European level is highly rudimentary and mainly ceremonial. The moment they are 'ready' – for all-European cooperation – they are already so deeply engaged in subregional integration that self-sufficiency makes for much less motivation. Of course, the exploitative, neo-colonial trade pattern already described will probably continue, even increase in volume, but that is not what is here meant by all-European integration.

A useful example in this connection is the all-European power grid, a plan long put forward by the Economic Commission for Europe. Due to the four hour difference in consumption peaks between East and West there is much to gain: $ 6 billion annually, or 75 % of the present East-West trade. It would be an excellent case of a peacebuilding structure where both parties contribute the same kind of thing and get the same kind of benefit – and even of a considerable magnitude. But Britain and the Netherlands have both been against – according to informed sources, because of pressure from Royal Dutch Shell who sees extra electric power made available through cooperation as a competitor to Western thermo-electric power plants based on oil. The most likely development is that

97

West will first find its own solution, and look for all-European cooperation only if there is no Western solution and if the vertical pattern so
often referred to is not effectively threatened.

In conclusion, let us for a moment go back to the distinction made between three possible models of future European development and imagine
some kind of all-European integration under all three. For *l'Europe des
patries* it would be flexible, but also, possibly, Soviet dominated – and
if the US were brought in to balance that, the institution would probably
not imply any kind of new departure. In *unicentric Europe* there would
be a new departure, back to the old pattern from the period before the
World War II when the USSR was the only exception to that pattern. An
in *bicentric Europe,* all-European cooperation would be hampered because integration has come so far in West and soon also in East.

The prospects do not look very good – except for those who confuse
treaties and arrangements meant to tidy up after a war finished 27 years
ago, and a neo-colonial trade pattern, with peace.

Chapter 8.
The military aspect

In a sense the thesis in this chapter is trivial: there will be a military side to the European Community. To avoid misunderstanding, we should state at the outset that the idea is not that the EC as such will develop a military wing. The military aspect to be discussed here would resemble some kind of European NATO. Nor is the thesis that any development of a Euro-NATO means the *dissolution* of NATO. Such a dissolution may or may not take place, but is neither likely nor important for the argument to be developed here. A *transformation* of NATO is all that is needed for the EC to take on a military character. By that we mean, roughly speaking, the following: the Western European military integration, with a centralized command, capable of at least some military postures and even action independent of the US. The latter does not necessarily mean action against the will of the US – it only means without involving the US. Thus, in the early years of the US war in Indochina the European NATO powers were not involved,[1] although with some few exceptions they were probably not much opposed either.

Again we cannot proceed by means of quotations from famous or less famous European statesmen. These may serve to illustrate, but not to demonstrate. About the future nothing can be proved, but predictions can be backed up by reasoning. It is this kind of reasoning that will be given below, and along seven different lines of thought.

1) *The participating countries are (almost) the same*

With the extension from Six to Ten the European Community and European NATO are not identical, but they coincide considerably. Most significantly: they coincide where the four larger members are concerned. Iceland is not an EC member – nor does it appear likely that she will become one – but it is not impossible that Iceland may detach herself from NATO. Three NATO countries of a more or less fascist nature in the Mediterranean area (Turkey, Greece, Portugal) are not EC members – but it is likely that over time they may become members. Then there is Eire, an EC but not NATO member – but not in and by herself sufficient to upset the relationship.

What this means is that there is no need for any formal link between EC and NATO: the link exists already, and at the highest level: a sharing of governments through which all information and decisions can flow. Informal links of any nature and at the highest level can easily be established at any point. More particularly, this means that bargains can be made whereby positions in the general field of security can be traded for position in the field of economic relations. Thus, from the viewpoint of the Six it is hardly audacious to assume that Norwegian membership in the EC is more important from the viewpoint of defense policy than from the viewpoint of fish, and that the former may certainly be worth some concessions to Norwegian negotiators in terms of the latter.[2]

To all this it may be objected that the coincidence between EC and Euro-NATO membership, although considerable, is not perfect. The answer, in turn, would be that other organizational forms can also be found whereby the EC would get a military face in the sense mentioned above. The two most important ones are Anglo-French cooperation and the framework provided by the Western Union, consisting of the Six and Great Britain. For either case British membership in the EC leads to a basic, qualitative change: whatever Britain does is now inside the EC family, and will inevitably be an important component of EC policy. Hence, any analysis must take into account several possible arrangements that may emerge,[3] probably sooner rather than later.

2) *The chain effects of integration*

Integration inside the EC has always had two basic characteristics: it has *started* in the economic field, and at the top; and it has *developed* at all levels and in very many fields. Any national organization, governmental or nongovernmental, in any one of the member countries is surrounded by integration, from major economic enterprises and the small beginnings in the field of trade union integration, to the many organizations reported in the *Yearbook of International Organizations*.[4] Another image of this is given in the very extensive network of lobbies established around the EC, of all sorts of organizations who have their offices for that purpose in Brussels.[5]

In the military field integration could be hardware or software oriented.

It can be oriented towards the weapons, the means of destruction themselves; or towards the men who are experts in using them, the soldiers of all kinds and ranks. Thus, in the field of arms industry the EC countries are by no means 'integrated'; the firms are not integrated, and the arms themselves differ. In broad terms, but more rightly than wrongly, one might say that as to hardware, NATO has largely been integrated by means of US (and some European produced) arms; whereas arms produced in Europe have been mainly for the country of production and for clients in their traditional sphere of influence and others – but certainly not for the US. Like European economic integration it has largely been built around US investments, capital and know-how.[6]

Is it reasonable to believe that the field of arms production will differ from all others in its efforts to find a 'European' platform? Or is it more reasonable to assume that much, much more integration in this field has already taken place than what meets the naked eye? Is it reasonable to believe that efforts to find a production basis in Western Europe more *independent of the Americans* will stop short of the field of arms? Or, is it more reasonable to assume that this motivating force will be as strong here as elsewhere?

Let us then turn to the software factor: exactly the same questions can be formulated. When foreign ministers coordinate and harmonize, within the setting provided by the EC – when all other ministers, practically speaking, do the same – is it then reasonable to assume that the ministers of defense and also the military staffs shall always and systematically insist that this setting is not for us? That we have another framework, NATO, which is not only necessary, but also sufficient? Or is it more reasonable to assume that an integrating environment will in and by itself *force* a *Defense Community* into being, regardless of what the intentions might have been at one stage or the other? Thus, to make just one point: to some extent problems of defense policy can be delegated to ministers of foreign affairs, but only up to a certain point. Beyond that, ministers of defense and their experts have to take over; and here *the EC as an independence movement of the US* will structure the relationships. But this is perhaps brought out more clearly in connection with the next factor.

3) *NATO: from hegemony to partnership*

A change in the structure of NATO has been taking place during the last few years. The point of departure resembled a pyramid with the US on top, the bigger European powers on the tier below, sometimes including the nuclear powers, France and Great Britain, the Security Council members only; sometimes also England; and after France partially left NATO, England and Germany only. The French effort under de Gaulle to establish an executive of nuclear powers did not suceed, and it is probably fair to say that the NATO structure has been ambiguous ever since (and was also before that). Under no circumstance can NATO be said to have been so clearly hegemonial as the Warsaw Treaty Organization appears to be; and it is probably correct to say that where the latter is an organization built around all the bilateral relationships (including stationing of troops) the USSR has with the Eastern European countries, the former is a much more multilateral organization. This difference, however, is only a difference in degree, not in kind.[7]

Whatever the changes were until years ago in the NATO structure, we can now see a slow transition towards partnership, between the US on the one hand and Euro-NATO on the other. Diagrammatically this might look something like Fig. 4.

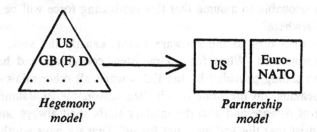

Fig. 4.

The diagram is, like most diagrams, too clear, but it serves to point out two phenomena. First, this process could not, and cannot, take place before Western Europe is brought more closely together. With thirteen European member states of NATO, the Six did not represent sufficient integration: the Ten do. Hence, it is to be expected that this process will speed up considerably with the expansion of the Community. Second, perhaps a small point in the total picture, but what about Canada? One line of thought might perhaps be as follows. In the hegemony model, Canada was one among several underlings; in the partnership it can fit in only if the non-European part is called 'North America', and then it would be painfully clear how much that big country is a periphery country under the US. There is only one solution: to leave NATO, at least partly – as did France when she was not accorded the special status she felt entitled to.

102

From the very early years of NATO the US has been complaining that the European allies do not carry a sufficient part of the defense burden. In the early years the answer might have been that they were not able; later it seemed rather to be that they were not willing. The reason might be simple although not necessarily expressed openly in such terms: a country pays in proportion to its share in real (as opposed to formal) decision-making. To shoulder the expenses in a more equitable manner would have to imply a partnership model of NATO. If the payments were slow in coming, so was the partnership; and if the partnership was slow in coming, then it was because 'Europe was not united' – as it was usually expressed. These three things are related to each other, and in a rather obvious manner.

But a second aspect to this is more important than sharing the financial burden. Is it reasonable to believe that when all over Western Europe there has been a movement going on, for years, to assert equity, equality, and parity with the US, the military people should simply stand still and say 'we are happy as we are, under US leadership'? Or, is it more reasonable to believe that exactly the same motivations and movements will also be found in military circles? The point here is not whether the US in fact exercised hegemonial power (except in the important field of nuclear strategy to be dealt with below). The point is rather that in a general Western European self-assertion movement the military also belong; hence, something must happen to NATO. This 'something' has two aspects: a closer integration of the European NATO-powers dealt with above, and a *Gleichberechtigung* between what emerges as the two parts of Europe.

4) *The rise and fall of the American empire*

The most surprising thing about the US empire is its relatively short duration. In a sense it started by exterminating most American Indians, and pushing the rest into reservations. It is probably more correct to say that the US empire started by beating another imperialist power, Spain, in Latin America and in South East Asia around the turn of the century. These are also the two parts of the world where US imperialism flourished and is now being beaten, starting with the Cuban revolution from 1958 on – leading on to the many confrontations in Latin America and, indeed, to the Indochina wars. If these wars of liberation and these revolutions had not taken place, the world would still be in the 1950s, politically speaking. As matters stand, the rise of the European Community has coincided with the fall of the US empire – and not merely by chance. US presidents who have talked much about the relation between the Vietnam war and the confidence of 'our allies' knew what they were talking about, and they were right: with increasing defeat, decreasing confidence, and still more defeat.

To this should then be added two other elements. It is too much to talk about moral and financial bankruptcy in the position of the US, but the signals point in that direction. As has been evident to the political *left* for many years, US society has heavy elements of *structural fascism* in its midst: a cool, technical, scientific fascism that murders and represses around the world (particularly in Indochina), and with a relatively clear racial address inside as well as outside the US mainland. It has mobilized thousands of scientists and technicians and workers in developing anti-personnel weapons, police methods, counter-insurgency of all kinds. It does not have the explicitness and the personal hatred and blood lust of the nazi aberration in human history, but for the victims – Vietnamese children, for instance – this must be of minor consequence. My Lai dramatizes it all but with the wrong emphasis: that was regular fascism, direct murder of civilians, eye-to-eye, not the much more significant indirect kind. By convicting Calley, the others were acquitted. The *Pentagon Papers* turned the attention in a more correct direction for a deeper understanding of the phenomenon.

What is new today is that the European political *right* also seems to perceive these phenomena, although they are more tactful and do not express this so openly to their US connections. Needless to say, to people engaged in any kind of independence movement – and the European Community is in part such a movement – revelations about your (real or imagined) overlord are by no means unpleasant. And the two feed into each other: the more revelation, the more fight for independence; the more fight for independence, the more search for revelations. Things that have been true about the US for decades, but never mentioned, surface as the European Community takes shape. We may even speak of a division of labor inside Western Europe: the left takes care of smearing the US, the right uses this climate of opinion to safeguard its military, political and business interests from US penetration.

In a sense, the whole thing is absurd and can only work because of the extremely short memory most of mankind seems to possess. After World War II all big powers gained legitimacy because they had beaten the nazis. Then, Britain and France got exposed in the final fits of their classical imperialism, with the joint Suez invasion as a last (so far) concerted

104

and spectacular effort. The United States gained legitimacy as a contrast to their allies. But then the turn came to the US – indeed – and the allies were not displeased. In the meantime Germany had been in cold storage; its sins being of a higher magnitude, partly in quantity and partly, it seems, because they were committed against Europeans. Today all three surface – England, France, and Germany together – in the shape of the European Community, trying to build up legitimacy as a contrast to the ally across the Atlantic.[8] They are not alone: the USSR, China, and to some extent Japan are also trying to appear innocent to their surroundings by contrasting themselves with the US.

As to the economic situation: it costs to defend a crumbling empire. This we see in the defense budgets, although they do not tell the whole story, as the militarization of US society goes much deeper. US business prefers to expand in Western Europe rather than at home (high labor costs, difficult trade unions, especially when race is involved) or in the Third World (particularly in the 'business-friendly' countries, usually dictatorships). Difficulties with balance of payments stem largely from overextension. One element in this overextension are the famous 320,000 US soldiers in Western Europe, but this does not prove that the motivation behind plans to withdraw them is simply and purely budgetary. Whatever the strategic equation held in the various fractions in the US and in Europe may be on this question is a matter to guess and write articles and books about. But the fact is that Western Europeans tend to believe in the withdrawal hypothesis, and that denials from US presidents are not taken very seriously. The symbolic value of rumors of US troop withdrawal is immense, although it is apparent that withdrawal must be accompanied by an increase in hardware. Such an increase may be of the automated type with sensors and automatic response aimed at destroying intruders (but not necessarily by means of nuclear land mines)[9] – in other words, be structural rationalization. This symbolic significance clearly was understood by de Gaulle. It means one more sign of the fall of the *pax americana;* one more green light to go ahead with the *pax bruxellana.*

5) *A shadow from the past: the European Defense Community*

The EDC was an effort to find a solution to the problem of how to rearm Germany without involving the Americans too directly. The Germans had to be controlled somehow: but inside an EDC, or under a more bilateral US-German arrangement within NATO?[10] The idea of a *Euro-*

pean Defense Community took shape, but it is rather obvious (in retrospect!) that such a Defense Community could not come into being without a Political Community. The debate in the Assemblée Nationale over the issue the night of 30 August 1954, when ratification was rejected, would hardly have taken place if there had already been a political community where such issues as 'French nationalism' could have been articulated in advance and compromises been developed – for instance awarding France a special status, more equal than the others, or some more escape clauses (dear to a nation who defines herself as different from all others).[11] Whatever was the reason, the motion was defeated and the EDC did not come about.

In retrospect we might point out that this was not only because of 'French nationalism' and the communist vote against, nor because there was no political community: but because integration in Western Europe had not come far enough in general, and the US had not declined enough either. Both these conditions are satisfied today. The significance of the EDC pre-history may then be as follows.

First: the EDC was signed by all Six, ratified by five of them, and defeated in France by a relatively slim majority only. Thus, very considerable political forces were in favor. These forces are not dead: most of them are alive and even lively.

Second: with the EDC a blueprint was made, a *Gestalt* was formed, an image of what could be. That image has to be revised in view of new political conditions and strategic doctrines, but it can still be compelling. We assume that however much the world changes, the people who developed this image do not necessarily change that much, but may still want to enact their old ideas.

6) *The problem of enriched uranium*[12]

Uranium as found in nature contains only 0.7 % U 235, the raw material for nuclear reaction. For use, it has to be enriched – up to 90 % to make an atomic bomb, 35 % to run a submarine, but only 3 % for a fuel plant. There are two problems to be overcome to enter the field of nuclear reactors: the first is to get the uranium ore, the second to enrich it. The first problem is solved easily enough: uranium is relatively abundant, and one of the 'associated states', Zaire (former Belgian Congo) is a major supplier.

The second problem is more difficult. Classical technology in the field, the gas diffusion plant (with gas or water cooling), is extremely expensive, very energy-requiring, and very big – which means easily detectable. For all three reasons, one may presume, Britain, Germany, and Netherlands all started experiments with the centrifugation technique whereby small containers with uranium are spun at 100,000 revolutions per minute to separate the heavier U 238 from the lighter U 235. The three nations joined together in 1970, signed an agreement and set up three pilot machines, one in Britain and two at Almelo in Netherlands – just across the border from Germany (by the 1955 Paris Treaty Germany is barred from doing this kind of thing on her own territory). Needless to say, by the accession of Britain to the EC this Anglo-Dutch-German company becomes an internal affair of the European Community.

It is difficult to evaluate what this will mean in precise terms, since much naivete is needed to assume that even a fraction of the relevant information is at public disposal in the EC countries. As to energy supply, the implications are probably clear.[13] The US supply of enriched uranium to Europe is expected to reach a saturation point in 1981 – and by that time the centrifuge should be able to deliver the goods to a Europe very poor in energy supply and very dependent on Middle East oil. The gas-diffusion project would make use of old technology whereas the centrifuge depends on new technology still being developed, which means that research and development spin-off effects from the project itself are considerable. The three countries are here breaking new ground; a number of scientists and technicians are not only receiving training but are also being forced into creativity. In the long run the centrifuge will be cheaper, and the requirements of electric energy would be only one sixth that necessary for the gas-diffusion method. Most significant in this connection: the centrifuge system can be installed in many small plants, and can operate on a much smaller scale than the gas diffusion method – some say two orders of magnitude smaller.[14] The only question is whether it works, not only technically but also economically: and here the leaders of the project seem most optimistic.[15] Incidentally, if this method should not work, there are still at least two technologies for third-generation processes in the field of uranium enrichment: a method based on ion exchange,[16] and one based on laser technology.[17]

The conclusion from this, and from the inspection controversy which went on for years between the UN International Atomic Energy Agency and the EC Euratom, is not necessarily that anything suspicious is going on in Almelo. But *if* there are forces in Western Europe that want an independent European nuclear force, an ENF, then some necessary conditions formerly not satisfied are now unproblematic. The US enrichment monopoly is being broken – one more (and important!) instance of the independence movement away from the US. Second, a new technology with first-hand research experience is being developed – with scientists and technicians who could easily be at the disposal of a coming European Defense Community. Third, technology can proceed and plants be constructed under the assumption that enrichment is for civilian purposes only. And finally: the size is so limited that when the experimental stages are over, miniaturization can proceed so far that detection will be extremely difficult. This method does not show up so easily on budgets, on energy consumption and for the naked eye – even the trained eye will have difficulties knowing for sure what is going on.

7) *Crises as catalysts*

All the items mentioned so far are *factors* to be taken into consideration, nothing more. They are also *facts:* there *is* this growing coincidence in membership; there *is* Western European integration all around; there *is* a general fight for equality relative to the US, a fight already finding some organizational expression in NATO;[18] there *is* a decline in the general US position in the world; there *is* the EDC pre-history; and there *is* a growing independence of the US in the field of enriched uranium. But even when these six factors are added together they prove nothing. Singly and also combined they are compatible with the continuation of NATO more or less as it is today. Extrapolating along these lines into the future, we still see mainly the same thing. The emergence of a really separate military community in Western Europe, built around Anglo-French cooperation, the Western Union and/or Euro-NATO – with or without nuclear capability – would be something qualitatively new relative to present trends. It would be a major discontinuity, and one discontinuity can often be explained in terms of another. Hence the crucial questions are what kinds of discontinuities would produce a military integration, and how likely are such discontinuities?

We should mention that military integration presupposes considerably more centralization than does economic or even political integration. Once a war has started and lasted for some time, it runs much on its own momentum, like business or regular, everyday political decision-making. But the big decisions in the beginning cannot be taken by a clumsy, six- or ten-edged machinery which needs considerable time to arrive at any decision. The fire brigade parallel, so dear to most military people,[19] points to one thing: reaction time has to be short even for mobilization

108

of the total machinery. Once mobilized, it tends to proceed on its own momentum. Hence anything similar to the present EC machinery would definitely be insufficient. To give EC a military aspect, the machinery will have to be changed.[20]

The discontinuities that could bring about major changes in the integration level, with much more centralized machinery for quick decision-making, would be *crises*, crises that are basic threats to the very existence of the European Community. Viewing the world as we have done in this effort to analyze the EC, we may discern four kinds of crises worth looking into:

- crises inside the EC itself
- crises in relation to the US
- crises in relation to the developing countries
- crises in relation to Eastern Europe

We have omitted 'other Western European countries' since they are not likely to produce crises, and also 'the rest of the world' since it it too remote. The other four, however, are meaningful in this context.

That there will be crises within the community, as in any other state, big or small, is trivial. Farmers' protests have already attained a certain level, for example. But apart from that, and with the exception of the strikes organized by the extremely well-paid Eurocrats in the Commission in order to get even better paid,[21] no action seems to be directed against the Community as such. In most countries in Western Europe, students have been revolting, many of them are marxists, none of them marched on the Commission. Far from being a sign of acceptance and of strength, this shows how poorly the EC is integrated into people's minds and actions in member states, how much it still lies far above the grasp of people in general. But this also has to do with the location of the Commission in Brussels with its extreme commercialism and low level of student activism. Would the Commission dare move to Paris, Rome, or West Berlin?

Whatever the reason, the period of grace will not last forever. Labor in the EC countries will join together, and will sooner or later organize European strikes, as a countermove to the European companies. The more politically conscious of them will sooner or later find out that a nucleus of Western European capitalism today is the Commission. Leftist students in Western Europe – on the continent, that is – will also sooner or later discover the reality of the EC, and not only define it conveniently away as a 'superstructure' on top of national and transnational capitalism.[22] Sooner or later they will discover that during the years they have used to analyze US imperialism to pieces, Western Europe's Right has built something very similar, right outside their own university windows. Again, sooner or later there will be marches on Brussels, literally and figuratively speaking. There will be stones thrown against the glass windows of the Berlaymont building – from that point of view an ideal piece of architecture, since it is all glass.

At least equally important will be the regional crises. The EC, with its programmatic high mobility of production factors, knows only one type of economic system: a capitalism where wealth accumulates in the center (where the production factors are moved), while the periphery is sapped of much of its natural, capital and labor resources and will have to depend on private and public charity in its many forms. The fisher-farmers in Northern Norway and the *braccianti* in Sicily will sooner or later find each other, although it will take time, for the whole Community is biased against them. They do not have pressure groups *together* in Brussels, only (sometimes) separately in their respective capitals; their resources are limited; their problems are so diverse that it is difficult to find a common demand, and so on. But some form will be found – as it always has been found, even in very repressive regimes. In the long run technocratic manipulation from above proves insufficient.

At this point there will have to be a response. The EC will have to develop a collective internal security system, based on national police (and particularly security police, like the CRS in France) organizations. This belongs to the logic of integration as much as cooperation among businessmen, lawyers and students. What is new, and would speed up the process, is the physical symbol of integration, the building of the Commission, and the possibility of marches on the Commission. Is the Belgian police supposed to handle such situations alone? Hardly: something more will have to be developed, and much more than today. This will not turn the EC into a police state, but may lead to a centralized security organization in a community which from the viewpoint of organization is less than a superstate, but much more than a regional organization. Hence internal crises and attacks may dialectically strengthen the centralist forces in the EC.

The second source of crisis would be in the US. Such crises would not weaken the EC: on the contrary, they would strengthen the hand of those who want to go further in detaching Western Europe from the US. Many types of crises are imaginable. The US is heavily overextended, and will still probably have to be beaten country by country in Latin

America – although the US may also learn to respond more subtly than has been the case in, say, Cuba and the Dominican Republic. Then there are internal crises. The US differs from the EC in one very important respect: *the US has part of the Third World inside its own borders*[23] – the US blacks, the Chicanos, the American Indians. From a Third World viewpoint this is a tremendous advantage: strikes against, say, General Motors can be coordinated and take place in mainland US as well as in its periphery. The Third World has no corresponding permanent representation in the EC. And the EC proletariat – the workers in Western Europe – have not shown any particular reticence to producing arms to be used against the real world proletariat, the masses in the poor countries. Nor has the EC regional periphery, the Italian South, the Norwegian North, etc. shown any inclination to see their battle in broader, more global terms. But in the US there is an increasing political consciousness in this direction, which may also be related to the fact that the Third World is so close – in the Caribbean and to the south of the Rio Grande.

Crises of any kind in the US tend to weaken US credibility further. More particularly, they lead to less faith in the US commitment in Europe out of a feeling that the US is a giant with clay feet, that it may show strong armor but be partly hollow, partly rotten inside. Thus, US soldiers have increasingly acquired an image where such elements as deserter, drug-addict, robot killer and traditional murderer mix and blend. Neither singly nor combined do these images inspire allegiance among allies, as mentioned above.

The third and major source of crisis lies in the developing countries. There are two basic patterns: countries as such detach themselves from the EC system, and masses in the poor countries revolt against their EC loyal elites; the national and the people's war of liberation. The second pattern is the most important here. Concretely it means internal war, directed against elites that are heavily dependent on the EC. At the same time, this takes place within countries where the EC has considerable and increasing investments, where an increasing number of Western Europeans are working in various capacities and where the EC also has considerable political investment. For the EC it is important to show that 'we are doing something different from the US'; any inclination towards a Vietnam in Southern Africa, any Cuba or Dominican Republic in Western Africa is therefore a political catastrophe.

Our thesis is that these revolts will come, they cannot be averted by clever politicking. They will come as a result of two factors: the vertical division of labor on the one hand, and the growing consciousness and mobilization in the world periphery on the other. The only way to avoid a confrontation, it seems, would be for the EC to have less to do with the Third World, or to engage in horizontal division of labor. The first is, if not impossible, at least very difficult when one is so heavily involved already; the second is impossible as long as the EC is basically capitalist. Hence, confrontation will come. The question then becomes: is it reasonable to assume that the EC countries will just sit and watch as revolts proceed, e.g. along Cuban lines or any other line known to this post-war generation?

The question can be met with a counter-question: what *can* the EC do? In the old days there was no problem: send the troops, or have them already stationed there. In the not-so-old days, the 1960s, residual *pax britannica* and *pax gallica* were still at work in East Africa, in Gabon, in Chad.[24] There was also the Congo action, using Ascension Island as a landing base. But these are structures from the past. When *Eurafrica* in the vague visions of the EC takes more form, revolt as well as counter-revolt will also take new forms, adapting to the patterns of integration. Or, are the old colonial powers supposed to protect their own nationals, in their old colonies, according to the old pattern? Even if this should be the case, with French troops protecting EC lives and investments in former Afrique Française and British troops protecting EC lives and investments in former British Africa there is a need for coordination. And that coordination is one more, and crucial, part of the military aspect of the EC we are talking about.

Before looking more closely into some of the possible coordination patterns, let us point out that two alternative approaches, both very important in the post-war years, now seem to be blocked.

The first alternative approach was to make use of *the US-as-the-policeman-of-the-world method*. This was a division of labor whereby the US did the dirty work – like wars in Indochina and counter-insurgency in Latin America – while Western Europe (and Japan) consolidated their economic penetration in investment-friendly countries (such as Brazil and Thailand). This was the *pax americana* pattern, now on its way out. Moreover, if the EC is in difficulties in Africa, why should the US help bail her out when the European nations did not come more actively to the assistance of the US in Indochina? The exception might be the very south of Africa, where US investment is so considerable that simple economic considerations would prevail over any *Schadenfreude* brought about by seeing the European brother in a similar situation. But in general what the US will send will probably not be

112

troops but journalists and TV teams to whitewash themselves by showing the dirt of others, in much detail and via telesatellite.[25]

The second alternative approach is *peace-keeping under the United Nations*. This formula would give legitimacy to a multilateral intervention in order to 'freeze' a conflict before it 'escalates'; i.e. stop a rebellion before it gets dangerous. But this possibility is much less likely today. It is possible that the UN operation in Lebanon was of that kind, as the 'UN' operation in Korea certainly was. But the world knows this technique by now, so the big powers have to use their own blocs if they want 'peace-keeping' operations to take place. This is what the US did in the Dominican Republic, the Soviet Union did it in Czechoslovakia; in neither case would it have been possible to get UN support for actions carried out by means of the satellites they could mobilize in either bloc.[26]

This pattern is not available for the EC, unless the EC should also try to develop a similar military 'integration' of Eur-Africa. But this development is improbable, because of the existence of the OAU. In Latin America an organization of Latin American states will have to be formed after the collapse of the US-dominated Organization of American States; in Africa the regional organization (as opposed to a bloc) already exists and offers considerable protection against efforts to make a new bloc, on a more gigantic basis. Any moves in this field should be watched with extreme care in the years to come since the EC might use her economic power to gain a military foothold.

The argument used above – that the US will not come to the assistance of the EC in the UN in such situations – also applies here: there will be no support for a UN presence from the US, as there was no support for a UN presence in Vietnam from the EC countries. And needless to say: there would be a Soviet and/or Chinese veto. In short, the EC would have to withdraw in face of a revolt, or else develop her own military response. The latter is an old European tradition and the more likely development.[27]

The fourth source of crisis relates to Eastern Europe. There are two basic patterns, quite different from the patterns just discussed relative to the Third World. Eastern Europe is squeezed between the USSR and the EC in a most unenviable way, in a pattern of double domination. We take it as axiomatic that Eastern Europe wants to be independent of either, and that in the longer run this will probably lead to an Eastern European Community, a *European Socialist Community* (ESC). In the short run, however, there is so narrow space for maneuvering between military-political domination from the USSR and economic-cultural pene-

113

tration from the EC some crises must be almost inevitable, even in the relatively near future.

Moves towards independence from the USSR may take well-known forms: the Czechoslovakian form of 1968 where most of the nation, it seems, wanted to stake out its own course; and the Hungarian form of 1956, which to start with was directed against the party elites. Just as for the relation between Third World countries and the EC the conflict border can lie between the country and the USSR, or within the country itself. The two forms are very strongly related. The first form will probably lead to immediate Soviet intervention; the second form seems more likely to lead to a wait-and-see tactic, as in the case of Poland December 1970. It would be in the Soviet interest to have revolts controlled by the Eastern European governments themselves – particularly if it becomes painfully clear that the revolts are spearheaded by workers, and even led by workers and intelligentsia who are party members.[28]

Then there are the moves to become independent of the EC, and independent of outside capitalist forces in general. Here only one of the two forms is of interest. There will be no EC military presence, probably no political grip over Eastern Europe either. But there will be a certain economic-cultural penetration, and any revolt will be directed against national elites who have permitted this penetration. We predict that there will be a new generation of Eastern Europeans loyal to marxist ideals rather than to communist party dogma and expediency. Many of them will turn against their parents, for being 'soft on capitalism'. They will learn what the youth of the West has learned about the stimulation of artificial needs, about consumer society and its poor quality of life, about the fragmentation of the mind, and of persons because of intensive division of labor, about increasing gaps between center and periphery in all respects because of the mobility of production factors, etc. They will not ask for more capitalism, nor for a return to the repressive, bureaucratic socialism of the past, but for something new – and they will fight for it. Some day this may even become an integrating force between youth in all of Europe. Is it reasonable to believe that the leadership in most Eastern European countries will yield without considerable pressure to such demands for reorientation? Gomulka certainly did not step back voluntarily. Since Eastern Europe has no other mechanisms of collective protest than violent outbursts (one reason why a free press and elections, however faulty, are in the interests of the leaders in order to avoid crises), the case of Gomulka will hardly be the only one. There will be more crises, and even frequent ones.

We shall not repeat here why we think the EC contributes to all these forms of crises simply by its glittering affluence, by the short-term 'economic growth' it offers, by its penetration. More important are the EC *responses* in the crisis situation.

First, we should note that the responses are likely to be increasingly Western European and decreasingly NATO or US, simply because the crises (or 'situations', in more diplomatic parlance) will be increasingly related to Western Europe alone. A sign of greatness, or at least bigness, is the ability to produce one's own crises around the world, without the US. It may be disputed who has the lead in openings towards Eastern Europe and the USSR, France or Germany or the EC as such. But politically speaking there is no doubt that the EC countries were the first out, not the US, and this is probably a major reason why it was so urgent for the US to be no. 1 in China. Thus, just as in East Asia, there hardly will be any Western European military presence, but a US one, there will be a continued and strong Western European military presence close to Eastern Europe – but hardly a US one. Spheres of interest, once more!

Second, our thesis is certainly not that instability in Eastern Europe – a Soviet invasion of Romania on the suspicion that she is leaving the Warsaw Treaty Organization, or a major student revolution in Hungary against revisionist tendencies – will lead to any kind of Western European military intervention in the short run. But it will strengthen the hand of those who want the European Defense Community, and want it now. A new Czechoslovakia August 1968 is what they would need to bolster their arguments; and all we are saying is that such events are likely to come precisely because of the growth of the European Community. The EC produces its own crises that in turn will tend to stimulate its own growth – both in the sense of deepening in the military and political directions and in the sense of extension to more members, particularly from Southern Europe.

Third, the final point: consider the end product, an EDC with considerable autonomy. In practice this means one thing: that the confrontation is not so much between Washington and Moscow, as between Moscow and Brussels-Casteau – a frighteningly short distance. Let us look at some of the implications of this possibility.

Some years ago, the major dimension for discussing this would be the German access to nuclear power – and this is still important. With NATO ever more quickly moving towards the partnership pattern, Germany moves up to the first rank, no longer eclipsed by the US. All kinds of speculations about the power configurations in the top triangle, England–Germany–France, may now be entertained. Let us here only point out that the situation is fluid; nobody knows what German government may come into power. If the thesis of this book is correct, then the German *Ostpolitik* will not succeed, partly because it does not have a solid political foundation (as seen in the *Bundestag* reaction to the non-aggression treaties), partly because the trade relationship is too neo-colonial, and mainly because of the integration race between West and East and the crises that will accompany this race. This may bring into power the kind of parties and groups who, like Adenauer, would turn a hostile back to the East and devote itself entirely to building the EDC. What reaction that would lead to in the East is more than obvious, for the integration race and the arms race are only two sides of the same coin, two different expressions of the same polarization. The Soviet Union would never believe that a change in the direction mentioned does not mean increased German access to nuclear triggers – and they would probably be right. For in the politics of Western Europe today Edward Heath, with his plans for a European Nuclear Planning Group, is far more typical than Willy Brandt[29] or the Scandinavians. As to the latter: they are not members of the Western European Union, which may therefore be the next instrument for the EDC idea.

Add up all of this: EC's need for internal security against the extreme left and the extreme right; EC's increasing ability to produce her own crises, unaided by the US (a new dimension of independence!); EC's coming need for a response when the Third World starts reacting to EC imperialism; the internal dynamism in the Western camp combined with the probable reaction of Eastern Europe – and the conclusion is not an optimistic one. In fact, the future looks so dark along the military axis that the optimist may be the person who hopes that status quo can be maintained.

Chapter 9. Pax Bruxellana:
The European superpower

That concludes our analysis of major aspects of this emerging superpower:

- the resource power (chapter 4)
- the structural power (chapter 5)
- the relation to the Third World (chapter 6)
- the relation to the socialist countries (chapter 7)
- the military aspect (chapter 8)

The conclusion in terms of tremendous resources and even greater structural power is trivial – it is only a reading of the present situation. The divisive impact on the Third World due to differential treatment in different directions of the compass; the polarizing impact on Europe as a whole due to the integration race; the classical division of labor according to capitalist formulas – these are also fundamental aspects of the present world situation. The only hypothetical element relates to the military aspect, but this is so closely linked to the other facets of this emerging superpower that it is hard to believe there will be no changes at all in the direction foreseen in the preceding chapter.

As asserted many times: this whole process is fundamentally and profoundly Western European – exactly what that imperialistic part of the world has engaged in for centuries, indeed back to the Roman Empire for that matter.[1] There exists a solid tradition to build on, and most Europeans – we fear – are not at all opposed to it. Many might agree that all this exploitation, fragmentation, and penetration add up to dominance of great parts of the world, and might have no major quarrels with the empirical and theoretical parts of the argument, only with the evaluation. 'So what?' may be the reaction – 'it is good for us, and eventually also for them. They will get the spoils of our growth, that is better than what they have now'. Visions of grandeur will intoxicate masses and elites alike. Images of a *pax bruxellana*, a world order with

117

its center in Brussels but also based on law and order according to well-known European recipes, are already rapidly becoming part of Western European belief systems.[2]

An old European tradition – and one far older than the imperialism practiced by member states in recent centuries – up to bloody, fascist wars only ten years back in history,[3] wars backed up by social forces that are still very much in existence. When did Europe last look like the European Community of today, like the Six? The closest would be the fragile and short-lived empires of *Napoleon,* and more interestingly *Charlemagne,* at the end of the first millenium of our era. At that time the eastern border was also the Elbe (but then further east, the Saale), and Böhmerwald. The Empire had a simpler form than the Six: what today are Switzerland and Austria were in, but Southern Italy was outside and Cataluña (down to Ebro) was in. The exceptions are actually present as political forces today: both Switzerland and Austria seem headed for very tight association agreements, and Cataluña would probably (with her high level of industrialization) have opted for the same independent of the rest of Spain, had she had the autonomy. Southern Italy is now as ever a step-child, not only of Italy, but of Western Europe as a whole.

The similarity is deeper than merely a question of extension: Western Europe pitted against Eastern Europe, and penetrating into the latter. Charlemagne's empire was divided into units ruled by counts – 'counties' – with considerable autonomy. This corresponds well to the map published by the EC, of a Europe of Six, without national borders, and with units referred to as Champagne, Hessen, Lombardia; rather than France, Germany, Italy.[4] It may well be that much smaller units than the current nation states will emerge, and ought to emerge, within the EC: but there is nothing new in the formula. Charlemagne ruled his empire through the counts controlled by envoys (in pairs, one layman, one clerical);[5] the EC has a different formula. Envoys are typically coming *from* the parts *to* the center instead of vice versa; the technocrats have taken the place of the aristocrats, the parliamentarians the place of the priests on the assumption that *vox dei* is now expressed through *vox populi,* and that *vox populi* finds its expression in the parliamentarians.[6] It has taken more than one thousand years of bloody European history to bring about these two changes, and the image is still haunting Western Europeans of today. But *plus ça change, plus c'est la même chose,* clearly seen in the name of the building in Brussels where negotiations for an extension far beyond Charlemagne's vision took place: the

Palais Charlemagne.

As Lord Walston expresses it:[7]

> The European Economic Community is an historical concept. If it succeeds, it will have profound impact upon the future of the entire world. It will mean, in effect, the eventual appearance upon the world scene of a third super power, comparable in population, economic resources and technical skills both with the United States of America and with the Soviet Union, and superior to both of them in cultural tradition.

True enough, even enemies of the EC may endorse the last statement. But few seem inclined yet to view the EC in such terms. It is also in the EC's interest that it be not so viewed, but be permitted to expand and consolidate before any total, global, threatening image of it as a superpower takes hold on the minds of men. The EC is still in an early phase. The conflicts mentioned in the preceding chapter as factors contributing to the growth of a military capacity are still only in their infancy. The European Community is spreading outwards like a set of concentric circles emanating from Brussels, expanding and deepening the membership, having profound impact on the US, the Third World and the socialist countries – and on the rest of the world as well. The initiative is decidedly in the hands of the EC since the Hague Summit Meeting and is likely to remain there for some time to come. The rest of the world is watching what is happening, and groping for short-term benefits in the form of trade agreements, association, even membership without looking into long-term consequences.[8]

With this as a point of departure let us now ask some more questions about the nature of this superpower, *embedded in an environment of other superpowers.* We start with some simple questions. What will be the name of this entity – how will it refer to itself, and how will others refer to it? Second, will it acquire more unifying symbols of power, such as one EC language, one impressive capital, one central person – as with the US: the language English, the capital Washington DC, and the US president as executive head and symbol of the nation?

Its name will not for long remain the European Communities or the more unifying European Community or anything like that, partly because this is too clumsy and partly because it is a misnomer: the EC will be closer to a state than to a community. The name will, in all likelihood, simply be *Europe,* as already used by conservative Britons (and others) in the proverbial expression 'getting into Europe' (meaning half of Europe). Jean Monnet's 'United States of Europe' USE, may be attractive, but we doubt it will be chosen. It sounds too much like someone imitating somebody – and would at most be the formal name.

The inhabitants will increasingly refer to themselves as 'Europeans', which they are, and the Europeans further east will have to refer to themselves as *East* Europeans, just as Americans south of Rio Grande have had to call themselves *Latin* Americans. Both terms will continue to have a second class connotation as long as the participants do not learn to drop the qualifying adjective and confuse this verbal game by also calling themselves simply Europeans and Americans. This will take time; the center defines the game.

When it comes to the symbols of a common language and an impressive capital (which overcommercialized, acultural Brussels is *not*) it has always been clear that the French would be willing to yield to a demand to dignify the EC by making French the official language and Paris the 'capital of Europe'. No such demand is forthcoming, for reasons made even more obvious with British entry.[9] There will be no common language; the only solution to the problem of a capital would be either to have it (as now) in one of the capitals of a smaller member state or to build something entirely new – a Brasilia for Europe, a 'Euralia' somewhere in the geographical center.

But when it comes to a central person, the situation is different. One symbol of a superstate, as opposed to a community, would be the clear emergence of a single person as the 'head' of the EC. By that we mean something much more than the present arrangement with the president of the Commission as a key person.[10] What formal status this person would have *inside* the EC would depend on the long-term outcome of the power struggle between the Commission, the Council of Ministers, and the Parliament, but this is less interesting. Our new key person could be the president of any one of them.[11] The basis for predicting the emergence of a strong one-person center – Senghor's 'unicéphalisme'[12] – would not rest on any reading of the power relation between these three components, nor on any guess about current personalities. It would rest on a much stronger basis.

When the EC emerges more and more as the third superpower, the EC more than its member countries separately will relate to the other two, and to the two superpower candidates, China and Japan. When member countries relate to them at the top level, heads of state or government are used. One of them can be delegated the task of dealing with other powers on behalf of the Community. There may even be division

120

of labor: the German Chancellor may deal with the Soviet Union, the British PM with the US, France with China, and so on – on the basis of theories of 'special relationship'. But such arrangements will not prove stable. There will be the suspicion that special relationships may also lead to special privileges. One solution might be to leave the task to a member country without any special relationship – but that would almost inevitably lead to friction between the delegate and the 'natural' member for contact. Hence neither arrangement is satisfactory.

If EC wants to rank with the superpowers there must be a person in the Community who can rank with the heads of the superpowers. This person will of course somehow be accountable to all member states. However, there are strong reasons to believe that he will not be much more accountable than the President of the US is to the various components in the US governmental structure, or the Soviet Secretary-General and PM are to theirs – because their ability to act upon agreements reached will have to be roughly similar. The EC cannot be much slower than the US and the Soviet Union if it wants to participate in the game.

In other words, we argue that a political entity, whether called a community or what-not, cannot be too different from the entities it wants to deal with. NATO does not need anything similar to a Head of State since it was never designed to deal directly with any superpower. The EC *does:* it is heading for participation in Brandt's quadrangle or Nixon's pentagon.

We further believe that this arrangement will come into being when two conditions are fulfilled: there is a felt need for such a person; *and* a person with sufficient stature and acceptability level is available. That is, we do not believe it is a question of anybody grabbing a power position and running away with the EC. Rather, it will be a question of the EC grabbing a person and making this person do what has to be done; a question of a role looking for an actor, rather than an actor looking for a role.

This theatrical-sociological metaphor actually opens for one final small, but important point: this is the structure the member states in general, and their representatives in particular, are familiar with. With the EC quickly resembling a modern nation-state more and more, with a national assembly (the parliament), a cabinet (the Council of Ministers), an executive[13] (the Commission), and a Court of Justice, one of the elements most conspicuously absent would be precisely a key top person. If the models offered by the strongest members are the strongest models, then this person will be more than *primus inter pares* (as in the Scandinavian countries, Benelux, perhaps Italy – relatively anonymous) and more like a state power in his own right able to imprint his political profile on the Community – as in Britain, France, Germany – not to mention in the superpowers. It is worth noting the general rule: the stronger the country, the stronger the power of the chief executive.

Concretely, as the EC grows, so will the stature of those who participate in its top organs. Member states will send higher-ranking officials to the Commission and higher-ranking ministers to the Council, starting with 'Ministers for Europe'[14] until in the end the president of either (or of the Parliament) could be even a former head of government. Of course, such a person will have a limited tenure, e.g. two years – but he will be the central person who can meet with opposite numbers among the other big – we will have the Charlemagne of our century.

So, a new giant is born, grows, and can throw its weight around. It is hard to believe that this will not lead to still some years of victories, to start with. In turn, this will lead to more euphoria; the traditional arrogance of European states will grow to the level of the super-arrogance to be expected from a European super-state.

What will be the role of this European superpower amidst other superpowers? How will it fit into the present world scene? So far, we have had much to say about the impact of the EC on parts of the world, but not about the new big power system emerging. Again the point might be that the system is not so terribly new. Europe had a concert system based on Five Big after the Vienna Congress, making the 19th century a 'century of peace' – to provincial European historians who conveniently forget the costs to other continents exposed to European imperialism, and to the 20th century exposed to delayed warfare.[15] Let us look at the global concert now developing – without the genius of a Metternich.

The relations between the five superpowers will be complex. There is only one relationship we feel can be accorded a certain stability: between the US and the European Community. In a sense that relation has already been sorted out. The Community as a union for economic defense has been operative; the partnership formula is at least verbally agreed to; and the partnership based on parity in NATO will emerge. Thus, we assume that OECD and NATO will be the two umbrellas under which this giant economic-military partnership will be negotiated and regulated in detail in the years to come. Neither organization will be made superfluous by the Community. On the contrary, they will grow; only their roles will change to mechanisms of conflict articulation and conflict resolution between the partners. Stiff economic competition will continue between them. It will take much time before (if ever) 'monetary crises' (as deep-rooted social phenomena are called when one looks at symptoms only) in the Atlantic area are overcome; there may even be a trade war now and then – but all within limits.

There are two possible exceptions to this state of peacefulness. The power pendulum over the Atlantic is swinging back towards Western Europe and away from the United States, just as it started swinging slowly away from London and towards Washington two centuries ago, arriving full force in the 1950s. Two expressions of power will be extremely hard for the US to lose, although we doubt this will lead to military confrontation. One concerns the *United States in Europe*, the US business empire. The other concerns the two spheres of influence wrested from the crumbling Spanish Empire: central and Northern parts of *Latin America* and part of *Southeast Asia* (particularly the Philippines). European penetration into these two sanctuaries, if deep enough, would cause tremendous resentment. How would the US react to concerted EC expropriation of the Coca- and Pepsi-Cola empires, if one were to substitute a less sweet, more sophisticated 'Euro-Cola'? How would the US react if and when European business overtakes US business in the two redoubts of US commercial hegemony? Again, we think the EC would move with extreme care in both areas, and watch closely and in minute detail the US reaction.

Will the US send the Marines? Not unless the expropriation (or more subtle outmaneuvering) of US business takes place after a communist election victory in Italy or France, in which case a Prometheus plan à la Greece 1967 could be possible. But in general, US–EC relations are uninteresting in this superpower context. The present generation of leftist youth in Western Europe has had its outlook on global politics so much moulded by US imperialism in Southeast Asia and in Latin America that a tendency to see the US behind everything evil and to expect the evil to escalate has developed – just as the preceding generation had a similar image of 'world communism' in general and the USSR in particular. As already mentioned both may meet in the idea that the EC is an alternative to either; both making either party strangely blind to the EC because of the overfocus on the superpower of one's choosing. One party is blind on the left eye, the other on the right eye: neither has a third eye, with which to see itself.

With no major confrontation between the US and the EC, the number of free actors at the superpower level is reduced to four. It seems unlikely that any other pair will have as strong positive ties for some time to come. The four can conveniently be classified as follows:

	EUROPEAN, white	ASIAN, colored
'CAPITALIST'	United States	Japan
	European Community	
'SOCIALIST'	Soviet Union	China

How will the relations be in this system?

One thing is obvious: in such a field of forces, any change between any two will have repercussions all over the system. Everything is too tight, too visible, too full of implications – real or imagined – for it not to be so. If two powers are on bad terms with each other, and one of the remaining two befriends one of them without immediately befriending the other, this will be seen as a hostile move by the other one. Examples are numerous: we need only mention the impact which US moves to establish contact with China had on the USSR and Japan in summer 1971.

There are only two stable patterns in this situation. Either all four-five have to develop positive relations and establish a global concert, or the system has to break down into two groups, friendly within, hostile without. The former is unlikely, but not impossible. The latter has two very clear forms: after World War II, after 1949, the split was along the 'capitalist'-'socialist' dividing line, till the end of the fifties when the 'eternal friendship' between USSR and China broke up. The US-EC-Japan triumvirate is still a possibility. But a much more fundamental split can also easily be imagined, between the Europeans and the Asians in this picture – to be explored later.

For even if the unlikely should become reality, that these five somehow established a concert to become the executive council of the world, this would not last. World reaction against them – and the rest of the world is the majority (although only as 2000 million against 1600 million) – would be one of justified fear of joint domination, with no leeway whatsoever for bargaining and riding on two horses. The reaction would probably be one of withdrawal and some acceleration of unification on the other side, the less powerful side – leaving the powerful to themselves. A trade union of the small against a concert of the big would be a predictable, long-term outcome – the world is less easily bossed than Europe one century ago.

Much more likely is a stable division of the five into two blocs. In this system we see the USSR and Japan as the weaker parties, not in the sense of military hardware, but weak in ideology and social structure. It

124

does not seem likely that the US or the European Community will change their liberal-capitalist nature this side of the Year 2000, although it may be substantially modified. They will remain essentially as they are, perhaps with more elements of Labour Party type welfare state'ism.[16] Without EC membership some of the countries might have moved in a more socialist direction. We also assume that the People's Republic of China has built into it a basic stability. It will certainly not revert to anything reminiscent of the past, neither to the European-US, nor to the Japanese, nor to the Soviet-dominated past. China is the only one of the four to have extremely negative, recent experiences with all the other three.

But neither the USSR, nor Japan is stable. Many reasons could be presented for development either in the US/EC or in the Chinese direction – for both of them. The very special social system found in Japan will not be able to survive the attraction from the other two (the USSR not being attractive any longer to anyone); and although each year brings Japan closer to a Western-type society, it is by no means certain this is where she will end up in a decade or two. The same applies to the USSR: the repressive, bureaucratic socialism now found in that country will not survive, but yield either to greater liberalism or for a new socialism, more of the Chinese type.[17]

One distinct possibility, and one well worth imagining, would therefore be that the USSR finds support in the US/EC and that Japan at the same time starts leaning towards China.[18] In our view, this process is in fact already under way. The SALT negotiations in the military field, and the heavy demands from socialist Europe for a Conference on European Security and Co-operation are all signs and signals of more than a détente – a search for some kind of *modus vivendi,* for a more active peaceful co-existence. As mentioned in chapter 7, we believe it will be problematic: that both the US, the EC, the small Eastern European states, and the USSR will be more concerned with internal integration problems, that the integration race both will split Europe and put Eastern Europe in a squeeze, and that even open conflicts may emerge from this. But an uneasy *modus vivendi* will result, not the 'unity of opposites' or the joint hegemony based on an alliance between imperialists and revisionists that China talks of.[19] The Soviet elite will import from the West the technology it hopes can be used to satisfy the demands for consumer goods as well as for production development till new formulas of development within the rigid Soviet framework have been developed.

Japan is in a deeper crisis, being a profoundly collectivist country yielding to Western individualism. Culturally, structurally, geographically

Japan belongs not *to*, but *with* China – and the argument can be put forward that the two will find each other in a marriage of convenience, an arranged marriage of a type not unknown in that part of the world. China has a message without a technology, Japan a technology without a message – what would be more natural than to join the two, and more profoundly than putting Quotations from Chairman Mao on Sony cassettes? Japan is extremely vulnerable to any nuclear attack, she cannot lash out against China once more. Also, a deep hostility towards the West in general and the US in particular now that Japan has out-Wested the West may come out into the open any day. The textile issue, Okinawa, the reaction when US recognized China de facto without even consulting Japan – these are only the beginnings. So far they have been masked by the pro-US attitude of the leading Japanese 'yellow yankee', Prime Minister Sato.

A regrouping of this kind would run against the cold war's traditional, ideological grouping. This may be seen as an advantage for it would constitute a complex combination of the forces with rich possibilities for changing alliances. European elites have always enjoyed this game, carried out far above the heads of the people except when things get out of hand and the peoples are hit badly, economically and/or militarily. There is no reason to believe that a European superpower will enjoy the game less. On the contrary: they will feel the world is becoming healthy again because they are in the center.

Thus, we envisage a complex process which will start out with some cold war elements and some efforts to build up a concert, the global executive. In this process the EC may have to pay for its superpower status by losing one permanent seat in the Security Council on the argument that a coordinated European Community should not be empowered to speak with both the French and the British voices. Actually, the EC may soon come into a situation where she will have difficulties balancing between a degree of coordination so *high* that international organizations will start arguing that *one voice also means one vote,* and a degree of coordination so *low* that all kinds of internal disagreement and rivalries come out into the open. However, that may be, we doubt that a cold war polarization or a global concert will be the lasting pattern. Rather, we find it much more likely that the superpower system, after some time, will stabilize along continental, racial lines, the Europeans against the Asians. In that case, the EC will have contributed to the pattern, making the system less flexible, more subject to simple polarizations, less open to maneuvers of a de Gaulle who suddenly sees a chance of coincidence between French national interests and a global interest in deplolarization.

That leads us straight into the last question, a highly legitimate set of objections often raised to the present kind of analysis: 'all right, you may be right that the EC has such effects as described – in the Third World, on the European scene, at the superpower level. But, (1) the EC is not alone in being like this, (2) the EC is only the sum of its members, no worse than they were, maybe even better, and (3) a world with three, four or five superpowers is no worse than a world with only two of them – maybe also possibly better'. These objections are important, and we shall try to pursue them as far as they seem worth pursuing.

(1) There is no doubt that the EC is not alone on the world scene in having policies of the kind described. The US and Japan are very similar, and together the three of them dominate very large parts of the world: US 'has' Latin America, the EC (the Ten) 'has' Black Africa (and with the Mediterranean policy even a total Eurafrica), Japan 'has' Southeast Asia. But three wrongs do not make one right: from the fact that others are bad does not follow one's own right to behave likewise. In addition to these dominance systems come the other empires: the USSR is herself a Russian sphere of dominance, in her Asian republics (Eurasia),[20] in Eastern Europe, and in the Arab World. Then, the Indian efforts in South Asia,[21] and China, if one sees China as an empire ruled from Peking. How correct this is we do not know – but it is hard to believe that the periphery of that enormous country is not exactly that, a periphery in the sense defined here. In short, much of our analysis can be used on these other empires, but that is not the issue here. The issue here is the European Community: that is what matters to Western Europeans, that is what we are responsible for – not somebody else's empire which it is comfortably easy to criticize, since we do not benefit from it.

(2) The EC *is* more than the sum of its members, Bismarck's Germany was also more than the sum of the German states. Even if it were only the sum, that sum is in itself so big, as indicated above, that it would imply a qualitative change in the world system. Thus, where formerly it was possible for the weaker and the poorer to play on controversies among the strong and rich in Western Europe, they now meet a much more united front. Where formerly Western and Eastern Europe were a joint buffer zone between the two superpowers there is now a totally different situation in Europe with two superpowers, one established and one emerging, uncomfortably close to each other. And where formerly Europeans benefitted from the decentralization the whole world talks so much about simply because they were not united, but split into even small coun-

tries like Norway, by now a very strong network of inter- and supra-national ties is being spun. In short, it does make a difference; a qualitative one, and the argument that the constituent parts were equally bad on a smaller scale – which is partly true – is a strange argument in favor of the European Community.

(3) But the *third* objection is still important: what difference does it make with more superpowers? Is it not a rather conservative argument to argue in favor of the 'good old days' with only two superpowers around? The answer to that is that there is no such argument, there is no glorification of the US–Soviet condominium. If there should be a glorification of anything in those terms, it might be of a world with 1400 instead of 140 countries; but that world is not here, and not in sight. The worlds that are here and are in sight have to be evaluated on their own merits, and the basic argument in favor of a system with two superpowers is that it seems less unstable than a system with more superpowers. The reason is simply that with increasing numbers there are more conflict configurations, more things that can go wrong. With two superpowers there is *one* overriding conflict and it *may* become institutionalized – as we have witnessed recently. With five superpowers there are ten pairs, and there may be trouble in any one of these pairs. Thus, Japan and the EC may one day be on a collision course, not necessarily militarily, but over who shall pick up the spoils from the US economic empire in Latin America, for instance. The more power they have behind a policy position, the more dangerous may the situation become; again not mili-tarily for the rich, but economically, for the masses in the poor countries.

In short: we see little or no reason to believe that the world becomes more peaceful with the emergence of the EC superpower. Some Euro-peans today seem to be mesmerized by the circumstances that the EC somehow has a front against the two cold war superpowers, and that right now it is only an economic, not a military superpower. But that argument rests on a failure to see economic penetration in the capitalist fashion as aggression and dominance stimulating countermoves that may in turn lead to militarization, and a failure to distinguish between hostility di-rected against US and Soviet dominance because one is against any kind of dominance, and because it stands in the way of one's own dominance. The former might be an instrument in the cause of peace – the latter decidedly not.

Actually a particularly unattractive feature of the EC is its timing. The first half of this century saw the rise of the two giants centered in Wash-ington and Moscow and the decline of the traditional Western Europe.

128

In the 1960s both of them are in disrepute, rejected by large parts of their own empires and by important segments of their own population – particularly by creative intellectuals on whom they also depend for renewal. But just as the world might think that the US and the Soviet Union, particularly the former, is declining, like Britain and France before them, a new empire is in the making, bigger than anyone before, hatched in Brussels under an entirely new non-military formula for empire-building. When the US gets rid of *her* imperialism and might even become a much more attractive society, the EC starts hers. But like other empires before it will sooner or later overextend itself, go one step too far and expose itself sufficiently for the weaker parts of the world to find weak spots to attack. And that is the topic of the final chapter.

Chapter 10.
Beyond the European Community

At this point the reader may feel the same way as have many discussants exposed to this analysis of the EC in the form of a lecture, a seminar talk, or a discussion contribution: 'OK, OK – I get the message. But what is the alternative, what should be changed and how, what can be done? Not that I don't agree with the author in much or even in most, but this is all so negative – what is the positive side of the message?'

This is a fair question, and an answer will be attempted in this final chapter. But let us first say that a critique need not always be positive. The alternative to Hitler was the negation of Hitler; the alternative to the US in Indochina is the US out of Indochina. That our critique now takes a more positive turn is because any parallel with Hitler fascism or US structural fascism[1] is rejected. The European Community is fundamentally, probably even irreversibly, capitalist, but it cannot at present be compared to the other two. A dialogue is not *a priori* impossible, but it has its limitations – and it should not be confused with 'working from the inside instead of from the outside'. A dialogue is an effort to influence others with words, and an implicit willingness to be influenced oneself, at least somewhat, by the response. To work from the inside is to accept most of the premises, and probably also to contribute much more than one is able to detract from the wrong policies pursued. To work from the outside may include dialogue, but may also mean actions directed against the European Community, and actions directed towards building up alternative structures.

One way of starting would be to indicate what aspects of a European Community might be acceptable even given the critique of this essay – or at least not too unacceptable. For this purpose we may use the division of the world into six parts.

First, our critique is not directed against integration of Western European states *per se*. On other occasions, arguments have been raised in favor of *associative structures* as a way of building peace;[2] and when the

130

EC is seen as an effort to bring together *states* in a traditionally war-torn part of the world, there is much good to be said about it. If the EC is seen as a way of bringing *regions* together the picture is less positive: capitalism leads to far too much accumulation in the centers and to continuous bloodletting of the periphery. Scotland, the Italian South, the Norwegian North will remain peripheries under that system; although they may be propped up by some compensatory policies, the system will not give them organic, self-sustained and autonomous life. Moreover, Britain *may* become the Scotland of the EC, Italy its Mezzogiorno, and Norway its North-Norway.

If the EC is seen as a way of bringing classes together, the picture becomes even worse: so far the EC has been a way of strengthening capitalism, because integration works more easily at the top than at the bottom. Even if this does not show up in increased income disparities, the power disparity has increased – as seen by the success of capital and the failure of labor (so far) to come together. The European Community is certainly not a mechanism for transcending class society, nor was it ever intended to be one.

However, this question is for European peoples to debate and to solve. Nothing is eternal, the EC class society included. What the present author would prefer is a European Community consisting of small, social units, like cantons. These would be bigger than municipalities but smaller than regions, free to choose their own social structure within a basically socialist and humanist framework, with a high level of mobility between them[3] – interdependent, but also self-sufficient so that they could survive a crisis among themselves. They would be tied together like cantons in a federation, with a high level of direct democracy both within and between the cantons. The superstructure would not be too strong, since that would increase the distance between decision-making and the common man; and the cantons would be defined so that none of them could dominate the other, in the sense defined here.[4] This vision is clearly very different from the European Community emerging today in Europe with its top-heavy technocratic superstructure. But again: this problem is for Western Europeans to fight out: it concerns nobody else. Western Europeans have the same right as others to 'integrate', but that term leaves a vast spectrum of possibilities open as to the concrete structure to be chosen.

What is not for Western Europeans alone to decide is the relation between any form of Western European integration and the rest of the world.[5] This concerns the rest of the world often even more than it concerns Western Europe because the latter is so strong. The foreign policy

131

of the EC is not for them alone to debate and decide. A flock of elephants in a chicken yard have a duty to move about with care. What the Western Europeans do to themselves at home is their own business, but abroad they have no right to

- *exploitation:* to secure raw materials and markets in East and South by all kinds of vertical division of labor;
- *fragmentation:* to split the rest of the world off from each other and deal with each part separately;
- *penetration:* to tie the elites of other countries to oneself.

Nor has the US any right to do so, nor has any other power for that matter. Hence, and that is the second point: the critique presented here is not directed against the European Community as an economic defense union against economic aggression from the United States. The only critique here would be that it does not go far enough. If autonomy is what is wanted, then the climate for US business in Europe should be made considerably colder. Efforts in the direction of cross-investment are not enough: that is only mutual penetration, not autonomy. Autonomy would be for the peoples in Western Europe, simulated by the impetus given by the whole debate about the environment issue and the quality of life, to ask much more basic questions: what kind of technology do we *really* want? What do we *need?* Such debates are not facilitated by a heavy technocratic structure that serves as an instrument for basically capitalist interests. The goal is clear and legitimate – but the range of means is much vaster than so far contemplated.

Third, as to the relation to other Western European states, the issue becomes more complex. Again, the argument would be that this is for candidate and member countries to decide. The decision must be taken by the populations in a referendum, and not in the disgraceful, feudal way this is being done in Britain. If the populations of, say, the present candidate countries vote in favor of becoming members, then that is their right. The terms of the membership are for them to fight out. Unfortunately, however, this is about the only fight there is: doubts about the global aspects of EC policy are rarely voiced.

Thus, we want strongly to emphasize that these three aspects of the EC have been kept outside the critique: internal EC relations, the relations to the US and to the other countries of Western Europe. This may seem a naive position: they are all three parts of the general EC pattern. A united Western Europe, stimulated by its competitive relation to the US, will have to be at least as capitalist as its member states, and then the rest follows. But even if this is empirically true today, it is not an eternally valid truth. Much can be said in favor of focussing attack as well as suggestions on the most detrimental aspects of EC policy from a global point of view.

Let us therefore turn to the concrete demands which, according to the type of thinking developed here, should be directed to the European Community. Since the three aspects singled out for critique in the preceding chapters were the policies towards the *less developed countries,* towards the *socialist countries* and the *military aspect,* the demands will fall in these categories. We shall put the military aspect aside for the time being since it has already been dealt with, and since it falls outside any critique of present EC as such. The demands, then, will be derived from the theoretical framework presented, in terms of exploitation, fragmentation and penetration, starting with fragmentation this time.

I *From fragmentation to solidarity*

Relative to the Third World this means
1. abolishing all preferential and differential agreements; abolish the whole system of associated states, treat all less developed countries the same way whether they are former dependencies or not, regardless of where they are located, and whether they are capitalist or socialist. At this point, the GPS can be seen as a step in the right direction, not because of what it does to trade composition (very little) but because of its more universal nature.
2. channeling maximum capital and assistance, without any strings attached, to build up strong organizations among the less developed countries and in the way they themselves want – building on such patterns as the Group of 77 and the Beograd-Cairo-Lusaka conferences.
3. having negotiations and deals in general with this organization of less developed countries rather than with countries or regional groupings. The UN and the UN organizations of various kinds should be used as the medium in which such negotiations may take place, as has been done, to a large extent, within UNCTAD.

Relative to the socialist countries this means
4. giving up all efforts to split one off from the others.
5. having negotiations and deals in general with the organization of socialist countries rather than with countries or regional groupings. In practice this means, today, CMEA. Again UN organizations should be used as an umbrella under which such meetings take place – as has been done, to a large extent, within the UN Economic Commission for Europe.

Admittedly, in both these cases there is the danger that the stronger within either group – countries like India and Brazil in the Third World and the USSR among the socialist countries – will dominate. But this is a different problem and should not be used as a pretext for the EC to continue her fragmentation. The EC is in the historically fortunate position that there is no single dominant power in its midst – the US is kept outside, and the three strongest members are not too unequal. The Third World and the socialist countries are not in that situation. Sooner or later this must lead to the emergence of an organization (not only a category!)[6] of the *Least Developed Countries* in the Third World, and to the organization (again, not only a category!) of the smaller, socialist Eastern European states – a *European Socialist Community*. Such developments are for these countries to decide on, and they will not be unproblematic. The EC has no right to interfere – and articulation of these problems should take place in a UN setting rather than bilaterally, between the EC on the one hand and Third World countries, or socialist countries on the other.

II *From exploitation to equity*

Relative to the Third World this means giving up the idea of using them as sources of raw materials and as markets for manufactured goods. Instead, the following practices should be developed:

6. higher prices for raw materials, probably as a result of concerted action and a strike on delivery.[7] This will, however, stimulate further search for synthetic substitutes, and may also freeze the international division of labor. In general it is a regressive method, but may have some virtue as a transitory device. Increased prices should be seen as 'negative tariffs'[8] compensating the poor countries for all the spin-off effects foregone in not processing the raw materials themselves.

7. much more import of goods genuinely manufactured in the poor countries with no quota restrictions. This can be done only on a basis of solidarity where some industries in the rich countries gradually step down to permit more import from the poor countries. At the same time import of raw materials should be increasingly discouraged.

8. instead of more exporting manufactured goods to the poor countries, much more free transfer of technology of all kinds. To withhold technical know-how that might, in principle and in practice, be of benefit to mankind so that the technology can be sold piece-meal and be used for bargaining in commercial and international negotiations should be

134

considered a crime – as it already is in the field of health.

9. changing 'multinational corporations' so that they become less asymmetric and less marked by vertical division of labor.[9]

10. strengthening horizontal trade among the poor countries themselves, regionally as well as universally.

Relative to the socialist countries this means

11. much more import of goods manufactured in the socialist countries. This can be done only on the basis of a genuine, all-European solidarity where some industries in Western Europe gradually step down to permit more import from the socialist countries in Eastern Europe.[10]

12. instead of more export of manufactured goods to the socialist countries much more free transfer of technology of all kinds.

For the socialist countries, the other points above are largely taken care of, because of the strength that has derived from their relatively early detachment from the capitalist orbit. They are less fragmented, have considerable horizontal trade, and are less penetrated.

III *From penetration to autonomy*

Essentially this is a question of counteracting the forces that tie the elites in Third World countries (and to a minor degree also in the socialist countries) to the EC elites, and the forces that divide the elites in the Third World countries from the masses in their own countries. Obviously this struggle will have to be fought above all in the Third World countries themselves. But there is also something that a different European Community, less bent on becoming world power, could do.

Relative to the Third World and (14, 15) the socialist countries this means:

13. a development policy that aims at raising the level of the masses. Instead of the capitalist and highly misleading GNP/capita measure of development that still has its backers among some economist and many politicians a meaningful measure of development should be used, something like the rise in the level of living of the bottom third or half of the population.[11] Development has to start from the bottom, not from the top. Each development project should therefore be evaluated in terms of its *short range* effects for the masses, not in terms of its *possible* long range effects through increased trade etc. Projects that quickly lead to a reduction of the distance between elites and masses will

also serve as a factor working against penetration. But this would mean that the EC would have to give up one of her most forceful tools of dominance.

14. a second aspect of an alternative definition of development would be the *possibility of forming one's own development goals,* and not simply imitate them because stronger nations teach local elites the 'true' meaning of development. Again, this has to come from the inside, just as the preceding point. But the EC could do something. Thus, the EC could encourage critical studies of the EC and the EC countries made by independent scholars from Third World and socialist countries, using *their* concepts of development. Today world consciousness is far too much formed by studies done *by* scholars in the rich OECD countries, *of* the rest of the world. And when studies are made the other way, the Third World experts are sometimes more Western than the West itself. And the EC could go further, even to step down from positions of arrogance and counteract superiority complexes by *learning* from Third World and socialist countries. For instance, what can be learned about integration of the old in society from African countries? About integration of city and countryside from Bulgaria? About reducing the fragmentation of man and society with excessive division of labor – from China? In short, dialogue and mutual learning instead of one way dominance!

15. and finally a point that actually would counteract all three, fragmentation, exploitation and penetration: opening the institutions of the European Community, at all levels, to the developing and socialist countries. More particularly, this means more than the type of arrangement made under the Yaoundé II agreement, with its special Ministerial Council and Parliamentary Assembly. It means opening up the Commission for Third World and socialist experts to prevent it from becoming an instrument for the preparation of even more penetration. It does not mean equality to the point found in UN institutions, for there is no denial of the right of Western European states to form a regional institution. But it does mean a denial of their right, as being among the richest countries in the world, to form a separatist, *exclusive* union all of their own.[12]

This type of program with its fifteen suggestions can now be discussed from at least three angles: how significant is it? how likely is its realization as a result of internal processes in the present EC establishment? and what strategies could be imagined to increase the likelihood of such policies if they are considered sufficiently significant?

136

It is not at all obvious that these policies are really significant. From the idea that vertical division of labor is wrong, because it is exploitative, it does not follow that a more horizontal division of labor between countries is right because it is less exploitative. If one policy is wrong it does not follow that the opposite policy is right. Both vertical and horizontal division of labor have interdependence, exchange, trade in common – and it may well be that a much more significant policy is self-dependence, or self-sufficiency. If the basic needs are those of the most needy, the primary needs of the lower parts of society, it is not at all obvious that these are promoted best by means of much trade, for instance. It may well be that the whole trade model is based on the old capitalist assumption that development starts at the top, 'trickles down', reaching the masses gradually.[13]

Of course, nothing is obtained by being excessively dogmatic on such issues, but we should point out that trade may imply a failure to utilize fully one's own resources. That is why so many innovations are made during wars, when trade is cut off and the population is forced to lean back on its own resources. The People's Republic of China, which probably holds a world record in satisfying primary needs for the masses and in a very short time, has very low foreign trade, and so on – although this certainly also has something to do with particular economies of scale obtainable within that vast country. In short, one should not make a fetish out of trade or any other form of exchange, but be equally or more attentive to policies of self-reliance.

Second, there is little likelihood that any internal dynamics of the EC system should lead to anything more than piecemeal changes in the directions indicated. The EC system is capitalist; and capitalism has always, in all its forms, been based on a division of labor between centers and peripheries, with accumulation in the former. It has always been based on underutilization of resources, including human resources, in the periphery; for that reason it was also highly compatible with the centralist tendencies in the nation states that emerged towards the end of feudalism. Some countries, the imperialist countries and their satellites, have had it in their power to place their periphery on the outside, in the colonies, creating a semblance of equality within their own borders because the periphery has been invisible. Is it likely that the population in these rich countries – capitalists, bureaucrats and workers alike – will voluntarily give up a system that benefits them so well? Or is it more likely that they will cling to doctrines and ideas which for all practical purposes are rationalizations of the status quo?

Looking through the list of fifteen relatively concrete suggestions made above we see quite clearly that they run counter to the two theses suggested at the very outset as two guidelines for understanding EC policies: the desire to recreate a *Eurocentric world,* and a *unicentric Europe,* founding a *pax bruxellana* on these two pillars. All that is suggested in the points above can be subsumed under one heading: they are steps in the opposite direction of equity, towards a less asymmetric world. Hence, they should be considered pious wishes, prescriptions rather than predictions. It is unnecessary to discuss each one in detail since this already lies implicit in the whole analysis in the preceding chapters – but the conclusion is clear: *new forces would have to be provided to turn the European Community in such directions.*

Where could such forces come from? More particularly, from the inside, from the outside (which outside?) or from both? This is the crucial question if one agrees with the basic value premises underlying the present analysis and with the basic conclusion. But the question is certainly not easily answered, particularly not since there is as yet so little empirical experience on what systematic efforts to bring about basic changes in the European Community might mean.

For simplicity of exposition we have chosen to present the little that can be said about political forces at this juncture under eleven headings, some negative, some positive.

1) *The present EC machinery is incapable of any basic change*

This is generally a safe statement about most bureaucracies, but seems *a fortiori* applicable to this one. The present machinery is so heavily tilted in favor of the Commission, because of its expertise, size and right of initiative, and in favor of the Council of Ministers, that the EC can largely be discussed in terms of those two components alone. The European Parliament is of minor significance, except, perhaps, on paper, and is likely to remain so for some time.

One basic aspect of the Commission is its isolation from the general society of the member countries. In a sense Commission members are responsible to no one; they do not have to face a lively party or parliament opposition, they have no press directed at them, they have no student or other youth groups working full time against them. They are attached to ordinary social life through the tiny channel of the Council of Ministers, for whom they seem to have little but thinly disguised contempt, and to the artificial life in commercialized Brussels. Unlike other bureau-

138

cracies, also unaccessible to direct pressure, they have not even much indirect pressure exercised on them.

One consequence of this very noticeable to an outsider[14] is the surprise of the Commission members when they are criticized, and their lack of training in coping with, even understanding, basic criticism. Some bureaucrats enjoy criticism even less than others; the Eurocrats seem to be among them. Many of them seem even honestly to believe that what they do is somehow purely technical; their isolation from regular life seems to have inoculated them effectively against understanding how deeply political every single act they perform appears to the outsider. To the Eurocrat the outside critic is 'political' and even 'emotional',[15] as opposed to the cool, technocratic Eurocrat. Even the most commonplace arguments – like doubting the value of GNP/capita as a development indicator, or doubting the theory that development starting at the top will sooner rather than later reach the bottom of society – take them by surprise. Yet no national politician or even bureaucrat who has followed debates from the late 'sixties will have failed to discover that nothing is unarguable in the field of development.

The Eurocrats move in their own circles. They seem to take for granted most of the assumptions on which the system is founded, and discuss details within that frame of reference. This is done in a language full of conservatively oriented statistics and technicalities.[16] In such systems the only hope for renewal would usually be the younger people or some very strong person on the top. But the latter is unlikely as a source of basic change because of the way in which the members of the Commission are recruited, their number and diversity which may lead them to neutralize each other into inactivity. The former will hardly lead to much, since the Commission has already a high incidence of people in the middle and older age groups, and the young are not homogeneous enough. Indoctrination of younger employees appears quite effective, or at least effective enough to give them the feeling, which they so often express, that 'with these museum pieces higher up one can do nothing, opposition has to come from the outside of the Commission'. In short, it is difficult to discover a true, concerted fighting spirit for anything but higher salaries for themselves.

2) *The new member states will not bring about a more radical orientation*

Some persons stake much hope on the entry of the new member countries. From the viewpoint of the Six, particularly of the Eurocrats themselves, this expansion must be a sign of dynamism, proving that the EC is alive and a center of major political attraction. It spells increased power for those who already have plenty of that commodity. However, it does not follow that extension will mean anything but just more of the same kind. There are the well-known speculations that Britain will bring with her a style of organizational behavior known as 'pragmatism'. It is difficult to know what this means. It may in fact be another way of expressing lack of any real perspective, rather than a praiseworthy dedication to a more experimental, non-dogmatic approach in world affairs. Whatever grand design the 'continentals' might concoct, Britain might then be able to sabotage it with a skilled mixture of scepticism and 'pragmatism'. More concretely, the idea could be that if it was difficult to arrive at decisions before, it will be almost impossible with Britain as a member – and three smaller new members next to her sharing some of that 'pragmatism'.

The argument carries some weight among those who believe that politics is only a question of decision-making. But throughout this essay we have argued that there is not much need for active decision-making inside or with the European Community: the decisions were already made long ago, centuries ago, and built into the structure which Western Europe built around the world. Those who founded the Community merely reactivated these old decisions and injected some new life into the impressive machinery of politics by non-decisions. The economic, political, cultural, etc. transactions carried out all over the world with Western Europe as a center are in no need of any formal decision-making at the very center to back them up: they simply exist and persist. When these countries wanted to – i.e. when their governments decided, with most of the local elites applauding, that they should join – it is because they like these non-decisions, and would like to see them continue with small modifications here and there. Pragmatism, then, becomes merely another word for status quo-ism – only that one prefers to state the conservatism more implicitly. Moreover, the representatives to EC from the new member countries will certainly not represent the opposition against the EC in their countries – but be 'good Europeans'.

Then, there was also another school of thought which emphasized a possible France–Norway alliance between the two countries which, more than others, have insisted on special national prerogatives. This may be true, but so what? There was nothing in, say, the Norwegian positions negotiated in Brussels that in any way, however slightly, indicated a less conservative approach to world politics. As for Britain, the part of the negotiations visible to the public concerns only the economic interests of special groups, which in Britain's case also would extend to the Commonwealth countries. Harold Wilson's 'opposition', for instance, is almost entirely parochial.

Then there is the school of thought that emphasizes the strong position of the social democrats in these countries.[17] We shall return to the argument below. Suffice it here to say that at present the major country, Britain, cannot be included in that category; and even if it could, it is, as mentioned, extremely difficult to discover anything in Harold Wilson's opposition to British entry that would point to new horizons in foreign relations. On the contrary, as for the new member governments, public silence on foreign policy seems to indicate not only basic agreement, but also some relief at sharing the burden of foreign policy with others.[18]

3) *More power to the European Parliament will not lead to basic changes*

A European parliament empowered to make politics, not only to pass comments or sometimes judgments on policies made by the other bodies, will not by itself lead to any changes. The parliamentarians might go in for exactly the same policies, or for even less progressive ones. The experience from the Consultative Assembly of the Council of Europe in Strasbourg is definitely not that it stands for more radical or even more innovative policies than those originating with the Council of Ministers or with the Secretariat. The same seems to hold true for NATO. This will not necessarily change with some changes in the constitution aimed to give more legitimacy to the top-heavy technocracy of the Commission. The overwhelming majority of any conceivable European Parliament in the near future will accept all basic aspects of the EC as it stands, because the European Community in its present shape is as basically Western European as are the Alps.

If there nevertheless should be any basic opposition, this opposition will surely either be trans-national, but on some internal EC matter of marginal significance to the environment of the EC; or about something basic, but limited to one or a few member states (like Danish-Norwegian opposition to Greece). After all, the parliamentarians are heavily fragmented: by party, nationality, language (including linguistic ability); they meet rarely, have much less contact with the issues than the experts in the Commission, and consequently have little time to build up an effective pressure group. British parliamentary tradition might possibly bring some more liveliness into this generally dull picture – but liveliness is certainly no guarantee for a less traditional and capitalistic approach.[19]

Some of this would change with direct elections to the European Parliament – a reform bound to come sooner rather than later, as a part of the general integration process. In that case the representatives would live their political lives in an atmosphere dominated by EC politics, and this might tip the internal power balance more in favor of the parliament. For those who identify democracy with parliamentarianism, this would be a change to the better. But from the outside, from the viewpoint of the peoples in the rest of the world, this remains an internal change with no necessary repercussions on foreign policy – at least not in a more progressive direction.

4) *Western European workers are in general not a radicalizing force for the EC*

This is a major reason for the negative conclusion to the preceding point. As pointed out repeatedly, EC foreign policy is the old policy of securing raw materials for processing, and markets for the processed goods, under some new guises – much of it even referred to as development assistance. Later on – and this has already started – this international division of labor will move up the scale, but always securing for Western Europe a place in the sun, on the top notches of processing scale. In the four-class system that emerges, three classes are not badly off at all: the elites in the center as well as in the periphery countries, *and* the workers in the center countries: the rich countries, the EC countries in this connection. The losers are the true world proletariat, the poor in the poor countries – maybe 70 % of the world population.

With whom do the workers in the rich countries identify? Above all with themselves – and why should they do otherwise? Marxist theory holds that the workers of the world should unite against the common enemy, the capitalistic enterprises which exploit them all. But 'should' is a norm, not an empirical account of what happens in reality. In reality, workers and workers' organizations are among the most reactionary forces in the rich countries when it comes to maintaining exploitation of the poor countries. In all the EC former colonial powers – such as in France, Netherlands, and Britain – workers could be counted upon to support imperialist policies, to produce the arms used to kill fellow proletarians in less fortunate corners of the world, to submit willingly to military service in the 'colonies', to demonstrate in favor of colonial policies. Labor

142

parties may have had more enlightened leaders, but their momentum seems to have been lost with the wave of juridical independence of the post-war period – for their social visions did not include deepor forms of colonialism.

But why should it? To be the factories of the world pays: not only for the owners, the industrialists and capitalists, but also for the workers to the extent they are able to get better shares in the fruits from joint exploitation of other countries. The elites in rich and poor countries are, by and large, at the same standard of living; but the masses in the two are certainly not. Had they been so, then joint action might have been possible. As already mentioned, in the US they are to some extent: the standard of living of some of the proletariat in the US – poor black Americans, Chicanos, American Indians – does not differ that much from the Third World proletariat. They can in fact be seen as representatives of the Third World in the very center of the capitalist system, partly taken there by force generations ago, partly migrating there. Joined with others in the Third World they can organize strikes against US-dominated multinational corporations – against mother-companies and daughter-companies at the same time. But in the EC countries there is no such Third World presence. In fact, the Third World is a Mediterranean away. It is not a bordering country, or an island 90 miles away, as living evidence of recent fight, like Cuba. In the EC only Britain presents a similar picture.

Once it was different: Western Europe had its Third World, called Eastern Europe. Today most Western Europeans would refuse to see things that way and prefer to see the situation as an 'East–West' conflict, between equals. And then there are no Eastern Europeans working in Western Europe, except for marginal Yugoslavia.

Nothing of the above is to deny that the working class may have a radicalizing influence at home, inside the EC, once it gets organized so as to cope with the heavy concentration of capital and technocracy in the EC center. Substantial efforts to bring about a more fair Western Europe will come from those who are under- rather than overprivileged inside Western Europe. The same holds for the world: that the population in the EC countries has so much to fight about at all, so much to distribute, is precisely because the classes stand together on the shoulders of toiling masses around the world – and enjoy that position.

In short, the European Community is tailor-made for the secondary (and tertiary) sectors of the economies of these countries. In general, the EC will be supported by those who work in these sectors – in the old

European tradition of viewing the rest of the world as second class. The joint Western European first class will hardly revolt on their behalf.

5) *EC opposition within the member countries will only grow slowly*

As already mentioned, this does not mean that there will not be a growing EC opposition. Apart from particularly conscious individuals with a global perspective (some intellectuals, some workers – many of them communists) fundamental EC opposition will come from those *whose interests suffer* or *whose values differ*, fundamentally. In the former category, the primary sector of the economy will play a certain role: farmers, fishermen and others. So far farmers have been the only ones to organize protests of any significance; others will follow. But the EC is rich: if the EC can use its considerable membership fee to finance a common agricultural policy, it is also in a position to steer world economic forces so that new positions, in industry and trade, can be created to compensate for underemployment in the primary sector. Or, in a position to pay the unemployed off, e.g. through the simple device of premature retirement. Chances are therefore that farmers and fishermen will be paid off one way or the other and not have any major radicalizing effect.

In this category, where the opposition is based on interests, are also most of the people in the periphery regions in the EC countries. Many of them work in the primary sector. Chances are that compensatory policies will also be found for them. With the diversified markets at the disposal of the EC for its world trade, the most recent products can be traded inside the EC itself and with Japan and the US; the less sophisticated can be exported to the socialist countries, and the least sophisticated to the Third World. Three tiers of markets can correspond to three tiers of production centers inside the EC countries themselves, to the point where the major industrial centers may produce in the first category, the second rate centers in the second category, and the products for the Third World may be produced in the First World periphery – to the benefit and profit of that periphery.

In short, we find it naive to believe that opposition from the EC periphery, almost certain to come, will have a radicalizing effect on global relations. Why should this periphery care more, or even equally much, for the world periphery as for themselves?

A much more likely source of radicalization will be those whose opposition is based on value disagreement rather than on interest disharmony. Who are they? In general terms, too general unfortunately, they are the

144

'youth'. About the Western European youth (and not only students) the following three statements seem to be more right than wrong:

- a higher degree of identification with the world proletariat (due to education revolution, due to the Indochina wars, etc.)
- a growing disenchantment with such basic values of the EC, as economic growth, accumulation, having rather than being, etc.
- a growing dislike for work in the type of organization (hierarchical, rigid) that the Commission represents.

These three factors are tendencies rather than absolutes, and they are unstable. In an economic squeeze with job scarcity, identification would probably turn inward; the same may happen to disenchantment with quantity of life and dislike for work in big bureaucracies. As the situation stands today, the EC institutions can probably mainly recruit only people who are Western European patriots with a generally conservative inclination (whether of the Tory or Labor varieties), hung up on 'economic growth' and with a sincere love for the type of 'career' the EC institutions can offer. With this recruitment profile, chances are that they will also be incapable of improving themselves, that they will commit a sufficient amount of gross errors due to lack of insight in how their own system works, and that these errors will have a radicalizing effect – not on them, but on the outside.

Thus, the EC may talk about world identification, 'quality of life'[20] and decentralization – but such precious redirections cannot be brought about by word magic alone, or by people who have never practiced anything but the opposite. There is little chance that the EC establishment itself will deflate this type of opposition. Generations are very different these days, and change rapidly; they cover short timespans only. Hence the hope of the present establishment would not be to win over the present youth, but to hope for a new generation of youth, as bent on world domination as they themselves are. Unfortunately, this is not entirely impossible.

6) *Inside the EC, work for increased consciousness is a major strategy for basic change*

In the experience of the present author, a relatively high level of awareness of what the EC means to the world at large is found only in the Nordic countries, mainly in Denmark and Norway.

145

For the populations in old colonial powers, the EC is in the general tradition of what they are used to, only carried out with other means. To those opposed to colonialism the EC was sufficiently new within that tradition to look more acceptable, because former colonies were now treated as equals. To those with less qualms about colonialism, the EC was also acceptable, precisely because it was not very new. But for the populations in a non-colonial power like Norway the EC was something basically new, to be evaluated against the background of the Indochina wars and all the insight in neo-colonialism developed during the 1960s. However, only a fraction of the opposition in Denmark and Norway was due to such factors.[21]

Second, to the populations in Continental Europe the argument of putting an end to the fratricidal wars with Germany on one side had considerable weight. In Scandinavia this was a slightly more remote concern – except for the present generation of political leaders, many of whom were resistance fighters during the war.[22] They fought in their twenties and rule in their fifties with the war thirty years away. They become Western European internationalists in a praiseworthy effort to build peace in that part of the world. Globally speaking they are provincial.

Third, the argument of collective defense against US penetration probably carried much more weight on the Continent and in Britain than in Scandinavia. Big European powers saw themselves as competitors to the US, and resented the defeat. For smaller powers on the fringe of Europe to be dominated by the major capitalist power was perhaps even preferable to being dominated by the lesser powers. It takes time to develop a 'European' ideology, and with the mind less 'Europeanized' there was room for a more global consciousness.

Finally, and most importantly: Denmark and Norway are small countries where the center is not very rich and powerful, and the periphery not very poor and powerless – relative to conditions further south. For people in Italy, France and Germany to see power accumulate and assemble in Brussels is only a minor extension of the power distance to which they have become accustomed: for people in Denmark and Norway it represents something basically new, with much more distance between the common man and the power center. This point is appreciated particularly by those groups in the two countries referred to in the preceding point.

For the present author it is almost incredible how low the degree of awareness of the EC is on the Western European continent.[23] The EC is an instrument greeted by the conservatives and used by them, and largely ignored by the radicals. European leftists, experts on blaming the US for the kind of policies the EC now engages in, are remarkably silent here. Among the reasons given are the following:

- the EC is built around a nucleus of US capital anyhow; hence the evil should be attacked at its US roots;
- the EC is only a superstructure atop a basically capitalist infrastructure, and it makes no sense to attack the superstructure alone – again, the evil has to be attacked at its root;[24]
- the EC is needed as a protection against US penetration; although it has some shortcomings, it is indispensable as an instrument of independence from the US.

The fascination with the US is clear from all of this. The present generation of European leftists already shows a blindness not dissimilar to the preceding generation. The preceding generation drew the lesson from the Second World War that evil comes when you are militarily unprepared, hence make alliances and arm yourself! To the present generation of young Europeans, evil comes from the US – and the US has certainly done its utmost to confirm and strengthen this hypothesis. But the hypothesis is also of great comfort to Europeans across the entire political spectrum; and under this strange consensus the EC has been permitted to grow and will still grow.

One conclusion from this is that there are tremendous reservoirs of untapped opposition. They will start flowing, once the US is off the headlines. This may be when the Indochina war is finally brought to an end and the US is not only defeated (it already is) but has even learned to enjoy, benefit from and probably also make a profit out of the defeat, as the French did. With the decline of the US, EC conscience and consciousness will probably be raised by stimulating discussions about the EC at universities, in high schools, in factories, in organizations all over Western Europe – never leaving it to the pro-EC establishment alone to spread its 'information'. There is no such thing as objective truth about such a many-sided phenomenon as the EC anyhow: so anybody has the right to participate in the information *process,* but everybody also has a duty to know the basic facts.

7) *Withholding working power from the EC might become part of a strategy*

Imagine one stands for the type of redirection, or basic change, of EC policy outlined above. Again, what is the preferable strategy – join the

147

institutions and 'work from the inside', or fight them 'from the outside'? The problem has been put before, but this time in a more precise form: which is better, to give to the institution one's working power, or to withhold it? The both-and answer is possible, but not for the individual, at least not at one and the same point in time. Nor is any individual answer very interesting except as an example: any strategy must be based on collective action.

Organized withholding of working power from EC institutions would have an effect even if there were no manpower shortage as a result. The European Community cannot do without qualified professionals – many of them in the social sciences, most of them at least potentially more radical in their world perspectives than the EC would ever be able to live up to. To very, very many young Europeans it may become clear that to work for the EC is not just any other job, but is to work for a very special system of world dominance. Needless to say, this applies not only to the EC but also to the countless organizations of which the EC is the political expression: the multinational corporations of various kinds, including organizations for cultural dissemination.

Imagine something like this were organized. What would be the likely result? This would not leave the EC as it was, but would either make it more conservative or more radical. In the first case the true nature of the EC would become even more obvious. In the latter case its true nature might be smoothened over, but chances are also that internal conflicts within the organization would have a certain paralyzing effect. In either case, consciousness would rise, and the political nature of the European Community become more clear. Moreover, some pattern of co-operation might develop between those on the inside and those on the outside, pushing the European Community out of the splendid isolation in which it finds itself today.

8) *Revealing commercial secrets might become part of a strategy*
A substantial part of Western European policy is based on military secrets, commercial secrets, patents etc. Behind these are innovations made by somebody, usually an intellectual, scientist or technician, who has sold his work product against a (usually quite good) salary. Leaving the military secrets aside in this connection, what would happen if innovators no longer played this game but said, as people in health and in more basic science have been saying for a long time: *what I have found*

148

is based on the experience of mankind, I have added a little bit, and it also belongs to mankind! It is not for the leaders of nations or firms to play with or bargain with; if it can be of any benefit then it belongs neither to me, nor to them, but to all!

The capitalist system would not be killed if this type of thinking became the basis of organized, collective action; but there would be some important constraints on its maneuvers in world politics. No longer could technology be used as bait for raw materials and markets; no longer would intellectuals be alienated from their work product, unable to see positive or negative effects of it, only highly able to see its salary and career implications – provided one behaves nicely. For intellectuals to break into the files, and the safes, a Daniel Ellsberg of the multinational corporation, and photocopy and publish what they find, would be a new pattern of behavior – to say the least.

Like the preceding point the potential of change is seen as located among intellectuals, essentially, as long as the focus is inside the Western European countries themselves. The reader may object that this is an elitist perspective, which is true. But it is not unfounded: we have given some reasons why we think politics of values and ideas will be more important than politics based on interests – inside the EC, that is. Secondly, an elitist perspective is better than no perspective at all; this is even more so since elites working against their own establishment, national or regional, may be effective because they are less substitutable than non-elites. But the likelihood of such protests, or their effectiveness, should not be overrated. In general it is to the outside we must turn in the search for forces capable of changing the European Community.

9) *The Third World as a source of basic change*

We have mentioned some possible Third World reactions before, and also argued that they may have a militarizing effect on the EC. Here let us look beyond that perspective, and see if the Third World can also force a real change in the EC – not only a military reaction.

This is certainly not impossible, but it will take time. What is needed, as argued above, are strong organizations of poor countries to force more equitable deals with the rich countries, to build up horizontal trade among themselves, and to be able to turn inward and do something effective for and with their own masses.

One possible source of change here would be young intellectuals, particularly in those countries within the EC sphere of influence, and more particularly in those with a second generation of intellectuals, more locally trained. One example might be the former British dependencies in East Africa. Here the first generation of intellectual leaders, those now in power, were trained at Oxford and Cambridge, at London School of Economics. Their horizon was the socialism or social technology of the 1930s, in India often referred to as 'laskiology' after the most prominent teacher – with political independence as the immediate goal. They are the opposites of the giants in the fight for independence, Gandhi and Mao, who found so much of the cultural and ideological basis for their fight on their own soil. For that reason they easily – although with some major exceptions – function as bridgeheads for penetration from the EC, while they are also swayed by the persuasiveness of the anti-US argument whispered in their ears by the European conservatives and trumpeted throughout the world by the European left.

They will not last. A new generation of African intellectuals seek other sources, not the least their own people and their own creativity, for a more genuine independence – and are much less likely to serve as bridgeheads.[25] As with Western European intellectuals, the framework of analysis is already there: the impressive literature developed during the last decade on the US system of dominance. What remains is to apply it to the European counterpart – as it is being applied to Japan by people in South-east Asia.

But Western Europe has long training in tolerating words as long as they are not followed by deeds: even Spain and Portugal have this ability.[26] Young Africans cannot withhold their working power, since their working power is not much in demand by the EC anyhow – moreover, they are less to be blamed if they are bought than are their Western European colleagues, since they have less to fall back upon. But even if there is a high attrition rate in the present level of East African campus radicalism there may be sufficient remaining to stir conscience and consciousness at all levels in African society, eventually leading to the two types of reactions mentioned in Chapter 9: national wars of liberation and people's wars of liberation.

Imagine that this succeeds, that the EC sees the writing on the wall, and panics because of the similarity with the reaction to US imperialism. What would they do? They would probably have to move in the direction of many of the policies mentioned in this chapter, in their foreign policy. At home they might turn to an intensely heated, inner-directed capitalism with ever-increasing exchange of goods in all directions inside the EC; or even towards something new, e.g. quality of life. If the latter should happen, it would find the European left by and large unprepared since their major preoccupation has been to criticize capitalism and its infrastructure, not to think of alternatives to the present society beyond vague slogans of socialism. The left's failure in that particular regard may play into the hands of the establishment again – and lead to a paternalistic introduction of 'quality of life' from above, with new directorates of the Commission for that purpose. With special Members of the Commission; promoted by the same middle-aged balding men, with the same lack of *joie de vivre*.

But however that might be, this is for Western Europeans to fight out – it does not in the same way concern the Third World. The argument here is that a strong reaction from the Third World may be what will eventually save Western Europe from itself – provided that reaction comes relatively soon, before Western Europe has built itself up to the same heights of power – not to mention arrogance of power – as somebody else did in the 1960s.

10) *The socialist countries as a source of basic change*

The same argument can now be repeated. If they yield to the short run temptations, the socialist countries will strengthen very old domineering traditions in Western Europe; if they stand up against the EC, they may contribute to a much better Western Europe – just as all the people fighting the US around the world have brought that country out of at least some of its smugness and conceit, and into self-criticism and to some extent even social reconstruction. Let it only be said that by 'yielding' is not meant 'recognition'. For the socialist countries not to recognize the EC, even *de facto,* is to try to play the same game as the Western powers did towards the socialist countries. Thus, it took the US 14 years to recognize the Soviet Union *de jure,* and 22 years to recognize China *de facto,* and nothing was helped by those delays. What is meant is not to yield to the three-pronged attack of exploitation, fragmentation and penetration.

Will the socialist countries do that, will they stand up against the EC? Probably yes. However, the socialist countries are far from uniform. China seems to have a positive attitude to the EC, dictated by the 'the enemy of my enemy is my friend in principle'; according to that principle, the EC must be a double friend, since it is seen as an enemy of the imperialists to the West as well as of the revisionists (social imperialists) to the East.[27] This is hardly a lasting attitude, however, but partly dictated by the special situation of isolation and conflict with both super-powers that has dominated the life of the young People's Republic of China.[28] Nor can Cuba's and Romania's claims to be included in the GPS-countries be seen as signs of accepting all the EC stands for, since such claims can also be interpreted as moves forcing the EC into the universalistic patterns argued above. In short, if only these countries pursue firm policies relative to the EC, this may have a very healthy educative effect.

11) *The rest of the world as a source of basic change*

So far our conclusion is that the most effective challenge to the EC will have to come from the outside, more particularly from the Third World and the socialist countries. This does not exhaust the external world; there are still some other sources of change. They do not seem so promising, however, from this point of view.

The remaining European countries, those neither socialist, nor EC members nor aspiring members, do not at present seem to amount to more than a scattered heap of nations incapable of formulating, let alone pursuing, a consistent alternative policy. But if they did, if they came together and pursued a policy less traditionally capitalist relative to the Third World and the socialist countries, then this would undoubtedly have some effect on the EC. It would almost force the EC into an effort to overbid in decapitalizing policies, a competition which might be very healthy for the world in general. Only these mildly socialist countries, like some of the Nordic countries and Yugoslavia, would be capable of en-gaging in this type of policy – not the US or Japan.

From US and Japan, competition in the traditional capitalist sense has, of course, been the rule. It is now their turn to protect themselves against the EC, by some of the same means as the EC uses against them. An economic alliance between the US and Japan, while highly unlikely, is not impossible. Such an alliance would not lead to any crisis since all three have a shared interest in the survival of capitalism as a system, but it would probably intensify some of the more crude capitalistic tendencies inside the EC, and for that reason be unhealthy for the world as a whole.

In short, not much should be expected from 'the rest of the world' in terms of radicalizing impact – the impact that could be good is not very likely, while the likely impact does not seem to be to the good.

That concludes the survey of possible countervailing forces. But this

152

does not lead to any conclusion. Where, then, does all this lead us? To try to answer, let us briefly retrace our steps.

Our point of departure was a Western Europe, devastated by the war, with strong opposition groups wanting basic social change, no longer the center of the world, and in the process of losing the military-political grip over her colonies. However, it was also a Western Europe capable of recovery with US assistance, even though the price for the Marshall aid was a deep US penetration into Western European economy. All this put the economic-political leadership of Western Europe into a strange inbetween position. On the one hand there was the desire to regain some of the control of the lost parts of the world, to the East and to the South – on the other hand there was the equally strong desire to get rid of the domination exercised by the US. The method was clear: to unite, to integrate, around few (but very concrete) issues, with few (but reliable and not too weak states) to start with. Later on, the exploitation of general world resentment of a dominant but declining United States was added to the political instruments, and with considerable skill.

Thus, the European Communities took form and are slowly becoming the European Community.[29] Waves of influence, of power, emanated from the Community, spreading outwards in geographical and political space. The Community proved itself dynamic in producing these waves, some of them real shock waves through the world economic, political, and social structure. Through skillful alternation between phases of extension and phases of deepening, EC as a superstate – and possibly also superpower – takes shape.[30] For the person who identifies a superstate as something that has supranational institutions similar to those of a big state, the EC is not a superstate[31] – but for the person who studies the total impact of the EC on the world, it is. Here is a new entity, certainly still incapable of making *new* decisions quickly, but highly capable of enacting the *old* ones every hour, every day, in practically speaking all corners of the world. With an extension to ten members follows, possibly, a network of 38 former colonies and 35 overseas territories – a total of 83. Many of them are small, but their geographical dispersion beats anything so far seen in the world, making the EC a global power, not a regional one like the present EC. That the sun never sets on this complex empire goes without saying. True, there is a heavy concentration on *Eurafrica*. But Mauritius on the Indian Ocean has already asked to join the 18 Yaoundé states – and then there are three countries in the Pacific Ocean (Fiji, Tonga, Western Samoa) and four in the Caribbean area (Barbados, Jamaica, Trinidad-Tobago, Guyana).

Nor does the range of EC power stop with this list. The European Community is not the greatest industrial grouping in the world, but it is by far the greatest trading partner. With five hundred years of lead in science and research over the peoples dominated by her, it lies in the EC's power to establish economic cycles around the world with a division of labor as favorable to the EC countries as in any colonial period. The EC can set up economic transactions so that research, financing, administration, and some of the most research- and capital-intensive tasks are carried out in Western Europe, whereas extraction of raw materials, labor-intensive production, production according to well established blueprints, and the better part of the consumption are taken care of elsewhere. Elsewhere – that means above all the Third World countries[32] and the socialist countries. The EC can do this because she has the resources to do so, *and* because the others think they depend on her. Hundreds, even thousands of years of Eurocentrism provide the background for this achievement, a power built into the rolls of history and of a magnitude far beyond the crude power possessed by the two superpowers that dethroned Western Europe.

But the power of the European Community is not less dangerous, it is only of a different kind. It is the power of an economic system that moves people, commodities, and money around, creating centers and peripheries, enriching the former and empoverishing the latter. True, there are welfare policies, there are elements of redistribution, of social democracy. The center hands some of its gains back to the periphery as subsidies and security benefits domestically, as 'development aid' internationally. But this is usually done so as to reinforce the grip the center has over the periphery.[33] Thus, the European Community engages in 'development assistance' in such a way that by far most of the money 'given' flows back to the EC countries, to EC firms, solidifying and expanding the power of multinational corporations with headquarters in the Center of the world and subsidiaries in the world Periphery.[34] The EC even subsidizes her own periphery, the farmers, in such a way that they produce an agricultural surplus that has to be exported, again at subsidized prices – competing in developing countries for the kinds of markets developing countries could take care of themselves.[35] And: the EC even introduces an extremely complex scheme of 'generalized preferences', apparently doing away with tariffs on semi-manufactured and manufactured goods from the Third World countries. But in the place of tariffs, quotas are introduced, reducing the possible impact of the system.[36] Moreover, only the most developed of the Third World countries (usually those that were most able to fight against colonialism) can draw some benefits from this scheme, for only they have any industry. In all likelihood the others will serve as well prepared 'infrastructures' for the subsidiaries of big multinational corporations,[37] they will carry out some routinized operation based on blueprints developed far up in the North somewhere, and the managers will know very well how to squeeze some benefits out of the 'generalized preferences'.

The policies of the EC relative to the socialist countries bear some resemblance to this. The socialist countries in Eastern Europe are, of course, autonomous politically relative to the EC – but perhaps not culturally. They seem to pursue the same goals with not too different means, and also enter into the capitalist orbit as suppliers of raw materials and buyers of technology.[38]

These are the waves emanating from the Community, spreading outwards in geographical and political space, carried by the old and new trade routes established by Western Europeans. *But in human affairs waves always generate counterwaves.* Social space reflects waves, it generates echoes that interfere with the waves coming from the center. The question is: where is the center and where is the periphery? The center are those who gain, the periphery are those who lose. The center are the elites in the EC countries; the EC workers who benefit from expanding markets for the industries they run together with EC industrialists, bureaucrats, and politicians; the farmers, heavily subsidized by the Community funds; the elites in the Third World countries who run the economic (and sometimes also political) subsidiaries; possibly also the elites in Eastern European countries who prefer an inferior position in the capitalist orbit to something like a cultural revolution at home that might threaten their own 'new class' position. *The periphery are the rest.*

They are the masses of the world, the poor in the poor countries for whom 'generalized preferences', or trade in general for that matter, are abstractions going on far above their heads, or invisible ties that make them vulnerable to market fluctuations as lethal as missiles. Raw material prices go down: and so do thousands in the real world proletariat, down in the gutter, in the slums, starving. The prices go up: and their lot improves somewhat, receiving a minor fraction of the surplus that accrues to the elites in their own country. Compute the average of a standstill for the masses and improvement for the elites: it is called 'economic growth'. Make a theory of it: it is called the 'science of economics'. Nowhere in the pretentious concoction of abstractions and statistics coming out of the Community are the primary needs of the lower half, or third, of the population taken as basic. And even that would be an abstraction. Rather, one could hold up against all the speeches and all the statistics the autobiography of one slum child, the innocent and ignorant victim of economic manipulations from the center of the world.

This is why there will be counterwaves: the EC system is not very different from the more fragmented system of empires that preceded it, nor is it very different from the other two giant capitalist systems that accompany it, the United States and Japan. In the early 1950s the US system was still expanding, filling a vacuum left by the Western European (and Japanese) losers of the war. Few would dream of a Cuba, an Algeria, an Indochina. And yet they all came, with tremendous force, small peoples, 'fifth-rate powers' or whatever expression some of the defense intellectuals made use of to demonstrate their own ignorance of world reality and poor understanding of power. The masses did not fight alone: they were supported materially by countries that had extricated themselves from the Western capitalist orbit at an earlier stage, and they were supported ideologically by intellectuals in all countries. The material support was also given with other motives in mind, the ideological support was often dictated much more by hatred of the dominators than by love for the dominated. But counterwaves they were, indeed: exposing, humiliating, even defeating the United States before the eyes of the world – like France before her.

Today the European Community is still on its way up. The waves are still emanating outwards, and there is little or no interference. The EC can still for some years to come present herself to the South as better than the US, and to the East as better than the Soviet Union – and even share with China some elements of a generalized anti-superpower ideology. The EC may also be able to fill a vacuum here and there, left behind by a retreating US, beaten morally and politically more than economically and militarily. The lack of opposition, even some applause from well penetrated elites with colored skins but white minds, with socialist words but capitalist thoughts and deeds, will all be registered as signs of success and reinforce the waves.

But then the counterwaves will come. They will be seen as the workings of agitators, as the machinations of other powers jealous of the EC success – and this may be partly correct. As the counterwaves grow stronger and start interfering effectively with the waves, each point of interference will constitute an argument for military strength, for internal security, for a *European* posture towards the East, for the possibility of rapid action in

156

the South. And as the repressive machinery grows, so will the counter-waves.

So, once more, what is the conclusion? Simply this: *the European Community, where its global role is concerned, is not the beginning of anything new, but the end of something old.* If the EC inspires anything at all, it is a strong feeling of *déja-vu*. Like its predecessors, the Charlemagne and the Napoleon empires,[39] it will in all likelihood be short-lived, and even more so than the US Empire – for increased communication and increased political consciousness around the world will have an accelerating effect on the counterwaves. Historically it may even have a positive function: it may serve to unify the opposition, progressive forces and progressive countries in search of other ways of organizing human society and our shrinking planet than by way of the classic EC approach. This does not come by itself, though, as day follows night – but will be the result of millions of quantum jumps in political consciousness around the world, accompanied by links of organized counteraction.

With the enormous extension of the EC now taking place, it is unlikely that some wisdom nevertheless will filter through from the past, from the ghost of Charlemagne or Napoleon, or from those responsible for the slaughters in Algeria and Indochina, for the interventions in Latin America, and so on: *do not overextend yourself*. The EC of Ten (with dependencies) is already overextended; that may be to the good because the weaknesses, the 'soft underbellies' will be exposed. But the hope one may nevertheless entertain is that the confrontation will be of short duration, and that the darkest elements of Western Europe will not be given too free a hand in the effort to proceed forward, from political, economic, and cultural superpower to military superpower. If that should happen there is no way of telling which disasters may follow. If they grow, as they seem to do, the European Community may also be headed for her Vietnam – for instance somewhere in the jungles, shrub, fields, deserts, villages, and cities of Southern Africa,[40] for instance sometime in the 1980s.

Such is the nature of power. The European Community has more structural power than anyone before her in world history, being as she is on top of a world-wide vertical division of labor, keeping the bottom of the world fragmented, separated from each other, and penetrating deeply into each one of them. *But this power creates counterforces.* The EC may hit back, using her resource power. *But her ideological power depends on a certain submissiveness, just as the remunerative power depends on dependency.* The poor countries of the world cannot match the EC here; but they can and they will inoculate themselves against this power, gradually developing the type of self-respect, self-reliance, and fearlessness that characterized the masses led by a Gandhi and a Mao Tse-Tung. This may be the most positive outcome of the European Community: one more display of Western, white dominance stimulating counterforces elsewhere, counterforces that may one day lead to a more equitable, more diversified world.

Epilogue:
After the referenda
in Norway and Denmark

After this book was written, after the Danish/Norwegian edition was out and the English edition had been set, the results of the two Scandinavian referenda became known. On 25 September 1972 the Norwegian people said no to membership in the European Community; on 2 October the Danish people said yes. In Norway, 46 % were for membership, 54 % against, with 78 % participation; in Denmark, 63 % for, 37 % against, and with 89 % participation. The Irish referendum in May 1972 gave the expected mandate to the government; while one of the oldest parliamentary democracies – England – has stood by the doctrine of the supremacy of Parliament and has pursued a persistent non-referendum policy. Hence, the likely outcome is that as of 1 January 1973, the European Community will have Denmark, Ireland, and England as new members, but not Norway. This will be the EC *a neuf,* at nine – not *a dix,* at ten. Clearly, the Commission will have to do some re-working of its statistics. All this has consequences, some minor ones for the text of this particular book, some major ones for world politics.

I have preferred not to correct the text, for the simple reason that the argument of this book was what the European Community was striving toward – not what they actually get at any one given moment. Obviously, the text will now not give a completely faithful image of the EC in early 1973. But Norway is small; the adjustments now necessary in chapter 4 about the EC resources are minor ones, except for shipping. Here the Norwegian contribution to the 77.3 million tons is about 20 million tons. Nor will the North Sea any longer be fully available as an EC lake. Apart from this, however, the Norwegian resources are not significant. And in terms of structural power, Norway now joins group 4a in chapter 5, together with Sweden, Switzerland, and Austria. The total number of territories in the potential EC system decreases from 83 to 79 – which may have some ocean floor implications. The total population is reduced by 3.9 million. Of these 3.9 million Norwegians, 2.6 million were voters, out of which 78 % voted – and out of these, 54 % voted against the European Community.

What does this imply?

Needless to say, the matter of EC membership was a more important issue for Norway than it was for the European Community. A 'yes' would have strengthened considerably all the forces in Norway which today support the modern, industrial state embedded in an emerging super-industrial superstate. In Norway these forces were located in the center, in the industrialized areas and the centers of administration. By and large, their vision of the future was clear: more of the same. Continued 'economic growth', tackling the problems of pollution, powerful multinational corporations, demands from less privileged sectors and peoples, etc. as they appear on the political horizon.

With the 'no' yielded by the referendum, however, these forces do not just disappear, for two reasons. First, they are strong, deeply rooted in the structure of Norwegian society as well as in Norway's relations with the world as a whole. Second, those who said 'no' are considerably less unified than the 'yes' people, at least today. They are more spread thoroughout the geographical and political periphery. In some years' time, it may well be that they can find a more common political platform, based on such elements as decentralization; a diversified economic structure not inimical to the primary sector; less insistence on economic growth and more on equality, justice, quality of life; more national autonomy, possibly even a neutral position in foreign affairs. But today the situation is fluid.

The 'yes'-forces may be able to make of the referendum a lost battle and still win their war. One strategy might be the trade treaty with an expansion clause. Another might be through the next elections with only 'yes'-candidates from the two party organizations clearly in favor of EC membership: Labor and the Conservatives. This could be combined with a change in the Constitution, so as to lower the threshold from a ¾ vote in favor of entry to a ⅔ vote. A third strategy would be to wait for a foreign policy crisis of some kind and then play on the security aspect of the European Community.

But the situation in Denmark and England is also fluid. In both countries the 'no'-forces are strong: in Denmark they are even located in the center of society, and in England they were almost able to win over Wilson's revisionism. The situation is different from that in the six current member states, where the integration has never been made a political issue at the mass level: it is something made by and for the elite. This may now change: there may be a growing awareness among people in the Six that the European Community is something else, something more than just a natural and inevitable attempt at harmonization and integration.

This then is the significance of the Norwegian vote: the first important rebuff suffered by the European Community. It was the first of the counterwaves predicted towards the end of chapter 10 in this book, and it came from the Norwegian periphery. Other such counterwaves will come. Norway has in all probability had a much more significant impact on the EC in voting 'no' than a handful of Norwegian representatives, in all essentials thinking and acting exactly like their colleagues in the Six, would ever have had.

For the EC, the loss of Norway means an incomplete configuration. We have mentioned shipping and a shared EC energy plan for the North Sea. More important is the security aspect: Norway as the only NATO member outside the EC (Turkey and Greece have their special EC association status, and also a special relation to the US; Portugal has solid backing for EC membership; Iceland is marginal in more than one sense). Moreover, Norway has two neutral neighbors in Sweden and Finland, and is now an atypical member of Northern Europe. In all probability this will tilt the balance for further 'Europeanization' of NATO from the Euro-group towards the Western Union, based on the more reliable military powers, the Six and England. Depending on internal movements in Norway, the result may well be a Norwegian withdrawal from NATO: but it may also be precisely the opposite, EC integration. And here the best advice would seem to abstain from any prediction.

Notes

CHAPTER 1.

1 See 'How the European Community's Institutions Work', by Emile Noël, *Community Topics* no. 37, May 1971, p. 4. Of course, this numerical measure is not a very good indicator since some regulations may be very minor indeed, others may be far-reaching; and a number can easily be inflated by splitting a more general regulation into any number of specifications.

2 The Werner Report is available as supplement to *Bulletin of the European Communities*, no. 11, 1970. As a typical expression of the intentions may serve this communiqué from the foreign minister meeting in Brussels 20 July 1970:

'The ministers expressed their determination to prepare the way of a united Europe... This united Europe remains the fundamental goal which must be attained as soon as possible... It is desirable to give form to the desire for political union... In order to bring nearer the moment when Europe can express itself with a single voice... It appeared to the ministers that it is in the area if the concertation of foreign policy that it would be best to make the first concrete efforts...'

3 It is important to make this point about 'intra-European tribal warfare'. Few people talk so readily as Europeans about 'tribal warfare' in other continents, particularly in Africa. A comparison with the Indian subcontinent may have a sobering influence on this type of thinking. There has been considerable bloodshed between Hindus and Muslims, but insignificant relative to the extent to which Europeans have killed each other. And if one looks at India alone the major fact is that this country with a population of the same order of magnitude as Europe has established a peace system far superior to the fragile mixture of passive peaceful coexistence and balance of deterrence found in Europe today. To establish a peace system in Western Europe alone is therefore only half of the Indian achievement.

4 It may also be argued that Germany and Japan, although more destroyed than the Western allies, were less defeated. The idea of 'strategic surrender' would be precisely the ability to surrender at the right moment, with old industries in shambles but the rebuilding capacity still not completely destroyed so that both Germany and Japan could rebuild completely shortly after the war and with quite new and modern equipment relative to, for instance, France.

5 In the West the Warsaw Treaty Organization is usually referred to as the Warsaw Pact.

6 As one example of a quote to illustrate this type of thinking, consider the following: 'The enlargement of the Community would create a framework for more

harmonious relationships in Western Europe. The relationships between Europe and the other countries of the world, particularly the United States, the Soviet Union and, one day, China, would become more evenly balanced. A Europe united would have the means of recovering the position in the world which Europe divided has lost', *The United Kingdom and the European Communities* (British White Paper on the Common Market, paragraph 61).

7 Gustavo Lagos Matus introduced this felicitous term into social science.

8 The resistance against Soviet-US condominium was probably first voiced by the Chinese, for instance as seen in a circular letter from the Chinese People's Committee for World Peace of 20 June 1963: '. . . neither the issue of world peace, nor that of European, Asian, African or Latin American peace and security can be decided simply by one or two big nations, since all nations, big and small, have the right to participate in the discussions and to decide on the vital questions which are common concern of mankind'. At that time, after the Cuban crisis and before the signing of the Partial Test Ban Treaty, it looked so obvious to most of the world that peace was something in the hands of the United States and the Soviet Union only. Today the statement quoted has an air even of triviality.

CHAPTER 2.

1 Reported in *The Times*, 9 October 1971, the press conference was on 8 October. As usual, Brandt also emphasized the role of the summit conference to be held fall 1972 as a major instrument.

2 In the tradition developed at Yale University in political science, 'domain' and 'scope' are the major dimensions for discussing problems of integration. However, as pointed out by many, the EC poses some empirical configurations that analytical tools developed so far perhaps do not handle too well. Thus, in the history of the EC it is not only integration of countries that is taking place, but also integration of the integration mechanisms – as, for instance, when the ECSC, EEC, and Euratom got common institutions as of 1 July 1967. In that sense the scope becomes more like a domain.

3 In connection with the staircase hypothesis: some might say that the steps will become smaller and smaller as time passes by; there will be fewer and fewer candidates for membership, and as the circle of members extends they will be able to agree on less and less. There may be some truth to this. Obviously, membership is limited, but as we shall argue later the upper limit may be quite high. It may be 14 countries, with four countries added to the Franco-German nucleus already in 1951, four more possibly added as of 1 January 1973, and the remaining four to be added by 1980. Moreover, these countries are in many respects so homogeneous that it may also be argued that as the Community expands so will its appetite for new tasks particularly in the purely political field, including defense policies – as will be argued in Chapter 8. In short, we do not think there is any firm basis for any clear-cut theory as to what the staircase will eventually look like.

4 The first point in the Preamble of the Treaty of Rome: 'Determined to establish the foundation of an ever closer union among the peoples of Europe'.

5 It may be argued that according to the Luxembourg decision a *de facto* veto also exists within the European Community. This veto, however, is not a part of

the constitutional structure, but something that developed in a particular situation and that may very well disappear when that situation no longer prevails. At any rate, there is a substantial difference between a *de facto* and a *de jure* veto.

6 For this presentation, in brief, of the history of the European Community we have made use of one of the publications of the Community: *Memento de la Communauté Européenne*, no. 25, 1970. Like most publications from the European Community it is clear, well written, well documented. As much as possible, such documents have been made use of in the following.

7 *Werner Report*, p. 12. In that connection the report also states: 'These transfers of responsibility represent a process of fundamental political significance which implies the progressive development of political cooperation'. Further, on p. 13 it is said: 'The implementation of economic and monetary union demands institutional reforms which presuppose a modification of the treaties of Rome'. These are very clear words. It is probably only in Denmark and Norway that adherents of the European Community express doubts as to whether a transition towards a much tighter political cooperation is really wanted, in order to assuage the fears expressed by the vocal oppositions.

8 For a communiqué from this very important meeting, see *Le Figaro*, 20 November 1970, p. 3. The most important points are: a decision to work out a common position in connection with the European Security Conference, a decision to have a meeting among specialists on the Middle East in order to have their views converge, a decision to appoint persons in each capital of the member states, one from the local foreign ministry and one from each of the five embassies, to be in charge of foreign policy consultation, a decision that the permanent delegates in the United Nations should try to find a common position before important votes.

9 Interview accorded to Robert Haeger of *US News and World Report*, June 1971. Here as elsewhere we make use of quotations from Willy Brandt rather than from big power heads like Heath and Pompidou. The reason is obvious: Nobel Peace Prize Winner Willy Brandt is generally considered the least power-oriented, the most peaceful of them; and what is here indicated is that even from him it is easy to find quotes that indicate an increasingly clear perception of a big power role for the future European Community.

10 According to *Die Industrie-politik der Gemeinschaft Memorandum der Commision an den Rat* (Brussels, 1970), 1258 cooperation or fusion agreements were made between enterprises in various EC countries in the period 1961 till first half of 1969 (p. 92). Particularly important are the agreements between Fiat and Citroën, between Commerz Bank and Credit Lyonnais, between Agfa and Gevaert, and the air industry consortium behind the production of the European air bus 300 B.

11 According to the *Yearbook of International Organizations*, published by the

Table A

	1962	1964	1966	1968	1970
Number of INGOs	216	233	235	261	275

(INGO: International Non-governmental Organization.)

Union of International Associations in Brussels, the figures for the last years look like Table A.

The growth is impressive because the number of EC-INGOs in 1956 was very low. However, in the next phase these organizations will no longer be international but transnational beecause they will correspond to the increasingly supranational nature of the Europan Community.

12 'Southeastern France' is in this connection known as Occitania.

13 In *European Community: The Facts* (Brussels, European Communities, 1971), p. 9 the number of people working in the Community institutions is given as 'altogether about 8,700', divided as in the text. Since then the Community has been growing, roughly maintaining the proportion.

14 Of course, it is difficult to tell precisely what the impact of the candidate countries in the EC might be in this connection. What is known is that British Foreign Minister Douglas-Home has said that Britain is completely behind the Portuguese effort to obtain association with the expanded European Community (UPI, date line London 8 March 1972). France has also expressed herself very clearly in favor of supporting an arrangement for Spain over and above a mere trade treaty (European Community, January 1972, p. 4). On the other hand, there will of course be opposition on political grounds both in the ideological and in the institutional senses (absence of real parties and free trade unions). Denmark and Norway might continue their line of opposition known from Council of Europe and to some extent also from NATO (the Norwegian foreign minister's action against Portugal at the NATO Council Meeting in Lisboa, June 1971). And voices of opposition against Turkey can also be heard, although Greece has tended to eclipse Turkey in this regard: 'Turkey has a fascist regime at least as vicious and repressive as that of the Greek colonels. All the left-wing press has been shut down ... the radio and TV network put under the command of a general, and left-wing writers and academics are being tried and condemned by ten military courts operating throughout the country. The Turkish Labour Party ... was banned soon after the coup ... Students awaiting trial have been brutally tortured with techniques similar to those used in Greece, and several of them subsequently executed'. *(Agenor, Jan.–March 1972, p. 5)*. This article is very critical of NATO and the Council of Europe in this connection, but does not mention explicitly the Turkish status as associate member of the EC.

15 As to the speculations about Portugal they are largely based on talks with members of resistance movements, as well as unpublished documents. Actually, inside Portugal there seem to be three currents when it comes to the major direction of orientation for Portugal: the colonialist tradition in various versions that still believe in 'Portuguese Africa', the old 'lucitanian tradition' that would base Portuguese future on the Portugal-Brazil axis, and the 'Europeans' for whom the European Community must appear as a very attractive haven of escape.

The second faction is of less importance, and of the other two the third seems to be gaining and the first losing. Thus, the debate is between three alternatives none of which presupposes any basic change in Portuguese structure, with the exception of some extension of the type of parliamentarism currently found in Portugal. The alternative would be a faction for a Portuguese Portugal, for giving up ideas of domination over others or absorption in larger settings and going in for self-reliance.

166

CHAPTER 3.

1 A more complete version of the power theory is given in the author's *The True Worlds: A Transnational Perspective* (forthcoming), *chapter 2*.

2 This distinction is used by such diverse authors as P. Sorokin *(Social and Cultural Dynamics)*, A. Etzioni *(A Comparative Analysis of Complex Organizations)*, and H. Morgenthau *(Politics Among Nations)*. For a comparison of the three approaches and a further development of them, see Johan Galtung, 'On the Meaning of Nonviolence', *Journal of Peace Research*, 1965, pp. 233 f.

3 See reference given in footnote 1.

4 In the theory of 'balance of power' (meaning military power) these two concepts of balance are often confused: sometimes one is talking of balance in a mechanical sense, sometimes a positive balance in the book-keeper sense, and sometimes of the latter as a future-oriented preparation for the former; in order to have something extra in case the other party should have a technological break-through.

5 The publications by the Institute for Strategic Studies in London, appropriately entitled *The Military Balance,* and widely disseminated throughout the world through excellent public relations activities, are important in this connection. They are read by all parties, and although they are probably not taken at their face value except by the very uninitiated, their psychological double-edged impact, partly as a typographical projection screen for world power, partly as a stimulus to expand this power further, is probably considerable.

6 For a complete presentation of this theory, see Johan Galtung, 'A Structural Theory of Imperialism', *Journal of Peace Research* 1971, pp. 81–118.

7 See the 1971 reference in footnote 1, chapter 4.

8 This is dealt with at some length in my paper 'Structural Pluralism and the Future of Human Society', *Challenges from the Future,* Proceedings from the International Future Research Conference, vol. III (Tokyo: Kodansha, 1970), pp. 271–308.

9 Thus, there is a consistent and relatively high negative correlation between indicators of socio-economic development, and the indicators of the emphasis on education of lawyers (relative to other types of intellectual training) in a given country. For an analysis, see Johan Galtung, 'Diachronic Analysis of Relationships between Human Resources Components and the Rate of Economic Growth in Selected Countries' (Paris: UNESCO, Human Resources Analysis Division, 1969), mimeo, 64 pp.

10 Between 1961 and 1967 for each dollar invested by the US in Latin America there were five dollars in the opposite direction. See CECLA VI E/3 May 1969, from UN Economic Commission for Latin America.

11 See the reference given in footnote 6, p. 102. The negative correlation between GNP per capita and the Gini index for income distribution is −0.90, and the negative correlation between GNP per capita and the Gini index for land distribution is −0.80.

CHAPTER 4.

1 The profile given below is taken from *European Community: The Facts* (Brussels, May 1971), p. 23. The data in the table, however, are from a mimeographed collection of tables (Information, The Enlarged Community in Figures, January

1972, Press and Information, Directorate A), with the exception of the data for the sources of gross domestic product that are taken from the same source as the profile, p. 22. It should be noted that the GNP for the Soviet Union is an estimate since socialist countries do not operate with this concept that more accurately represents economic activity in capitalist countries. The data reported in the table are from 1970, the data in the profile from 1969.

2 The kind of statistics given here were also expressed very clearly by EC politicians in connection with the ceremony in the Egmont palace, Brussels 22 January 1972 when the accession treaty opening the way for Britain, Ireland, Denmark and Norway to join the European Community was signed. Thus, according to *International Herald Tribune* 22–23 January 1972 (p. 2) West German Foreign Minister Walter Scheel spoke of the expanded Community as 'the greatest trade power in the world', with a population of 260 million and a gross national product of $ 564 billion – 'exceeded only by the USA'. Actually, Scheel is here using data for 1969.

In *Frankfurter Allgemeine,* also for Saturday 22 January, Scheel is also emphasizing that EC is by far the biggest trading power in the world, and that the extension of the European Community means that the EC share in world trade will rise from 40 % to 54 % of the total international exchanges, including exchanges inside the European Community. (On the same first page of *Frankfurter Allgemeine* there is an article by Bruno Dechamps, 'Erweitert – jetzt vertiefen' – playing on the staircase hypothesis.)

In short, the European Community stimulates exercises in comparative statistics, particularly among the economic superpowers.

3 Figures taken from *European Community: The Facts,* p. 21.

4 This, of course, is the vision of the world repeatedly put forward by Zbigniew Brzezinski. However, that vision presupposes an identity of basic interests in protecting capitalism, and a similarity in fundamental social structure between the US–EC on the one hand and Japan on the other which hardly corresponds with deeper-lying aspects of Japan. For some indication of factors to be taken into account, see chapter 9.

5 Figures taken from Zbigniew Brzezinski, 'America and Europe', *Foreign Affairs,* October 1970, p. 19. It should be noted that Germany is number 3, and that Willy Brandt has had a keen understanding that technological expansion may more than compensate for the territorial contraction.

6 We are thinking of the dispute between the Federal Republic of Germany and The Netherlands. However, in our interpretation the basic point about that dispute is that it defines the North Sea continental shelf as disputable between coastal states, and thereby firmly reinforces the right of the coastal states to divide it among themselves. If any prediction is safe in this world, then it is that later generations will look back at these decisions in anger, since there is no absolute principle that separates the North Sea bottom from any other ocean bottom.

7 According to *The Times,* 23 August 1971. More recent estimates are considerably higher; 15 %, even 60 % of the total EC oil consumption later in this century.

8 For an analysis of this, see *Dagens Nyheter* (Stockholm), 12 September 1971.

9 This, of course, is the basic theme behind the *Pacem in Maribus* conferences initiated by the Center for Study of Democratic Institutions, Santa Barbara, US, and

168

the Government of Malta. It is also a principle adopted in UN resolutions, but not yet worked out in any legally clear form. The Pacem in Maribus continuing group for policy research is now located at the International Ocean Institute of the Royal University of Malta.

10 Another way of expressing the impact of the extension from Six to Ten would be to say that the merchant marine increases 173 %, coal 81 %, electricity 57 %, export to third countries 41 %, industrial production 33 %, steel 25 %, car production 24 %, etc. The population increases 36 %. This expansion is done without military conquest − in the days of military conquest anything of this magnitude would have been accompanied by a major war. One may then speculate that a corresponding amount of energy must have gone into this expansion − millions of small details of negotiation and persuasion at all levels, public and private, bilateral and multilateral. But there is no measure of this total input − only of the output (data from *European Community*, 3/1972, p. 1).

11 Data from ICAO, *Digest of Statistics*, 1969, Montreal 1971.

CHAPTER 5.

1 It should be pointed out that cross investment, for instance by building up an empire of Shell and BP gas stations in the United States to parallel empires that carry the names of ESSO and Texaco, is not the only way of obtaining some kind of balance between two expansive economies. Another method would be a horizontal division of labor, for instance with one party focussing on gasoline and the other on oil and related products, and then exchanging. And then, a third approach is to build down mutual dependence and go in for self-reliance − and anti-trade directed policy.

2 The idea of a 'peace structure' is explored in the first part of Johan Galtung, ed., *Co-operation in Europe* (Oslo: Universitetsforlaget, 1970). Another version is given in Johan Galtung, 'Europe: Bipolar, Bicentric or Cooperative?', *Journal of Peace Research*, 1972, pp. 1−26. A basic point in this theory is that peace is not necessarily proportionate to 'international cooperation', but depends on the type of cooperation. Only if this cooperation is symmetric, based on equality, will it be peace productive in the long run.

3 Again, the crucial point would be the extent to which the relationship is egalitarian. After some oscillations of disagreement it does not seem unlikely that France and Germany will find an equilibrium point that will make the famous *pont des invasions* in Northern France − which five German armies have made use of — now used for the last time.

4 The European Community is interesting in this regard. Traditionally peace in the sense of *absentia belli* has been built at the expense of the burden of an arms race and the threat that a precarious balance of power may no longer function. The EC uses another formula: not the equality of opposing, equal forces, but the equality of intensive cooperation, even fusion, at the economic and political top of the participating societies, combined with fragmentation lower down.

5 So far, however, this mutual penetration has not been very successful. The tendency has long been for US business in Europe to grow faster than fusion of European business in Europe. Moreover, at a crucial point in the deliberations subsequent to the dollar crisis August 1971 Commissioner Ralf Dahrendorf said: in GATT (24 August 1971) that the US investment in Europe had increased from

$ 1.1 billion in 1958, to $ 10.2 billion in 1969 and probably $ 13 billion in 1970 —whereas the Six only invested $ 3.3 billion in the US.

6 I am indebted to Helge Hveem for felicitous expression.

7 The magnetic power of an emerging power center, still fresh and untainted by evident power abuses, is considerable. Thus, ILO officials report a decline in the interests of many member states in ILO because of a strong feeling that the real center for decision-making in that particular field is Brussels. In this connection it must also be remembered how the European Community plays up to the Euro-centered thinking of all Western European elites, a pattern of orientation now reactivated after the years of Western European disunity, with United States, Soviet Union and the Third World as major foci of attention, and the UN and its specialized agencies as the media in which a more global orientation was articulated. The rise of the EC will therefore almost certainly lead to a decline in the UN.

8 According to an article in *Asahi Evening News* (April 18, 1972, p. 1) the basic mechanism behind 'mounting friction' is 'a levelling-off of Japan's exports to the US and a switch in its export production capacity eventually to sail to Europe'. Just as there was a textile crisis which was singled out as a major item of contention between Japan and the US, Japan is accused by the EC of dumping oxalic acid, a dye ingredient, in the EC countries, and of dumping polyester and 'several types of ball bearings' in Britain. The powerful Japanese Ministry of International Trade and Industry(MITI) tries to avoid any open confrontation and 'is calling on the electronics manufacturing, automobile and chemical industries in particular to adopt and follow export programs to avoid friction in overseas markets'. Another question is to what extent Japanese industries follow suit, but 'some auto-makers are starting to shift concentration of the European sales to countries which do not produce autovehicles'. Obviously, this is an interesting test of liberalism in the field of trade: it works as long as there is no major threat to major producers, but when a firm like Voigtländer collapses because of competition from Japanese camera makers it starts getting more serious (likewise with Pollar ball-bearing factory).

9 In *Asian Drama*. One difficulty with Myrdal's conception is that his 'hard state' looks a bit too much like the particular pattern of public sector-private sector relation practised in Sweden during the years of social-democratic leadership. The hard states of Eastern Europe are certainly considerably harder, with very few mechanisms of institutionalized conflict articulation between the private and the public sectors, since the theory is that there is no built-in contradiction between the two sectors in socialist countries.

10 It is still too early to see to what extent Western European countries outside the EC, even outside the Six for that matter, will undergo a deteriorating trade composition. For Norway there are signs in that direction.

11 The data for this table are taken from the Commission publication *The Enlarged Community: Outcome of the Negotiations with the Applicant States*, pp. 43 ff, or from the British White Paper, paragraphs 117 and 118. Of course, what will eventually happen to the 20 former dependencies of the United Kingdom remains still to be seen. But the other figures should be unproblematic insofar as the Yaoundé Convention already exists defining the AASM countries, the 18; and the dependent territories of Norway and the United Kingdom are 3 and 19

170

respectively. When it comes to the dependent territories of the Six original EC members, the P.T.O.M. and D.O.M., we have given them as 13 in number. In doing so the Anglo-French condominium of the New Hebrides-Nouvelles Hebrides has been counted among the British dependent territories. Actually, almost all the former 'dependent territories' were French, with the exception mentioned, and Surinam and the Dutch Antilles. It should also be pointed out that special provisions apply to the cases of Gibraltar and Hong Kong (counted among the 19), that there is a special protocol on the Faroe Islands (section 72), special provisions for Greenland (section 74), and that there is a protocol on Svalbard (Spitsbergen) – giving Norway an 'option of excluding the island of Svalbard from the scope of the Treaties' (section 80). Actually, what all this means is that there is still some scope for extension in the future even in the category 'dependent territories'. And then there is the category 'independent developing countries situated in Asia': India, Pakistan, Ceylon, Singapore, and Malaysia who are not at present candidates for association agreements, but only for 'appropriate solutions' of 'any trade problems' (section 49). How this will develop in the future remains to be seen, but the Indian attitude to the European Community seems at present relatively cool.

The population figures given in the table are in most cases from *Demographic Yearbook*, 1967, except for the European Community itself.

12 Uolevi Arosalo and Raimo Väyrynen, 'Industrial and Financial Oligarchy: Present Structure and Some Trends' (Paper presented for the 5th Nordic Conference on Peace Research, February 1972, revised version in the *Journal of Peace Research*, 1973).

13 Adapted from Table 5 and Table 11 in Arosalo & Väyrynen, op. cit. There may be a slight underestimation of EC based corporations since there is a residual category of 'others' that may include one of the smaller EC countries. However, most of 'others' is Canada, Switzerland, Sweden.

14 Adapted from Table 9, Arosalo & Väyrynen, op. cit.

15 Adapted from Table 29, Arosalo & Väyrynen, op. cit. Data originally from Kjell Skjelsbæk, 'Location of Headquarters of International Organizations', *International Associations*, 1970, pp. 36–37.

16 It should be pointed out, though, that many of these 'international' organizations are in fact EC-organizations (see footnote 11, chapter 2, above). With the progressive change of the European Community towards a super-state these organizations will no longer be 'international' but simply ordinary EC organizations, and that will reduce the number of 'international' organizations within the EC. Thus, a part of the high number of headquarters of IGOs and INGOs in the EC can be seen as a sign that the European Community is weak rather than strong. I am indebted to Kjell Skjelsbæk for pointing this out. On the other hand, what remains is more than sufficient to warrant the conclusion drawn.

CHAPTER 6.

1 Thus, more than half of the 18 AASM states are among the 25 recently defined 'least developed' countries in the world. The average GNP per capita of the 70 million inhabitants of these 18 countries was in 1968 only $ 89. And that is of course a basic point: since most of them have been under French colonialism, since this colonialism did not produce better results, any new system introduced

would have to be qualitatively different from the preceding system if changes are to take place. Hence the argument of the chapter is that no such fundamental qualitative difference can be said to have taken place. Incidentally, there are three criteria for being 'least developed'; a national income of less than $ 100 per capita per year, an illiteracy rate of more than 80 %, and that less than 10 % of the national income derives from industry; in other words a very low level.

2 These figures are taken from Helge Hveem, 'EEC-samarbeidet og utviklings-landene', in Susan Høivik, ed. *10 innlegg om EEC*, (Oslo: Universitetsforlaget, 1971), p. 55. In the publication by the Commission of the European Communities, *European Development Aid*, p. 25, these figures are given as 7.1 % and 6 % respectively, for the period 1958–69. The significant similarity, i.e. that the associated states show less increase in export to the EC than developing countries in general, is more important than the dissimilarity in precise order of magnitude. However, it is also possible to present statistics differently: if France is taken out of the EC and the three former Belgian dependencies are taken out of the AASM, then the annual increase is 16.3 % – showing that there has been a spread of the trade from former French dependencies to the EC as a whole. On the other hand, (ibid., p. 26), export from the associated states to the EC consists almost exclusively of raw materials, with 21.8 % of the dollar value consisting of copper, followed by timber (13.8 %), coffee (10.5 %), cocoa (8.5 %), ground-nuts (3.9 %), and then the lesser percentages. But this is not seen as problematic in the pamphlet; the reason why Europe 'should face particular responsibilities' is that Europe contributed to 'awakening vast areas' and to 'setting off the population explosion' (ibid., p. 7).

3 See Hveem, op. cit., p. 56.

4 This increase, according to *European development aid*, p. 24, is 5.6 % annually for the period 1968–69. In other words, it is below the 6 % annual increase reported in the same pamphlet in exports to EC. More significant, however, is the information that whereas in 1960 the export from the developing countries to the less developed countries was 22 % of EC's import, in 1968 it was only 17 %. Of course, much of this is due to the increase in trade between the Six, but the corresponding percentages for Western developed nations were only 21 and 18 – in other words, a smaller drop. The data are taken from the Danish newspaper *Information*, article series on the European Community and the developing countries, March 1971.

5 The third EDF, currently running, is $ 900 million. See Hveem op. cit., p. 58.

6 Thus, at the Universities Social Sciences Council Conference, Makerere, Uganda, 14–17 December 1971, the Kenyan minister of finance argued in favor of a Yaoundé type of association for Kenya (and implicitly, for the other East African countries), with the argument that this would make EDF money available. No theory of vested economic interests for present or future East African elites is needed to explain this. Any planner would have a short-term interest in having funds made available for some of his products, and this interest may by far outweigh any long-term considerations, particularly when the immediate and urgent needs are so pressing as in most developing countries.

7 The GPS has later on been extended to comprise a couple of more countries, and socialist countries like Cuba and Romania have requested to be included on the grounds that their economic structures should warrant it. This is, of course, a

172

major test of the universality of the system as opposed to its possible use as a political instrument, as reward power.

8 One of Tinbergen's main results is that a rational world plan, with optimum utilization of the production factors found in the various countries, would tend to allocate to less developed countries the type of industries that represent early periods of Western European industrialization: textiles, simple iron and steel products, and so on.

9 The basic point in this principle is to utilize the factors of production on which the country is strong, e.g. raw materials, or labor, or capital. What Tinbergen did was to make a country analysis of the factors of production available and a commodity analysis of the factors of production needed, and then a model for optimum allocation – in our view without taking into account spin-off effects.

10 This point is made very clearly in *Le Monde Weekly*, April 15–21 1971, p. 5:
'But why have they chosen preferences instead of an aid programme? The most obvious reason is that this will benefit foreign firms established in the poor countries, which are better equipped to take advantage of the opening up of the markets of the rich countries.

The system of special preferences will thus enable the international companies to profit from both the cheap labour of the poor countries, as a factor of production, and the high salaries of the rich countries, in terms of purchasing power.

To this redistribution of activity within the international firms must be added a redistribution of economic activities on a world scale. The rich countries tend to specialize in the most advanced capital-intensive tehno-countries tend to specialize in the most advanced capital-intensive techno-logical sectors. By 'abandoning' the other sectors to the poor countries, this trend towards an ever-increasing specialization will be intensified.'

11 We have in mind here the letter from Sicco Mansholt to the President of the Commission where this term, 'quality of life', appears. The element always present in the policies of the European Community is a clear distinction between policies for the first class members and policies for the rest of the world. Thus, the conclusion from the famous Colonna Plan fits with Mansholt's program (as yet merely a slogan): 'quality of life' for member states, 'quantity of life' for associate members and other developing countries.

12 This question has been raised by Paul Streeten in an article in *New Society* (13 April 1972, pp. 60–62, 'The kind of selfhelp poor nations need'. His point is that trade preferences are now somewhat dated as a major agenda point, and that 'developing countries need to look to their institutions, and to work together'.

13 The information is taken from Antonin Wagner, *EWG und Dritte Welt* (Freiburg: Imba Verlag, 1971), p. 128 (original data from Tarif Douanier de Communautés Européennes, July 1963, up to date September 1966). It should be kept in mind that coffee, cocoa and ground-nuts are number 3, 4 and 5 respectively in dollar value in the exports from the associated states to the EC (1967–69 average). In other words, even many years after the Treaties of Rome the EC maintained a system, relative to developing countries, so hostile to even the lowest level of processing.

14 Wagner, op. cit., pp. 29–32. However, even though the effective tariff protec-

tion for the EC was high, it was generally speaking still higher for the United States and for Japan. For an evaluation of this, one should take into account that the US has much more of the Third World in its very center, e.g. in the Deep South; and Japan is traditionally anti-liberal in her trade policies.

15 Wagner, op. cit., p. 125 – with some recalculation. The original source is the annual report for the World Bank for 1970.

16 Thus, it is difficult not to attribute some importance to theories about the significance of climate, and to theories that put social structure and cultural content into focus. Particularly important in a more complete theory of development might be the interplay between such factors, making some countries highly vulnerable to outside influence, even to dominance and colonization.

17 For that reason, a system of technical assistance has even been set up to explain and implement the rules in developing countries; in other words, one more profession for the world elites!

18 According to interview with Peter Neersø, Kontakt, special issue 1971/72 on EEC. Such is the general pattern. Nor is it possible to conclude from the many memoranda of the Commission about policy towards developing countries, such as the 'document de synthese' of 27 July 1971 (SEC(71) 2700) with its accompanying volumes and the memorandum of 2 February 1972 (SEC(72)), that anything like a fundamentally new development policy is being contemplated.

19 According to the UN Yearbook of International Trade Statistics, 1968 the percentage of the total export from more developed countries to other developed countries rose from 68 in 1957 to 76 in 1968: a clear tendency for these countries to concentrate more on themselves. On the other hand, the corresponding percentage for the less developed countries decreased from 24 in 1957 to 20 in 1968. In other words, not only are the percentages much smaller, but the former is increasing and the latter decreasing – whereas total world trade is increasing.

20 Mentioned by the Secretary-General of the UN Economic Commission for Africa, Dr. R. Gardiner, in his paper to the African World Order Models Project Conference, Kampala, December 1969.

21 This is spelt out in detail in chapter 3.

22 For an analysis of this, see Johan Galtung, 'A Structural Theory of Imperialism', Journal of Peace Research 1971, particularly pp. 101–103.

23 In his important article, 'East African Associates and the EEC', East Africa, 1971, pp. 7–13, L. L. Kato points out that the European Community used its relationship with the Yaoundé associates as a norm, disregarding the UNCTAD resolution 'that emergent countries were no longer obliged to offer counterconcessions to developed countries and that the EEC should not press for reverse preferential treatment' (p. 8). The EC argued that any system not involving inverse preferences would constitute discrimination against the Yaoundé associates. Kato also mentions (p. 5) that East African imports from EC more than doubled in the period 1963–1967, whereas East African exports to EC declined in the same period. For general information about the relation between EC and Africa, see P. N. C. Okigbo, Africa and the Common Market (London: Longmans, 1970).

24 In N. N. Kitomari, 'East Africa's Association with the EEC', (paper presented at the Social Sciences Council conference, Makerere 14–17 December 1971) it is pointed out that the decline of the trade balance between East Africa and the

174

EC continued: 'in 1970 East African imports ... increased 24 % ... while exports ... increased 13 % (p. 4). Kitomari points out that the EC insisted on quota restrictions because no country should be treated more favorably than the AASM states 'because of their special relations with France and Belgium in particular and the EC as a whole' (p. 8). It is further pointed out (p. 17) that there are so many manufactured products East Africa could export to EC without tariff walls and quota restrictions, but 'goods in this category are not currently exported by East Africa as well as the majority of the developing countries'. Kitomari, incidentally, also seems to feel that the major attraction of the EC is the money England might contribute via EDF and EIB – so this is where the major reward power is located in the system.

25 The significant point about 'negative tariffs' is to overcome the idea that the debate on tariffs can stop when tariffs are brought down to zero. Any measure that would facilitate the import into industrial countries of goods from Third World countries would be the equivalent of some kind of 'negative tariff', but particularly important in this connection would be export subsidies, as well as gradual reduction of subsidies rich countries give to primary production, and particularly to production of foodstuffs at home.

26 The major mechanism here is the vested interest that elites in associated states will have in maintaining some kind of special privilege, however small.

27 The Group of 77, as it is still called, now in fact has 96 members, the five most recent ones being Bahrein, Butan, Fiji, Quatar, and Cuba.

28 The figures are taken from R. Gardiner, op. cit., p. 6.

29 In more collectively-oriented countries it is always assumed that if one is abroad, on mission, then it is on behalf of one's own country. This would probably apply with more ease to countries like Japan and China with a more fundamentally collectivist orientation, than to Eastern European countries that seem more dominated by traditional European individualism, and hence in need of forceful patterns of control of individual delegates, lest they defect to the West.

30 The number for Congo according to UN officials; the number for Libya according to Adrian Pelt: *Libyan Independence and the United Nations* (New Haven: Yale University Press, 1970), p. 671.

31 A shorter economic cycle would bring Nature, producers, and consumers geographically closer to each other, and also socially closer so that any one who participates in the cycle – on the extraction, processing, or consumption sides – knows fairly well what is going on and is not merely a part in a world-wide cycle over which he has no understanding, let alone any control. Another aspect of this is the idea of self-reliance, of utilizing the resources at hand, including local expertice, instead of waiting for an economic cycle to be set up from the world's metropoles.

32 In the current movement for technology assessment (see, for instance, the *Futurist*, December 1971, which is dedicated to this), emphasis has so far been on new technologies compatible with the new norms against pollution and depletion; i.e. technologies that not only maintain but also restore natural balances. It has also been associated with the idea of cheap technology, which easily means second-rate and old-fashioned technology, for instance of the labor-intensive kind. Without arguing against these purposes, we should point out that what is needed in developing and developed countries alike is a technology that is less dividing,

175

less stratifying, less exploitative; a technology that introduces machines and modes of production that distribute the amount of challenge and also the degree of inconvenience, dirt, noise, health hazards etc. more evenly among the participants in a production system. Unfortunately, marxists who attribute great significance to the mode of production seem interested only in ownership of the means of production, not so much in other social relations technology induces.

33 We are thinking of the publication by the *Club of Rome*, the whole Forrester tradition out of MIT culminating in the book *The Limits to Growth*, the famous *Blueprint for Survival* by British ecologists, and so on. Characteristic of all this is the concern, sincere, with the problems of the rich man in the rich countries. Thus, the working classes always lived in noise and dirt, always had to eat substandard foodstuffs, much of it more or less contaminated. What is new is only that these conditions have now reached the middle classes; and since this class is listened to more than the working classes in the rich countries, not to mention the masses in the poor countries, ever were, this has now become a major world concern. Which does not mean that the problems are not real, only that they were also very real before.

34 It is difficult to find in the arguments by Harold Wilson and others in the British Labour Party against the European Community any clear views about policies towards the Third World, towards the socialist countries, the danger of the European Community ever becoming a new military power, and so on. There is some indication, as in his speech to Labour's special Common Market Conference (*The Observer*, 18 July 1971, pp. 1–2) but the dominant theme is New Zealand butter, etc. See also *International Herald Tribune*, 27 April 1971, p. 2. On the other hand, it is easy to find argumentation on a rather different level, e.g. against the harmonized standards for detergents developed by the EC (see *The Times*, 2 May 1972).

35 See 'Empiricism, Criticism, Constructivism: Three Aspects of Scientific Activity', in *Essays in Theory and Methods of Social Research*, (forthcoming).

36 Two arguments are particularly significant in this connection: first, the European Community has a cumbersome decision-process which makes it more difficult to change rules and procedures – although it must also be admitted that once they are changed, they affect more countries. Second, there is less opportunity for playing the more progressive among the member states off against the less progressive. And then, in addition: imagine the European Community should develop, over a decade or two or three, in the direction of a real superpower. In that case its formidable size would be a basic impediment for any country, group of countries, or group inside countries, wanting to extricate themselves from superpower dominance. They might well prefer to carry out the struggle against smaller units, just as we assume that the Vietnamese peasant would prefer 50 disunited American states to the present US reality in the form of bombs dropped in a way and in a quantity that only a superpower can afford.

CHAPTER 7.

1 This is expressed very clearly in the famous Arusha declaration, where among other things it is stated: 'If every individual is self-reliant the ten-house cell will be self-reliant; if all the cells are self-reliant the whole ward will be self-

176

reliant ... and if the Regions are self-reliant, then the whole Nation is self-reliant, and this is our aim'. In other words, not only self-reliance as the stated goal, but also the theory that it has to be built from the individual up, in concentric circles – which makes self-reliance depend fundamentally on each individual's self-respect.

2 On the Latin American side this takes the form of intergovernmental declarations like the 'Declaration from Buenos Aires' of 29 July 1970, where the need for an institutionalization of talks at a high political level between Latin America on the one hand and the European Community on the other is underlined. Guidelines for all kinds of cooperation – bilateral, subregional, regional – are to be worked out. For a concretization of this, see the following footnote. For more information about the relation between Latin America and the EC see 'Las Comunidades Europeas y America Latina', supplement to *European Community*, June 1970.

3 Thus, the first non-preferential trade agreement between the EC and a Latin American country was with Argentina (signed 8 November 1971 in Brussels). Argentina supplies 38 % of the meat imports for the EC, and the EC will lower levies on 'frozen meat imported from Argentina for processing'. Argentina, in return (for delivering raw materials) will phase out its import deposit system for some EC exports, make concessions in ocean transport and 'create favourable conditions for foreign investment in Argentina' *(European Community,* December 1971, p. 3). Thus, the agreement is a typical example of a very old pattern which presupposes an intimate harmony of interests between the EC and the Argentine elites agreeing to a treaty of that kind.

4 For a detailed account of this, see Johan Galtung, 'Europe: Bipolar, Bicentric or Co-operative?', Appendix. The best and most up-to-date material is probably found in 'The European Economy from the 1950s to the 1970s', Part I of the *Economic Survey of Europe in 1971* from the ECE Secretariat (ME/GEA/72/D.1), particularly chapter 2. Also see Helmut Klocke, 'Comecon Relations with the EEC', *Aussenpolitik* (German Foreign Affairs Review), 1971, pp. 427–446. The trade between the EEC and the CMEA countries actually does not account for much of the EEC trade. But exports increased from 3.9 % of the total amount in 1958 to 6.9 % in 1969, and imports from 4.2 % to 6.2 %. The percentage share Italy had in total EEC trade accounts for much of this (foodstuffs).

As is well known negotiations between CMEA and EEC countries should have been at the Community level already from the beginning of 1970, according to Article 113 of the Treaty, but 16 December 1969 the EC decided to postpone the limit till 1 January 1973. What will actually happen then remains to be seen – there are already talks of a further postponement of eight months. In the meantime bilateralism is prevailing, particularly at the initiative of the French and the Germans — bilateralism usually pays of better for the big. A possible compromise would be to let the substance remain at the bilateral level, and then have some formalities towards the end at the sub-regional level – unless (what we would both hope and predict) the two economic blocs, EC and CMEA, recognize each other and constitute together some kind of umbrella for all the bilateralism.

5 These non-attributable 'informed sources' are located in Eastern European capitals as well as in the UN Economic Commission for Europe.

6 Trade is then only seen as one component in an increasingly complex web of transactions.

7 A journey from Northern Greeece into Southern Bulgaria is interesting and important in this context since both are parts of Macedonia, and are ecologically very similar; but the socio-economic systems, although not very dissimilar before, are today highly dissimilar. The strong aspect of Eastern European socialism can be seen clearly in that context: the disappearance of the lowest layer of society, the lumpen-proletariat mixed with prostitutes and beggars. When it comes to Poland, Polish researchers (in a conference at the Polish Institute of International Affairs, November 1970) put it this way: 'after the war the gap relative to France in the level of development was perhaps 60 years, relative to England 75 years. Now it is more like 20 and 25–30 years, respectively. One factor creating this development was the almost complete discrimination from Western Europe right after the war when not even penicillin was exported to Poland. This discrimination had the effect of forcing Poland into a higher level of self-reliance'.

8 According to several speeches by the Soviet leadership, particularly Brezhnev, spring 1972.

9 It was pointed out by an American lawyer, S. Pisar, in his paper 'The enlarged Common Market and the Socialist Countries of Europe: Political, economic and institutional dimensions', *Semaine de Bruges,* 1972, that the major difficulties are institutional rather than ideological. Thus, the socialist countries insist on bilateralism, that 'state monopolies intrude into the conventional procedures of trade, and suddenly cast an unexplained veto based on national policy considerations', that they cannot 'outbid competing Western firms which function under the umbrella of bilateral intergovernmental agreements', that 'they are unable to negotiate directly with the end-users of their products', and that 'they cannot hold equity in local companies' (except in Yugoslavia and Romania) (pp. 13–14).

10 Polish sources claim that Western cars are good, but not necessarily sturdy enough, and that the resale value of a Polish-built car in Poland is actually higher. And, whereas a Fiat produced in Poland cost (fall 1970) 182,000 zloty, the Warszawa car cost only 130,000 and was 'tougher'. The Soviet-produced Fiat 124, Lada, is also sturdier than the original.

11 For a more complete presentation of this, see Johan Galtung, 'Europe: Bipolar, Bicentric or Co-operative?', *Journal of Peace Research,* 1972, pp. 1 ff.

12 'Subregional' refers here to any part of 'Europe', meaning 'all of Europe'. The most important subregions are, of course, those defined by NATO or WTO memberships, or those defined by OECD–CMEA membership.

13 By this is meant a relation of equity. That formula is very broad, however: it covers the competitive mutual exploitation found in EC–US relations, a truly horizontal division of labor that might be worked out if the political will existed between capitalist and socialist Europe, and a non-relation of mutual isolation. The important point is that a 'bicentric' Europe rules out any dominance of one part by the other.

14 These were the forces that in the 1950s would think in military-political terms, in terms of the peoples in Eastern European countries rising against their governments and the West giving a helping hand; and the forces that during the

178

1960s would think in terms of making Western Europe more attractive from a consumer viewpoint so that peoples or governments, or both, in Eastern European countries, singly or combined, would strive for the best possible deal with the European Community. 'What we could not obtain before with military-political means we might obtain today with economic-cultural means', as it was expressed in a debate at the Institute for Strategic Studies' Annual Conference, Evian, September 1970.

15 Some of the most interestingly analyses of the relation over time, between the EC and the socialist countries, are carried out by Jerzy Lukaszwski, for instance in his articles 'Le traité germano-sovietique et l'Europe des Six', *Le Monde*, 2–3 October, 1970. Also see the volume edited by him, *The People's Democracies after Prague* (Bruge: De Tempel, 1970).

16 The number of diplomatic missions accredited to the EC is today about 90.

17 The point about multilateral recognition of the DDR is argued in chapter 7, 'The German problem: some perspectives', in Johan Galtung, ed., *Co-operation in Europe*.

18 It is still too early to have a very firm opinion about what happened in the *Nordek* negotiations. If all Nordic countries had been sincere in a desire to build a strong economic region in the North, the Soviet Union had supported this and the EC had agreed to some kind of free trade area with this region, then this might have constituted an alternative to current policies pursued by Nordic governments. Precisely for this reason it might have been important for some, even most of the Nordic governments to destroy that alternative: and that was possibly the major function of the *Nordek* negotiations. The Norwegian and Danish governments could then go ahead with the EC, and Finland could prove her loyalty to the friendship treaty with the Soviet Union.

19 The most important things that happened at this meeting seem to be the following: The session was held in Bucharest 27–29 July and agreed on a program to be implemented stage by stage over 10–15 years. At no point is there any open decision to become an integrated actor towards the outside with a common policy towards all third parties. But the program is so comprehensive that this may nevertheless be the result. Thus, it was decided:
   - to coordinate national economic plans;
   - to extend cooperation in planning;
   - to improve cooperation in reciprocal trade;
   - to develop much further trade with non-CMEA socialist countries;
   - to develop the transferable ruble into an international currency;
   - to cooperate in construction work, and water conservation;
   - to improve the legal principles behind their cooperation, in order to insure the most advantageous legal conditions;
   - to equalize the level of economic development of participating countries;
   - to attain a higher level of social labor productivity, with maximum mobilization and effective utilization of each country's efforts and resources;
   - to expand further the reciprocal trade in machinery and equipment;
   - to build joint coal-mines, and have joint prospecting for minerals;
   - to standardize standards;
   - to strengthen cooperation on supply of fuel and raw materials, on sophisticated technical equipment, consumer goods and foodstuffs;

− to increase cooperation in science and technology in general, particularly in bio-physics, conservation of nature, atomic power-generation, new computing facilities, program control systems for metal cutting, etc.

(from *Soviet News*, Press Department, Soviet Embassy, London). Altogether this would result in a level of cooperation so high that one could talk of integration, although with 'respect for state sovereignty, independence and national interests, non-interference in the internal affairs of the countries, complete equality, mutual advantage and comradely beneficial assistance'. However, there is nothing corresponding to the common agricultural policy of the EC. Nevertheless, it is almost bound to come, and ultimately much, much more − even union. (Professor A. Rumyantsev, *Categories and laws of the political economy of Communism*, p. 293). But long before that CMEA will have full negotiating authority, with something corresponding to the Council.

For an interesting analysis of CMEA, see Kormnov, Dyakin 1971: 'Specialization and cooperation in production and integration of CMEA countries', *International Affairs*, September 1971, pp. 11−18.

20 This extension is supposed to take place in June 1972.

21 This problem is currently being explored by Jarda Tusek, School of International Studies, Columbia University, and research fellow at the International Peace Research Institute, Oslo, winter 1971−72. Jerzy Lukaszewski, in 'Western Integration and the People's Democracies', *Foreign Affairs*, 1968, pp. 377−387, develops ideas along such lines. One important point he makes is how nationalism in Central Europe plays a role in 'the perpetuation of Soviet control there'. He argues in favor of a 'multinational Central European assembly'.

22 There is a certain symmetry within the capitalist part as well as within the socialist part, in the sense that both traditional superpowers are to some extent balanced off. At the same time there is a certain symmetry between the two parts. Any other arrangement is highly asymmetric. However, this type of balance-thinking should not overshadow the significance of the much more peace-building effect that can be obtained through real cooperation; symmetry should only be seen as a prerequisite for equitable cooperation, not as a pretext for some new type of 'balance of power' thinking. The latter can only lead to an integration race. Actually, one of the first to point to the danger of this integration race was Amitai Etzioni, in 'US & Europe, Limited', *Columbia University Forum*, 1963, pp. 7−8.

CHAPTER 8

1 But in the early years of the French war in Indochina the European NATO powers were involved. We are thinking of the infamous NATO resolution of 17 December 1952 where it is stated that the NATO Council (including such countries as Denmark and Norway):

'recognizes that resistance to direct or indirect aggression in any part of the world is an essential contribution to the common security of the free world; expresses its whole-hearted admiration for the valiant and long-continued struggle by the French forces and the armies of the Associated States against Communist aggression; acknowledges that the resistance of the free nations in Southeast Asia, as in Korea, is in fullest harmony with the aims and

180

ideals of the Atlantic Community; and therefore agrees that the campaign waged by the French Union forces in Indochina deserves continuing support from the NATO governments.'

This decision actually followed an *exposé* the preceding day by the French Foreign Minister, Robert Schuman, who is also regarded as the father of the European Community. It might also be mentioned that at the same NATO Council meeting, a resolution was adopted urging rapid ratification of the European Defense Community Treaty by the six countries concerned. (*Keesings Contemporary Archives,* 12733.)

2 This view is expressed by Mathis Mossberg in an article, 'Norge, EEC och NATO', *Dagens Nyheter,* 14 December 1971. His conclusion is: 'could the strategic considerations eventually lead to the Six being willing to pay for the cohesion of the NATO alliance by finally yielding in the fisheries question and giving the Norwegians what they want?' Not *all* Norwegians got what they wanted in the fisheries question. But relative to the original position of the Commission, negotiation results were considerable: the right of other EC members to fish in Norwegian waters considerably curtailed, whereas Norwegians can market their fish products as any other EC member country throughout the EC. This does not prove Mossberg's thesis of a *quid pro quo* in this connection, nor will it ever be easy to prove it – but the hypothesis is a strong one.

3 Of course, a basic factor brought into the European Community by England will always be its nuclear force. Since both Edward Heath (in his Harvard University speech 1970, before he was elected) and Lord George-Brown (in his memoirs) indicate that they favor some kind of European Nuclear Force, this factor should not be underestimated. Lord Chalfont ('The Dangers of a Nuclear Europe', *New Statesman,* 16 April 1971) has a very critical analysis of this type of thinking, emphasizing among other things that pooling together the four British nuclear subs each with 16 A2 Polaris missiles and the 36 French Mirage IV with nuclear bombs might be a good indication of superpower status, but certainly not a force that can be used for a nuclear strike. However that may be, it is hard to believe that Heath and Pompidou mainly discussed New Zealand butter at their well-publicized summit meeting June 1971.

4 See the data reported at the end of chapter 5.

5 The best known analysis of this is Jean Meynaud and Dusan Sidjanski, *Les groupes de pressions dans la Communauté Européenne,* (Brussels: L'Institut de Sociologie de l'Université Libre de Bruxelles, 1971). Unfortunately, the 700-page analysis contains relatively little data in a quantitative form, but the total amount of activity reported is highly impressive.

6 This dependence on the US is, of course, particularly true for England, among other reasons because of the special form nuclear cooperation has between US and England; and it is particularly untrue for France.

7 Thus, United States has troops stationed in several European countries, members and non-members of NATO. But the most significant test of differences and similarities would be what would happen if NATO as such should collapse. This could happen only because the member states so wanted it, and this in turn is likely to happen only provided there is a major change of government in member states. The case of Greece gives some indication of the likely development in that eventuality. In other words, in that case NATO might relatively soon be-

181

come a set of bilateral arrangements with the United States. One way of forestalling that, as argued in this chapter, is the relatively quick emergence of a European NATO as a partner to the US part of NATO, before NATO is seriously threatened because of the decline of the US. The latter seems now (Spring 1972) to be an inevitable consequence of the Indochina war: either the US is defeated, in which case the decline is obvious; or the US is able to prevent defeat, but forced to use means that would be inacceptable to world public opinion, comprising the establishments even in many NATO countries.

8 A British conservative MP, Mr. Selwin-Gamma, expressed in the debate about the future of the European Community at the *Semaine de Bruges* March 1972 how it was the task of the European Community to put the 'dynamism of capitalism at work', but to avoid the 'ugly American capitalism'. For others this might be a difference in degree that goes up and down and sometimes is negative, depending on time and place.

9 As one example of the automated warfare now being developed, see the article 'War by Automation', in *Boston Sunday Globe*, 4 July 1971; p. A-3.

10 The problem was actually stated, in the debate in France, as an alternative between EDC on the one hand and a *Wehrmacht* on the other. Thus, Adenauer said very clearly: 'let us assume the improbable – that France, contrary to expectations, rejects the EDC. We shall then reject, in any circumstances, any attempt to offer us rearmament under humiliating conditions – that is, a German Army under some kind of tutelage. I am concerned to make this clear once for all. There will be nothing for it but a German national army side by side with the French national army and other European national armies. It cannot be said with sufficient emphasis that the alternative to the EDC is a German national army.' *(Keesings Contemporary Archives, 13653.)* In fact, the improbable became reality, the EDC was defeated and the German Army emerged, de facto under US 'tutelage'. The issue divided the French National Assembly, and particularly the socialist party, with Guy Mollet (then Secretary-General of the party, later on playing a leading role in the war in Algeria) in favor of the EDC and Jules Moch strongly opposed. It is interesting to note that Eisenhower, at that time President of the US, in a speech 16 April 1954, pronounced himself strongly in favor of the EDC as a basis 'for consolidating Western defense, and leading to an ever-developing community of nations in Europe'.

11 The famous vote that put a stop to the EDC was 319 against the EDC, 264 for in favor, and 12 abstentions. Socialists and radicals were split down the middle, communists and gaullists were against, and MRP as well as the independent republicans were in favor. But the arguments against were very mixed: from Jules Moch arguing that the EDC would stimulate an increase in the arms race because Eastern Europe would feel even more threatened, via the mixture of nationalism and fear of German rearmament found in the very strong statement made by Herriot, to the clear-cut nationalism of General Aumeran: 'ratification will put us in the same ranks as two vanquished peoples and three small nations' *(Keesing's Contemporary Archives, 13754).* With such arguments, very different political forces inside France could come to the same conclusion as to the external situation. But it is also clear that these forces will not be able to join together and formulate a coherent alternative policy if the issue should come up again.

12 Most of the data and the arguments in this section are taken from the article 'Enriched uranium: Europe must choose', *European Community*, February 1972, pp. 52–53, by Paul Kemezis.

13 In a well-informed article, 'Atomic Power: Europe's Last Chances', *Agenor*, no. 12, p. 58, it is taken for granted that nuclear power will be the major source of energy in the EC countries towards the end of this century.

14 Report presented at the 19th Pugwash Conference on Science and World Affairs, Sochi, October 1969, by J. H. Watson: 'Centrifugal Uranium Isotope Separation and Nuclear Weapon Proliferation' *(Proceedings*, pp. 354–361).

15 *International Herald Tribune.*

16 This method was developed by a Japanese scientist and reported in Tokyo newspapers April 1970.

17 According to report in *International Herald Tribune*, February 1972.

18 Thus, the Euro-group inside NATO is a committee of the defense ministers of ten of the European NATO countries. France does not participate because of her particular relation to NATO; Iceland and Portugal are not participants either. This ministerial council meets twice a year in connection with the NATO Council meetings, and then there are meetings at the level of the Permanent Representatives. There are also six working groups, out of which France participates in two. The Euro-group recently announced that they would increase their total defense spending in 1972 by more than $ 1 billion, in addition to the existing $ 1 billion program over five years for the Euro-group, announced in December 1970. To what extent this really means more money for NATO or a restructuring of the budget is more difficult to tell. But the latter is more important in this connection, since our argument is not so much in terms of an arms race as in terms of an integration race *at the present stage.*

19 The essential aspect of the fire brigade parallel is the idea that the world is 'normal' when there is no 'trouble', and that 'trouble' serves as a trigger to stimulate military forces into reaction. For less conservatively minded people the fire brigade parallel is false because it calls for action only at particularly critical points — not for continuous action to improve, in an evolutionary or revolutionary way, a world where absence of 'trouble' is often the real trouble.

20 Interesting in this connection is the most recent meeting of the Western European Union Assembly, as reported in *European Community*, January 1972 (p. 8). Lord Gladwyn's report, acceted unanimously by the assembly, argued for a political Europe, with a Western European armaments agency to coordinate European weaponry, built on the framework of the WEU and the EEC which could act as a valid partner for the United States in the NATO alliance. Then there was the Boyden report (the votes were here 49 for and 4 against) which argued in favor of the Eurogroup of NATO as the best forum for closer European cooperation. For our own reasoning it does not matter so much what kind of balance is struck between the Eurogroup and the WEU, for neither report expressed any desire for the classical NATO organization.

21 Thus, in November–December 1971 Eurocrats wanted an 11.6 % increase in salaries and the right to bargain directly with the Council, and not with the Commission *(European Community*, January 1972, p. 6.)

22 However satisfactory such definitions may be from an abstract marxist point of view, they may fail to come to grips with political reality. Thus, to claim that

Hitler was a phenomenon of secondary importance because nazism was only an expression of objective economic forces, an effort to protect capitalism, may also be satisfactory to the abstract mind, but is hardly good political analysis since it is too narrow to understand a major phenomenon. But we hasten to point out that the only factor connecting these two cases is that they are both products of dogmatic marxist analysis. See T. Abel's analysis of John Strachey's *The Menace of Fascism*, in Abel's *The Nazi Movement* (New York: Atherton Press, 1966), pp. 195–202.

23 I am indebted to Archie Singham of the University of Michigan for making me aware of this important point. Both Britain and France have non-European foreign workers, but they are not part of the population in the same sense as in the US.

24 The expression 'residual pax britannica' was introduced, I think, by Ali Mazrui of the University of East Africa, Kampala.

25 Which, incidentally, would be mainly owned by the United States.

26 For an analysis of the relationship between universal and regional peace-keeping, see Asbjørn Eide, 'Peacekeeping and Enforcement by Regional Organizations', *Journal of Peace Research*, 1966, pp. 125–145.

27 In this connection one should also remember that Western Europe has an enormous number of former colonial officers and other officials who would not dislike being called upon to offer their advice, and even more concrete services. Several of them have been active as advisors to the US government in the Vietnam wars, and they have undoubtedly drawn the conclusion that this is the way it should not be done. Conservative in their ideological outlook, the likelihood that they would contribute in time to any fundamental understanding of how exploitative policies sooner or later lead to open conflict is very low. Deprived of any structural theory of the conflict, they would have to introduce the hypothesis of 'foreign agents', agitators, etc. And from that point on it seems highly unlikely that some coordination between such elements in the former colonial powers will not take place, in order to be prepared for all possibilities.

28 When, after all, the revolt in Poland in December 1970 led to so much more change than the students' revolt in March 1968, this may be precisely because a socialist government would pay more attention to workers than to students. In a sense this is strange, for in a socialist state both categories should be equally legitimate.

29 For some analyses by Western European 'defense intellectuals' of this type of problems, see Ian Smart, 'Future Conditional, The Prospect for Anglo-French Nuclear Co-operation', *Adelphi Papers* (London: Institute for Strategic Studies, 1971) and François Duchene, 'A New European Defence Community' *Foreign Affairs*, October 1971, pp. 68–82.

Actually, even Willy Brandt came out quite clearly in the famous TV interview February 1972, saying that 'as the political cooperation develops it is logical that these states will also develop a defense policy' – and later on confirmed this (rather trivial) statement. But there is a long pre-history, out of which we shall only mention some examples.

Thus, Hans von der Groeben, Commissioner for Germany from the beginning till 1 July 1970, produced in 1969 a program for Europe, from the present customs union, via economic and monetary union to a military union, an arma-

184

ment union and a security union (Adolph Rasten, *Fællesmarkedet – et politisk magtspil*, Copenhagen, 1971, p. 153). So far only the second step is about to be implemented. But the significant factor is that the EC has in its midst people thinking along such lines.

When Kurt Georg Kiesinger was chancellor, his party CDU launched a plan (June 1969) for a European political union to coordinate foreign policy and defense policy, with a Defense Council. And Henry Kiessinger, in an article in *Foreign Affairs* July 1962, was also among the early spokesmen for a European nuclear force, including the British.

Edward Heath, in Zürich 17 September 1971 (commemorating Winston Churchill's Zürich address): 'It is inevitable that progress towards a common foreign policy will be accompanied by increasing cooperation on defense' (*International Herald Tribune*, 18–19 September 1971, p. 1). And the extreme right, the para-military neo-fascist organization *Europa Civiltà* in Italy, argues in favor of an 'organic Europe – with nuclear weapons' – and the neo-fascists are on their way up. Of course, they will not have direct political influence. But if they represent an extremist position relative to which a small and heavily circumscribed nuclear element within, say, the Western Union, will look modest, even liberal. The major function of extremist movements is precisely their indirect influence in changing political debate and political points of reference. For a general account of the development of fascist tendencies in France and Italy, see the report 'Creeping fascism', *Agenor*, June/July 1971, pp. 3–7.

The reader who wants all these possibilities spelt out by 'an advance weapons systems consultant', should see James B. Edwards, 'A United Europe?', *Ordnance*, September/October 1971, pp. 124–25. The author, a consultant to the US Navy, argues in favor of a first-rate tactical and strategic nuclear capability for United Europe, in favor of an arms race with United Europe spending 7 % of her GNP, forcing the Soviet Union to spend 30 % 'which would ruin their economy totally –/and/ destroy the last hope of – improving their miserable standard of living.' It is difficult to move around in any Western European establishment without finding echoes of this type of thinking. And this also applies to the US. The integration race finds a spokesman in George Ball (*Newsweek*, 24 April 1972, p. 56) who clearly feels that 'though the drive toward unity in Europe has large objectives quite unrelated to the cold war, they know that, even in East–West terms, it is indispensable. Only unity can check the fragmentation and rivalry that Russia hopes to exploit in its drive for political ascendancy'. Incidentally, some of the contours of coordinated European military production are already taking shape. Thus, French anti-tank weapons are to be introduced into the German *Bundeswehr* and replace US systems (*Der Spiegel*, no. 9, 1972), and a European aviation company, *Panavia*, producing fighters for the Italian, German and British air forces is taking shape in München (*Europa Magazine*, March 1972).

To all this let it only be added that although the enlarged EC comes nowhere near the two superpowers in military potential because they do not possess nuclear deterrents of anything like the same order of magnitude, their conventional forces are of the same dimension. The Soviet defense expenditure is about the double and the US defense expenditure three times that of the EC members (or the European alliance members); and the latter actually had a higher defense

185

maanpower than the US (2.9 million as against 2.7 million) in mid-1971. For a good survey of such figures, for whatever they are worth, see *Strategic Survey 1971*, p. 26.

CHAPTER 9.

1 However, the Roman Empire does not constitute any type of model or historical analogy in this connection. The Roman Empire *integrated* the East and West of Europe (and more than that). If there was a split it was along a North–South axis, between *cisalpina* and *transalpina*, not along the East–West axis that emerged soon after the decline and fall of the Roman Empire. On the other hand, the Roman Empire has given Europeans and others an image of empire formation, an image of how center-periphery relations can be organized that has left an indelible imprint on both Europeans and non-Europeans exposed to this image.

2 A significant part of the Western European belief system seems to be that Western Europeans are fundamentally good, also to others, except when there are 'tragic mistakes'. One of the most disconcerting impressions one can get from talking with the people working in the Commission in Brussels is precisely the self-confidence with which they assume that the European Community is an instrument of peace because it has a certain front against either superpower of today. Thus, the more or less clear visions of a unicentric Europe, and the Euro-centric world, are always coated with thick layers of peacefulness in the semantics surrounding the issue, but with low level of analysis.

3 Ten years ago the bloody war in Algeria was barely ended. From that it does not follow that the EC or her member states will commit the same type of action in a near or remote future. But in the recent past such actions were committed very often. For the future to be different in this regard, at least one essential factor must have been changed dramatically. In our view, the factors that have remained constant are so many and the factors that are changing so few, that the burden of proof rests on whoever says nothing can be inferred from the 'sins of the father' – particularly since we could point out that even the politicians who committed these atrocities a decade or two ago are still active in Western European politics today.

4 The map is published in the major information pamphlet in English: *European Community: The Facts* (Brussel, May 1971), p. 2.

5 See *Atlas Historique* (Paris: Librairie Stock, 1968), p. 118. Actually, Napoleon's various coalitions also bear some similarity with the European Community of the Six, especially the fourth coalition of 1806/07 if the Confederation of the Rhine is included (the fifth coalition of 1809 is already too big, including Spain as a satellite and the Grand Duchy of Warsaw). Both Charlemagne's and Napoleon's empires have one important similarity with the present situation: the *Drang nach Osten*, the penetration of the East. But there is also one important dissimilarity: in the first two, France dominated; in the EC, there is a French-German axis, sometimes of rivalry, sometimes of condominium. Is that the major result of eleven centuries of European history – the emergence of Germany next to France? Arnold Toynbee has another perspective (*European Community*, December 1971, p. 9): 'However, the Community of the original Six differs from its

two precursors in at least one vital point. Charlemagne's and Napoleon's empires were put together by conquest, and, for this reason, were ephemeral, since Europeans are allergic to unification by force. By contrast the Community is a spontaneous association based on equality, and it therefore has good prospects of enduring'. One needs a very Eurocentric perspective that one would not normally attribute to the author of *A Study of History* to omit any reference to European lack of allergy when it comes to trying to unify, or split, others by force, not to mention that the 'spontaneous association' may have something to do with an effort to keep the markets conquered that way. Toynbee is actually a leading producer of ideological statements for the European Community, like: 'The Community collectively has an important role on the world's stage, since no individual member has the capacity to conduct the full scale of operations required in a global society'. As usual the concrete nature of that 'role' remains unspecified. Or this *(The Times*, 12 October 1971): '(Europe has) remained disunited ever since the collapse of the Roman Empire in the West in the fifth century A.D. Europe's post-Roman political history has been dramatically different from China's; for China has been a political unity for most of the time since 221 BC'.

6 If the reader will permit this 'parallel' (which like all historical 'parallels' serves as a heuristic and as proof of nothing) to be extended a little further it might be pointed out that the Catholic church will in that case be precisely *catholic:* the united population of the EC countries. If the parliamentarians are even elected through direct elections, many would say that one more very important step towards the superstate will have been taken. In our view, however, what constitutes a superstate is its impact on the outside more than its internal anatomy, and the precise similarity between that anatomy and the anatomy of the regular nation state.

7 Lord Walston, *Farm Gate to Brussels,* Fabian Research Series 288 (London: Fabian Society, 1970). Unfortunately, after this wide perspective, his presentation narrows down to agriculture and agriculture alone.

8 The debate in Ireland may serve as an example here. Among the pro-arguments were four clear points: to avoid any firm border between the six counties of Ulster and the twenty-six counties of the Irish Republic, to get the full benefits of CAP for Ireland which produces foodstuffs relatively cheaply, to enter a new important political configuration on, at least formally speaking, equal terms with the British overlord, and to get closer to the rest of Western Europe, becoming less of an appendix of England. There was, of course, also the negative pro-argument of not having any walls erected between Ireland and the country on which she depends in so many respects. Similarly, the were four significant contra-arguments: that reunification of Ireland will be lost as an issue because of general absorption into the European Community, that CAP together with the Mansholt plan would favor big farmers but make migrant workers of the small farmers, that Ireland would forever remain a producer of raw materials and foodstuffs, and that Irish culture would be destroyed due to the impact from the outside. All these arguments are important, but it is significant that global thinking is conspicuously absent. This is not strange: the world is structured in nation states that are systematically trained to think in terms of their own interests, and there is no demand placed on governments or peoples of nation states to think

in global terms even though their policies may have the most global perspectives and intentions.

9 Instead, there is the likelihood of considerable bickering between the British and the French as to what shall be the major official language, since there are two 'super-languages' among the official eight languages of the expanded Community.

10 Whatever the formal situation is, the person most known to people in general is the President of the Commission, not the President of the Council of Ministers. This may be partly due to the difference in tenure, possibly due to the relative size of the public relations establishments of these two parts of the European Community, but mainly, we feel, due to a clear understanding of where basic power (as opposed to formal power, which becomes real power only in some particularly acute situations) is located.

11 Pompidou has already announced (in his press conference 21 January 1971) a relatively detailed plan precisely in this direction, based on ministers for Europe in each government of the member states, serving as links between the governments and the Community. The Council of Ministers will then become the future European government, and the Commission more or less reduced to a secretariat.

12 This was Senghor's rationale for the coup that took place in Dakar in December 1962, ousting the Prime Minister on the basis that Senghor felt that the 'bicéphalisme' between President and Prime Minister led to inactivity.

13 Of course, the parallel between the EC and the modern nation state is far from perfect; it is also intended to be imperfect. There is nothing quite corresponding to the Commission. But Karlheinz Neunreither, in 'Transformation of a Political Role: Reconsidering the case of the Commission of the European Communities', Paper presented for the IPSA Round Table, Louvain 15–18 September 1971, argues convincingly that the Council of Ministers will emerge as the future institution similar to a government.

14 Pompidou, see footnote 11.

15 The basis for referring to World War I as a delayed war out of the 19th century would be that it was so much concerned with Europe's inability to house a united Germany in its midst, and World War II obviously arose out of World War I, as a reaction to the defeat.

16 There is also the distinct possibility that the European Community, top-heavy as it is, may continue, with both extension and deepening, but without really touching the younger generation in the populations of the member states. They may simply disregard it, and go in for much more decentralized types of living, building their own institutions at a subnational level *and* at a transnational level, but in that case much more universal than the narrow confines of the European Community would permit. For an elaboration of this view, see Johan Galtung, 'European Security – An Era of Negotiation? Society and Power during the 1970s' (London: *Adelphi Papers,* Institute for Strategic Studies, 1970).

17 In saying so, we are not necessarily taking the view that Chinese socialism is 'genuine' socialism, and Soviet socialism not. One aspect of socialism is its humanism, one aspect of humanism is its respect for the individual. This respect does not seem well protected in the structures currently developing in China: the focus seems much more to be on equality and equity.

18 This is developed further in Johan Galtung, 'Japan and Future World Politics', (Oslo: PRIO, mimeo, 1972).

19 In Europe the same fear is expressed by Albania, the only country to refuse to participate in the European Security Conference.

20 One particular aspect of the Russian dominance over the Asian republics in the Soviet Union is demographic: a continuation of the Tsarist policy of populating these territories. According to the last Soviet census this policy is implemented on a relatively large scale.

21 The South-Asian subcontinent has certainly not yet taken its shape. The Indian Union, if it is an empire ruled from New Delhi, is a benevolent one with some notable exceptions like the Nagaland. Relations to small peripheral countries like, first of all, Bhutan and Sikkim, and then to Ceylon and Nepal, and for that matter also Kashmir, are more problematic – to say the least. Potentially, relations to Afghanistan, Pakistan, Bangladesh, and Burma may also become contentious in the future. There are also other possibilities, of some type of South-Asian confederation, like the ABC (Afghanistan-Burma-Ceylon) triangle envisaged by Gandhi's successor, Vinoba Bhave. The latter may rank low in probability today, but as mentioned: South Asia is still taking shape after centuries and millenia of outside oppression.

CHAPTER 10

1 By structural fascism' we mean a system that in its consequences is destructive of particular groups of individuals, like people of other races or other classes '(gooks' or 'kulaks'), but with no fascist ideology, attitudes, personality syndromes, or anything of that kind. One way of building up such a system is through a technocracy based on highly alienated technocrats and scientists who only carry out very limited jobs without asking questions.

2 In *Co-operation in Europe*, Chapter 2.

3 For one vision of a society of this type, see Johan Galtung, 'Structural Pluralism and the Future of Human Society'.

4 For an indication that this vision of relatively domination-free relations between countries is not entirely utopian, see relations between Scandinavian, or Nordic, countries of today.

5 One still almost takes for granted that it belongs to the prerogatives of nations to discuss and decide over foreign policy just as much as over domestic policy – regardless of the fact that the former often affects others not represented, and profoundly so. Of course, participation in international organizations serves as a constraint on this liberty, but that is not the same as having the people affected present. The way the world is developing, national parliaments will probably have to accept the presence of foreigners when foreign affairs are discussed, not only in the form of diplomats listening to the debate, but in the form of representatives with a right to intervene. So far, there is no sign that the European Community would be less in-group oriented.

6 See footnote 1, chapter 6.

7 We are thinking of the OPEC action, the Organization of Petrol Exporting Countries. However, as argued before, they were successful because their action affected only prices, not the trade structure.

8 The Tanzanian-American economist Reginald Green has given a program with

189

some interesting ideas (quoted from Helge Hveem, 'EEC-samarbeidet og utvik-lingslandene', in Susan Høivik, ed., *Ti innlegg om EEC* (Oslo: Universitetsforlaget, 1971), pp. 71 ff.). Green thinks in terms of better prices for raw materials and foodstuffs and increased access to the markets of the developed countries, as well as a decrease in the subsidies that the developed countries give to their own production in these fields. Further, clear preferences must be given to processed goods form the developing countries, and the export products from developing countries must be subsidized up till 25 % of their value as a logical parallel to protective tariffs for products produced for the home market. Further, discriminating, closed economic regionalism between developing countries must be accepted as a necessity, as a development strategy for the developing countries, but regional associations of metropoles and satellites must be abolished. We feel considerable sympathy for all these points, particularly for the latter: the world is so biased in favor of the rich countries, which means above all the former colonial powers, that the bias only can be corrected with a new bias working for some time.

9 For some ideas in connection with changes of multinational corporations, see *The True World*, chapter 8.

10 However, just as important as a more equitable trade structure would be better all-European cooperation organizations in the fields of industrial cooperation, finance, transportation and communication, education, health, environment protection and so on. For a list of suggestions, see Appendix 1 in 'Some Institutional Suggestions for a System of Security and Cooperation in Europe', *Bulletin of Peace Proposals*, 1972, pp. 73–88.

11 I am indebted to Otto von Krye, fellow participant in the World Order Models Project, for referring to this type of measure as an indicator of development, or at least of a major aspect of development.

12 It does not help in this connection to argue that African states also have formed an exclusive union of their own, the Organization of African Unity. It makes a lot of difference whether the countries joining together are among the richest or the poorest in the world; and this makes the similarity between the two organizations only formal, not material.

13 For a brilliant analysis of the difference between this conception of development and another conception, see 'Marginality and Ideology in Latin American Development', by Roger Vekemans and Jorge Giusti, *Studies in Comparative International Development*, 1969–70, pp. 221–234, particularly p. 226, 'Trickle down theory, an economic hypothesis'.

14 The impression derives from several debates under various conditions with people from the commission, high and low. Thus, when Ralf Dahrendorf, assuming that he is 'Wieland Europa', complains about the lack of perspective in the Commission he may be right *(Die Zeit*, 9 and 16 July 1971). But he is equally silent on the concrete content of this 'role' 'Europe' is to play, the broader perspectives, as most others. His 'Possibilities and Limits of a European Communities Foreign Policy', *The World Today*, April 1971, is not very concrete either. All Dahrendorf wants is much more discussion, 'I wait excitedly for the day when instead of the Bundestag emptying when its European delegates address it debate will be as intense in the German parliament about the future of European problems as it is now on a number of other subjects' *(The Guardian, 23/8/71)*.

190

15 The term 'emotional' is interesting in this connection. People in position will often be highly empiricist in their approach to social affairs, and empirical language is very rich and non-emotional. Non-empirical language is often less articulate, since values are given much less nuances than data. The man in position and the man in opposition, hence, will appear overly cool and overly emotional to each other.

16 By 'conservatively oriented statistics' we mean statistics that serve as operationalizations of conservative conceptions, particularly of development. Examples of such statistics would be GNP per capita measures without also mentioning dispersion measures, measures that emphasize trade and exchange in general without mentioning internal development, and so on. For many people such statistics will appear as completely value-neutral, objective, because this is the only type of development they can imagine. But there are no neutral statistics, any statistic chosen leads the attention away from something and in the direction of something else and hence represents a *choice*.

17 With ten member countries and a probability of 50 % for a social democratic government in each one of them, the chance of a social democratic government in all at the same time is about one promille. To this it may be objected that social democrats in, say, seven or more countries may be enough to change the policies; this increases the likelihood to about 18 %. But the likelihood of anything non-conservative − social democrat, socialist or communist − being in power is certainly much less than 50 % in many of the countries. Moreover, the higher the likelihood of a social democratic government, the more conservative the social democracy, with the British Labour Party and the German SPD being among the most conservative. On the other hand again, if by social democracy is meant Bismarck welfarestate-ism, and some keynesian planned economics, then this belongs to general technocracy just as much as to social democracy, and is in no need of election victories to dominate the EC. In this connection we should also emphasize that in the present European Parliament the 142 members are divided between 53 in the group of Christian Democrats, 36 in the group of social democrats, 25 liberals and 18 from the Democratic European Union, and then ten who are not placed in any group (seven of them from the Italian Communist Party). There seems to be a very long march ahead if a majority of social democrats is the goal (data from *European Community*, March 1971).

Agenor also points to this lack of socialist criticism of the EC in 'Revolution nationale ou transnationale', no. 18, 61−64. It is pointed out that leftist thinking has not given sufficient attention to transnational action − 'il n'existe pas de stratégie socialiste devant le fait transnational' (p. 62). Among its four main goals *Agenor* lists 'to contribute to new thinking about a strategy for the left in the European dimension' and probably contributes more than any other group. Whether the critique it offers is radical enough is another matter. Thus, the communiqué from the 'colloque syndical' organized by the Confederation Européenne des Syndicats Libres dans la Communauté in Luxembourg June 1970 is very little removed from what is found in EC practice already, except for the strong insistence that migrant workers be treated like workers in the EC countries. It remains to be seen how strong the workers' support for resolutions of this kind will be in a economical squeeze.

Quite typical of this type of 'opposition' is Michel Rocard, for instance in an interview in *Agenor* (January–March 1972) where he mentions five tasks for socialists within the EC: to 'limit the impact of liberalism elsewhere in the Community', to 'use safeguards against any attempt to sabotage a socialist experiment', to 'follow an anti-imperialist line in its relations with the rest of the world, and above all the United States', 'a division of labour among member countries that leaves each autonomous', 'strengthening the conditions of socialist forces, parties and unions, throughout the area'. In short, nothing about the Third World, nothing about the socialist countries – and the whole interview filled with remarks about the US that could also be directed against the EC. But Rocard argues against Servan-Schreiber's analysis of Europe–US relations.

Of course, more radical socialists exist, but the present author must also admit that he is unable to see the contours of any alternative, or of new political forces, in the final chapter, 'Die sozialistische Alternative', in Ernest Mandel's otherwise impressive *Die EWG und die Konkurrenz Europa-Amerika* (Frankfurt: Europäische Verlagsanstalt, 1968). And the same applies to many who do not pretend to have an alternative. As an example the pamphlet *The Truth about the Common Market 1970*, by the Common Markets Safeguards Campaign, can be used: not a word about Eastern Europe, not a word about the Third World as a whole (except 'our Commonwealth partners'), not a word about the world as a whole.

18 We would imagine that this argument could apply to two types of members of the European Community: former colonial powers that have suffered considerable *atimia* and do not quite know what to do in the current world, like Britain, and small countries that are used to combining national sovereignty with domination by others, like Norway. In the case of Norway one might even talk about a country in search of a master: after 400 years under Denmark, 100 years under Sweden, then 40 years strong orientation towards England lasting till the end of World War II, then 25 years or so with an equally strong orientation towards the United States lasting until the current decline of the US. For a Norwegian leadership suddenly to be alone in the world would be a completely new experience; this is where the European Community comes into the picture. There is one element of change along this Denmark-Sweden-England-United States-European Community axis, however: as Norway grows, so does the master – in size, in power potential, in everything.

19 On the contrary, a lively parliament may serve to obscure politics even further, because it looks so fascinating that people start believing in the idea that a democratic parliament actually means a democratic country. And then there is the problem of the power of the Parliament. The relative power of the Commission and the Parliament can to some extent be expressed in the well-known relation between the 2,448 regulations enacted by the Commission in 1970 (mostly relating to CAP), as opposed to merely 15 oral questions, with or without ensuing debate, in the parliamentary year 1969–70. There were also 477 written questions to the Commission and 30 to the Council – but written questions do not offer a chance of real control of the executive branches. Rather, they will often be turned into an opportunity for the executive to inform rather than to enter into a political dialogue.

20 See footnote 11, Chapter 6.

21 See, for instance, the survey reported in Kjell Landmark, *Ikke gi det bort* (Oslo:

192

Pax, 1967) – carried out by the International Peace Research Institute, Oslo during the first EC debate in Norway in 1961–62.

22 Thus, for Norwegian Prime Minister Trygve Bratteli the German-French reconciliation argument is used very often. The debate is actually not about the validity of this argument, but about its relevance, and its relevance depends on one's world horizon. Age seems a major factor here, with the politically conscious of the younger generation thinking much more in global terms, those of the middle generation in Western European terms, and those of the older generation, possibly, in Nordic terms.

23 The impression derives from several discussions in various groups in most EC member states.

24 This argument derives easily from marxist thinking. It was presented by Professor E. Altvater at a conference in Berlin January 1972.

25 The impression derives from various discussions in East African countries.

26 A basic impression from Spanish intellectual life is the possibility of having conferences and meetings where everything can be said almost as anywhere else in Western European countries, but in addition to the general understanding that there should be no translation into action, there is also the idea that there should be no effort to reach larger audiences.

27 This Chinese attitude is hardly stable, but to a large extent due to China's over-isolation from the world. With more participation in world affairs, and with more confrontation with EC policies around the world, ths attitude is likely to change, and this will polarize the big power complex further.

28 See footnote 7, chapter 6.

29 'The merger of the Institutions – in July 1967 – is no more than a first step towards the setting-up of a single European Community, governed by a single Treaty which will replace the Paris Treaty (establishing the ECSC) and the Rome Treaties (establishing the Common Market and Euratom)'. (Emile Noël, 'How the European Community's Institutions Work', *Community Topics*, 37, p. 2.) Thus, the EC is at present somewhere between communi*ty* and communi*ties*, vascillating in its own terminology between the two. But this step is only a small one among many leadirfg towards higher levels of unification. From a theoretical viewpoint it is interesting to see how the EC is an exercise not only in integrating countries but also in integrating the institutions integrating countries.

30 Our conclusion to the global role of the EC is very different from those given in the chapter 'Conclusions', by Stanley Henig, in *External Relations of the European Community* (London: Chatham House, 1971), pp. 64–71. Henig's major point is that 'external policy has evolved as a result of actions taken in response to external stimuli. Even though there was no original basic doctrine, there is now as a result a broad theory for the external relations of the European Community'. His view is one of stimulus, response, and institutionalization, leading to complaints about 'slowness and duplication of work' and that the Commission is so tied by internal compromise that it cannot negotiate at all with the other country' (p. 66). Such conclusions are natural when foreign policy is seen as the outcome of deliberate decision-making only. For other analyses, see Ph. P. Everts, ed., *The European Community in the World*, Rotterdam 1972 and particularly Gerda Zellentin, *Europa 1985*, Europa Union Verlag, 1972.

31 Public opinion research, incidentally, shows that changes towards supra-national

institutions have considerable support in the populations of the member states. In January/February 1970, 13,000 persons were interviewed in the Six, England and Denmark (where the interviews took place in July/August). For the populations of the Six, the answers were very clear: 65 % in favor of a further development of the EC to a political community and to a 'united Europe', only 10 % against; 60 % in favor of directly elected parliament, only 11 % against; an 52 % in favor of supra-national government, 20 % against. In England the majority was against on all questions, in Denmark the majority was in favor of the first two, but against the latter – a clear indication that people differentiate between the power of a parliament and the power of a government. These data were reported in Norway by K. Hongrø and N. P. Gleditsch, in 'Sterk EEC-opinion for integrasjon', *Dagbladet* (Oslo), 16 August 1971.

32 However, it is pointed out by C. A. Cosgrove and K. J. Twitchett, in 'The Second Yaoundé Convention in Perspective', *International Relations*, 1970, pp. 679 ff., especially p. 687 that 'without the association umbrella, however, most of the Eighteen would probably not have maintained their position /in the trading pattern/'. The same authors are of the opinion (p. 688) that efforts by the 18 to achieve some modest level of industrialization e.g. in the field of textiles will easily be stopped by 'important and vocal interest groups within the European Community, who, if threatened, will almost certainly press for protection from the competing products of the Eighteen'. Moreover, their chances of developing trade among themselves is an up-hill fight 'due to the paucity of viable intra-African communication networks and the existing patterns of commerce, /making it/ easier for almost all the African states to trade with Western Europe than with each other'. But this is actually trivial knowledge today: this is only what colonialism was, and is, about. Also see R. H. Green and Ann Seidman, *Unity or Poverty* (London: Penguin, 1968).

33 This grip is also used for political purposes, as pointed out by *The Times*, 24 November 1962: Germany wanted to make use of EEC benefits to deter African associates from recognizing the DDR.

34 Helge Hveem, 'Mangelfullt om u-hjelp', *Dagbladet*, 29 April 1972, points out that about 78 % of EDF means end up in European Community firms. Only EC firms can participate in these projects.

In his *Europe at Six and Seven*, Emile Benoit was of the early authors in saying that (p. 247) '(the EC) clearly aimed at ultimate political unification in some form – not necessarily a federation, but some type of political togetherness which would make isolationism and political neutrality inappropriate policy for any member'.

A leading African political scientist, Professor Ali A. Mazrui, accuses the EEC of 'dividing the world into a white bourgeoisie and a colored proletariat' ('The International Class System', *New Statesman*, 21 September 1962). Mazrui expresses similar thoughts in 'African attitudes to the European Common Market', *International Affairs*, January 1963.

35 As *Agenor* summarizes the effect of CAP on the less developed countries: 'The Six are paying their farmers to produce what farmers in the rest of the world can produce better and more cheaply; and then paying again to sell it off at dumping prices to steal the markets of the developing countries in other areas' ('Farm Policies for the Rich', *Agenor* no. 16, p. 53). To this should be added

that such policies make the heavily subsidized farmers in the EC countries partners in the exploitation of the Third World countries, as workers so easily become through division of labor.

36 The total loss in revenue due to GPS is estimated to perhaps $ 100 million or on the average $ 1 million per country. As pointed out, that does not necessarily mean $ 100 million to the developing countries or to cut the prices of their products. It should also be pointed out that Japan is actually more generous in her scheme, allowing an increase of 10 % instead of 5 % per year *(European Community,* January 1972, p. 22).

37 In the period 1958 to 1968 about 1,000 million dollars were transferred in the two EDFs. The distribution of the money is highly revealing. Best known is the small percentage (around 1 %) to industrial development. Less known is the *decreasing* percentage given to education, from 19.9 % to 10.0 %, and the *decreasing* percentage given to health, from 8.8 % to 4.6 %. Always high was the category infrastructure' – 44 % and 38 % respectively – and 'modernization of agriculture (read: mainly more efficient production of raw materials) – from 25 % to 45 %.

38 Lukaszewski, in his *Le Monde* articles (2–3 October 1970) points out very clearly the changes in the Soviet view of the European Community. The famous 17 Theses (on the Common Market) from 1957 predicted a rapid disintegration of the capitalist world; the 32 Theses of 1962, prepared for the conference of communist parties held in Moscow in August–September that year do not. We agree with Lukaszewski that the Soviet Union will sooner or later recognize the inevitable and withdraw the non-recognition of the EC as they lifted the Berlin blockade and withdrew the missiles from Cuba in earlier decades. But that is very different from the present willingness to play the role of supplier of raw materials and markets.

39 Adolph Rastén also points to some similarities between the Treaty of Rome and the visions entertained by the German geopolitician Karl Haushofer in the 1920s, as well as the *Neuropa* of Hitlerism and the visions of the *Kaiser* (op. cit., pp. 148 f). But apart from Hallenstein's talk about a Europe from the Atlantic to the Urals, today's EC leaders seem only to think in terms of Western Europe – à la Charlemagne (after whom even a prize for 'good Europeans' is named).

40 For an account of the involvement of the member states of the EC in the Cabora Bassa dam, see 'Aid and Arms for South Africa's Racists', *Agenor*, no. 19, p. 5.

9780367710989